FREDERICK DOUGLASS:

The Colored Orator.

BY

FREDERIC MAY HOLLAND,

Author of " *The Reign of the Stoics*," " *Stories from Robert Browning*,"
" *The Rise of Intellectual Liberty*," *etc.*

REVISED EDITION

HASKELL HOUSE PUBLISHERS Ltd.
Publishers of Scarce Scholarly Books
NEW YORK, N. Y. 10012
1969

First Published 1891

HASKELL HOUSE PUBLISHERS LTD.
Publishers of Scarce Scholarly Books
280 LAFAYETTE STREET
NEW YORK, N. Y. 10012

Library of Congress Catalog Card Number: **77-92969**

Standard Book Number 8383-1004-4

Printed in the United States of America

PREFACE TO FIRST EDITION.

THE invitation to write this life was readily accepted, partly because I hoped it would in some degree reduce the color-prejudice, with other prejudices also, and partly because I have always felt an admiration for Mr. Douglass, which has increased as I have come to know him thoroughly. His consent was cordially given in a letter, where he says: " If you can say anything of me that the public does not already know, by all means tell it. I am sure you cannot say anything of me which will not be pretty strongly colored, but go ahead." Shortly before departing to Hayti he was kind enough to answer many questions which I put to him in his house, on Cedar Hill, and to relate anecdotes which will be new to my readers. He also lent me ten of his unpublished lectures, and so many other manuscripts and rare pamphlets, that I have been able not only to mention but to quote more than a hundred works by an author not admitted to a place among the forty-six thousand writers of English enrolled by Allibone.

The list of published speeches, etc., in the Appendix has been made as complete as possible by inquiry in various directions. Much valuable information was obtained from Mr. Frederick Douglass, Jr., whose scrap-books gave me abundance of material about the later years of his father's life. By far the most difficult part of my work has been that relating to the decade just before the war; and here I was greatly aided and encouraged by the letters of reminiscences contributed by Miss Sallie Holley, Mrs. Lucy N. Colman, and another lady who knew Mr. Douglass in Rochester. For these and other extraordinary opportunities I am very grateful.

More generally known sources of information, like the files of the " Liberator," have, of course, been examined thoroughly. Among the most valuable of books to me has been the " Life of Garrison," by his sons, who kindly supplied advance sheets and permitted me to make copious extracts. This favor I should have been glad to repay more fully, but unfortunately there were some serious differences of opinion between their hero and mine, under circumstances now but little known to readers generally. Here it becomes my plain duty to try and vindicate Douglass, even at the expense of a great philanthropist whom all delight to honor. Desire to do sufficient justice to important questions has suggested some comments on the Harper's Ferry tragedy, socialism, and the Southern problem ; but it did not seem necessary to do more than give the orator's views about prohibition, the tariff, and the merits of various candidates for President; and I hope I have not shown myself too party-colored.

F. M. H.

PREFACE TO SECOND EDITION.

To this edition I have added an account of the last five years of the life of Mr. Douglass, and especially of his speeches at the World's Fair. I have also been able to show his position on the Hawaian question, to complete my list of his publications, to correct several mistakes, for instance on pp. 45 and 229, and to give what may be a more accurate estimate than my previous one of his peculiar greatness.

F. M. H.

April, 1895.

CONTENTS.

(v)

FREDERICK DOUGLASS.

CHAPTER I.

THE SLAVE.

"It has been a source of great annoyance to me, never to have a birthday," says Mr. Douglass, in a private letter. He supposes that he was born in February, 1817; but no one knows the day of his birth or his father's name. Such trifles were seldom recorded of slaves. His mother, Harriet Bailey, was one of the five daughters of Isaac and Betsy Bailey; and as slaves were not often permitted to own a sur-name, this must have been one of the old families of Maryland. Grandmother Betty was especially honored for her skill in planting sweet potatoes, as well as in making and handling nets for taking shad and herring. When we find further that the village where she resided still bore the aboriginal name, Tuckahoe, we may believe that it was from her, that her grandson derived those high cheek bones, and other peculiarities of physiognomy, which often caused him to be mistaken for an Indian in later life. His first master sometimes called him "My little Indian boy," and his whole history shows that he sprang from a race of warriors, who had rather die than be slaves. His oratorical power should be ascribed to his African descent, or to his European parentage. He himself attributes his love of letters to the native genius of his mother, who was the only colored person able to read in the whole village. This rare accomplishment suggests the probability that she had once been something more than a field hand. Her son saw her so seldom, however, and lost her so early, that he may have overestimated her ability, in consequence partly of gratitude and partly of a popular theory, about the preponderating influence over great men of gifted mothers, which long investigation justifies my calling extravagant. Inheritance of genius has come, in actual fact, at least as much from the father as from the mother ; and in the most illustrious instances it has come from both sides. I suspect that there is some foundation for the rumor, that the father in this case was a noted politician. White he undoubtedly was, for the son was of much lighter color than his mother, whose " deep black, glossy " features, are said by him to have resembled those of King Rameses the Great, on page 157 of " Prichard's Natural History of Man."

She called him Frederick Augustus Washington Bailey ; but after his escape he took the name which he has made famous. She had an older son, Perry, and four daughters; but none of them, I think, was endowed with his peculiar genius. Perhaps there was a different father. Her services were too valuable for her to be permitted to waste her time on her children, and Douglass does not remember having ever seen her before he was six years old.

His earliest memories are of his grandmother's log cabin in his native village, Tuckahoe, on the bank of the Choptank River, in Talbot County, on the eastern shore of Maryland. The floor and chimney were of clay, and there were no windows, nor any bedsteads, except rails flung over the cross-beams. Food was coarse, but it was abundant, and the little boy was never scolded for playing in the dirt, or getting his clothes wet, or not learning his lessons, or using his knife and fork awkwardly. In fact, he had no lessons, or knife and fork, and scarcely any clothing, to be troubled about. Year after year went by, during which he was as free and happy as the squirrels he saw running up the trees, or the minnows for which he used to fish in the mill-pond. His grandmother was always kind, and the only cloud upon his path was the fear of being taken from her, as his brother and his sisters had been. He dreaded to find himself growing taller, and at last the terrible day came.

One summer morning, before he was seven, she took his hand in hers, and led him, or carried him on her shoulder, over the twelve miles which lay between Tuckahoe and the house of their master, Captain Anthony. This man owned three farms in Tuckahoe, and about thirty slaves ; but his time was mainly occupied in managing the estates of Colonel Lloyd, who had a thousand slaves and twenty or thirty different farms. All the overseers were under the control of Captain

Anthony, whose plain brick house stood near the
stately mansion of Colonel Lloyd, on the latter's
home plantation, on the banks of the Wye, which
flows into Chesapeake Bay, about thirty-five miles
southeast of Baltimore.

At the " great house " the Lloyds lived in such luxury as the little boy had never dreamed of ; but the
suffering outside was almost indescribable. Most of
the slaves were driven out into the field at the first
sign of dawn, with lashes for those who came last ;
and they were kept there until it was too dark to work.
The mending and cooking were done during the night,
and the food was carried out to be eaten in the field,
where the babies were nursed, when the mothers
could not be spared time to go home. There
was no public opinion in Talbot County to hinder
the worst of cruelties. Our hero saw his Aunt
Esther receive from his master, because he was
jealous and she loved another slave, thirty or forty
stripes, each of which drew screams and blood. One
of his cousins once walked the twelve miles from
Tuckahoe, to show how a drunken overseer had
gashed her shoulders with his cowhide, and struck
her such a blow over the head with his stick as left
her face covered with blood. Her master only told
her to tramp back at once or he would take the rest
of her skin off her back himself. Such floggings
were frequent, and a slave who tried to escape one
by running into the creek, was shot down there by
the overseer, on the very plantation where the little
Frederick was kept. His wife's cousin, a girl of
fifteen, was beaten to death in her sleep by her mistress for being unable to hear the cry of a baby who

had kept her up night after night. Murders of slaves
were frequent on the Eastern Shore, but there was no
punishment and little blame. The worst sufferings
of the slaves, however, seem to have come from lack
of sleep and food. The men and women were given
about a quarter of a pound of pork, or a little fish,
daily, a peck of coarse corn-meal per week, and
nothing else, except a little salt. The corn-cake was
full of bran, and covered so thickly with ashes that
no Northerner could eat it. Bed there was none,
only a blanket for each adult. The children had no
blanket, nor any clothes, except a pair of shirts of sack-
cloth for each child every year. Whole flocks of
little boys and girls, from five to ten years old, might
be seen running naked around the " great house," or
huddled together in the sun during the frosty days
of March.

The little Frederick had to sleep on cold nights
with his head and shoulders in a sack, and his feet
had cracks big enough to hold a penholder. His
share of the mush, which a dozen children at Captain
Anthony's ate like pigs out of a trough on the kitchen
floor, was so scanty that he was often pinched with
hunger. He used to run to pick up the little bones
which were flung out for the cats, and he often fought
with the dog for the crumbs which fell from the
kitchen table. The very taste of white bread was
unknown to him ; but he was fascinated by the sight
of those snowy biscuits, baked in a quick oven, out
of unleavened flour, which he saw carried to the
Lloyd's table, and he made up his mind that he would
have some to eat every morning when he was a man.
This ambition has been so far satisfied that precisely

such biscuit have been regularly set before him for his Sunday breakfast at Cedar Hill.

The worst of it was that the cook, Aunt Katy, often whipped him or made him go all day without food, except a wretched breakfast. One night, when he had been treated thus and was too hungry to sleep, he managed to steal a few kernels of Indian corn and roast them in the fire. Just as he was about to eat them, his mother came in and took him in her arms. She had walked twelve miles to see him, and her indignation, at hearing that Aunt Katy threatened to starve the life out of him, was loud and fierce. He ate the large ginger cake she gave him, and felt prouder, as he sat on her knee, than a king on his throne. He soon dropped off to sleep, however ; before he awoke, his mother had to go back to her work ; and he never saw her again, for he was not allowed to stand beside her dying bed. These visits had been rare, for it could only have been under unusually favorable circumstances that she was able to travel the twenty-four miles in a single night.

These scenes show what was the early life of "Cap'n Ant'ney Fed," as he was called in the jargon of the plantation, where the sign of the possessive case was a luxury unknown to the slaves. He was switched into repeating the Lord's Prayer, but had no other religious training, except the information that " God up in the sky " had made white men to be masters and black people to be slaves, and that He knew what was best for them all. The child could not believe that the slaves were as well off as they ought to be, and he used to sit and wonder how slavery could exist if God was good. His trouble often made him weep, and his perplexity was increased by observing that God had not made, by any means, slaves of all the blacks, or slave-holders of all the whites. Light broke in upon his troubled mind as he found that some of his fellow-slaves had been stolen from homes where they were free, and others were children of fathers and mothers who had been thus brought into bondage. Clearly it was man who was responsible, not God. The little boy's Aunt Jennie suddenly disappeared with her husband, and it was whispered about that they had run away to the free States, and would henceforth be free. Before he was eight years old he made up his mind that he would, some day, do what they did. No wonder, for, as he said in 1855, he became "just as well aware of the unjust, unnatural, and murderous character of slavery when nine years old, as I am now."

Among the few bright spots in Fred's plantation life was the kindness of his master's daughter, Mrs. Thomas Auld, still called "Miss Lucretia" by the slaves. When he had a fight with another slave-boy, and came home roaring with pain, and streaming with blood from a wound which left the sign of the cross upon his forehead, it was she who washed away the blood, put on balsam, and bound up the wound. When he was unusually hungry he used to go and sing under her window, and she would give him a slice of bread and butter. It may have been her intercession which saved his boyish spirit from being crushed into submission to his lot, and gave him the key to the prison door.

In the summer of 1825, soon after he had begun his ninth year, she told him that he was to go to Baltimore, which seemed like heaven to the slaves on the Eastern Shore. The next three days were the happiest he had ever known, and were spent mainly in the creek, where he was trying to wash the dead skin off his feet and knees. "Miss Lucretia" had told him she would give him a pair of trousers if he could get himself clean. He had no home to regret, and he hardly dared to go to sleep, for fear he might be left behind.

Early on a Saturday morning he was able to look for the last time, as he hoped, on the plantation, as the sloop carried him over Chesapeake Bay towards Baltimore. He arrived there on Sunday morning, and was kindly received by his new Mistress, Mrs. Hugh Auld, sister-in-law of Lucretia's husband, Thomas. "Miss Sopha," as the boy called her, gave him a comfortable bed, good clothes, and palatable food, while he had nothing harder to do than to run errands and take care of her son, little Tommy. All three soon grew very fond of each other, and she even granted a request, made under circumstances described thus, in a speech made at Belfast, in 1846 :

"I remember the first time I ever heard the Bible read, and from that time I trace my first desire to learn to read. I was over seven years old ; my master had gone out one Sunday night, the children had gone to bed. I had crawled under the center table and had fallen asleep, when my mistress commenced to read the Bible aloud, so loud that she waked me. She waked me to sleep no more. I have found since that the chapter she then read was the first of Job. I remember my sympathy for the good old man, and my anxiety to learn more about him led me to ask my mistress to teach me to read."

She complied gladly and was soon looking for-

ward to see him reading the Bible. Her joy led her
to tell her husband, but he at once forbade any more
lessons, telling her that learning would spoil any
nigger, and that if this one should ever be taught to
read the Bible, there would be no keeping him a slave.

This was said in Fred's hearing, and it proved the
best lesson he ever had. He heard that knowledge
would prevent his remaining a slave, and at once he
made up his mind to get all he could. " Miss Sopha"
not only taught him no more, but would snatch away
any book or newspaper she might see in his hand,
while she took great care never to leave him alone
with anything he could read. He turned the street
into a school-room, and made his white playmates his
teachers. He always carried Webster's spelling-book
in his pocket, and also bread enough to pay the hungry little boys he met for giving him lessons. He
used now and then to ask these white boys if it was
right for him to be a slave, and they always agreed
with him that it was not. Finding them interested in
the " Columbian Orator," he bought a copy with fifty
cents, earned by blacking boots in the street. Here
he found a dialogue between a runaway slave, just
recaptured, and his master. The negro demonstrated
the injustice of slavery with such power that he was
emancipated. Think how eagerly this was read by
the boy of thirteen! He entered with equal zeal into
the denunciations of oppression by great orators, and
especially by Sheridan in his demand for Catholic
emancipation. The speeches of Chatham and Fox,
too, in behalf of America, helped him to understand
the rights of man. He was all ears when he heard
any one speak of slavery, and the heat which his

master and other white men showed against Abolitionists, made him very curious to know who they were.
Evidently they had something to do with slavery, but
what could it be ? At last he found out from one of
the city newspapers, probably in February, 1833,
when there was much agitation, that they had been
sending petitions to Congress, asking for the abolition
of the slave trade between States, as well as of slavery
itself in the District of Columbia. Thenceforth he
knew that he was not without friends upon the earth.
This idea assumed a practicable form, when an Irishman repaid him, for helping to unload a boat full of
stones, by telling him that he need only go North to
be as free as anybody.

His confidence that he would finally gain both
freedom and knowledge was much increased by an
interest in religion, which became very strong before
he was fourteen. At this time he used to pick up
stray pages of the Bible in the gutter, and wash and
dry them, in order to pore over them in secret. His
leisure was now mostly spent either in attending
prayer-meetings, or in holding private worship with
a good old colored man, who prayed almost without
ceasing, even when on his dray. The boy taught the
old man how to make out the hard words, and, in
return was shown something of their meaning. Both
felt sure that the Lord would call Frederick in due
time to preach the Gospel ; and the exhortation " to
wait in trust and patience until the good time came,"
may have done much to keep him from making a
premature attempt to escape. His master tried in
vain to break up the intimacy by threats of the lash.
The young church-member resented bitterly the

persecution, as he called it ; and when the cholera smote Baltimore, in 1833, he thought that the Lord was punishing the whites for holding his people in bondage.

One reason that Frederick did not run away then, was that he wished first to learn how to write a pass for himself. He had now exchanged his easy life, of waiting on "Miss Sopha" and little Tommy, for regular work in Mr. Auld's ship-yard. He noticed that the carpenters marked each piece of timber with a capital letter, S. L. A. or F.; and he soon found that these were the initials of the words "Starboard," "Larboard," "Aft," and "Forward." While the men were at dinner, he taught himself to make these four letters. Then he challenged the white boys to "beat that," and thus made them show him other letters. Thus he "learned to write on board fences, making some of his early capitals with their heads downwards and looking the wrong way." By and by he managed to copy the italics out of the spelling-book. He even ventured, at great risk of a flogging, to take the old writing-books which Master Tommy had brought home from school, and copy off line after line in the vacant spaces. He secretly carried a flour barrel and a chair into the kitchen loft, where he slept, and there he used to work late into the night, copying from the Bible and the Methodist hymn-book.

While the young slave was preparing himself for freedom, he became, in consequence of the death of "Miss Lucretia" and her father, the property of her husband, Captain Thomas Auld. His new master soon quarreled with his brother in Baltimore, and took his chattel away. This was in March, 1833, when Captain Auld had taken up his residence at St. Michael's, a fishing village on the Bay, about forty miles from Baltimore. He had taken a second wife ; and her father, a rich slave-holder named Hamilton, lived a few miles away. The kitchen at St. Michael's was not very bountifully supplied ; and the appetite of the growing boy was keen enough to tempt him to theft.

Whatever scruples the young aspirant for the ministry felt, were quieted by this ingenious argument. Captain Auld's meat continued to be his, after it was taken out of one of his tubs and put into another ; so there really was no stealing. As for the neighbors, they were accomplices in deliberately robbing the laborer of his reward, and he was justified in protecting himself against starvation at their expense. Another way in which he used to supply himself with food was letting loose his master's horse. The animal would always dash off to its former stable, on the Hamilton plantation, five miles off. The groom would have to be sent to bring him back, and he would return with bread enough to make him comfortable for a day or two. He gave additional offence by constantly speaking to Mr. Auld, or of him to Mrs. Auld, by his old title, "Captain," and not saying "Master," as was desired by the wife especially. Of course, this led to frequent whippings.

Mrs. Auld was a devout member of the church, and Thomas became one at a camp-meeting that August ; but Frederick's new brother disappointed all his hopes of better treatment than before. He ventured, soon after the conversion, to help teach a little Sunday-school. A dozen old spelling-books and a few Testaments were collected. Twenty children came together the first day, and the young teacher thought he had now found something worth living for. Scarcely had school begun on the second Sunday, however, when in rushed a mob, headed by Master Thomas and two Methodist class-leaders. The scholars were driven away with sticks and stones, and forbidden ever to meet again, for they were black. Frederick was told that he wanted to be like Nat Turner, who led a bloody insurrection in Southampton, Va., 1831, and that he would get as many balls in his body as Nat had, if he did not look out. He had seen slave girls treated with unusual cruelty by a pious mistress in Baltimore, and he was soon to have new proof of how little could be done, even by religion, to lessen the essential wickedness of slavery.

The completion of his industrial education was intrusted by Brother Auld to Brother Covey, a devout neighbor, famous for success in breaking unruly slaves. The morning of the first of January, 1834, found the poor boy trudging along, with his little bundle at the end of his stick, to the new master with whom that year must be spent. Covey, too, was a Methodist, and made his slaves hear a great deal of religious talk on Sunday, as well as a short prayer every morning and a long prayer every night. Frederick was depended upon to lead the singing, but he often failed to do so ; for such worship seemed to him a mockery. He was no longer starved, but he was overworked systematically, and often kept in the field until almost midnight. It was never too hot or

too cold for out-door work—it could never rain, blow,
snow, or hail too hard. The longest days were too
short, he says, for his master, and the shortest nights
were too long. Covey relied mainly on hard work
for breaking slaves. When he chose to set them an
example, he would " make everything fly before him."
He was an experienced overseer, and had peculiar
skill in watching his slaves, when they thought him
far away, and creeping out upon them unexpectedly.
They spoke of him to each other as " the snake," and
felt as if they were always under his cruel eye.

The lash was only a secondary feature of his plan ;
but it was not left out. Frederick had been with him
but three days when he was sent, on one of the
coldest mornings of January, with a pair of oxen, to
bring in wood from the forest. He had never driven
oxen before, and these were scarcely broken in.
Covey himself would not have dared to take them
into the woods, until he had let them work off some
of their wildness in the open field. The young
driver was told to go to the woods ; and thither he
went, without daring to make objections. The oxen
ran all the way over the fields, pulling him along at
the end of the rope with which he was ordered to
keep them from running away. When they got in
among the trees, they took fright, and rushed about
wildly, so that he expected to be dashed to death.
At last they stopped, entangled in saplings, and
with the body of the cart, the wheels, and the tongue
lying scattered about. It took hard work to get the
pieces together and release the oxen. On their way
out of the wood they ran away once more, despite a
heavy load, broke the gate into splinters, and nearly

crushed the driver between the wheel and the post.
It was noon when he reached the house, but he was
sent back at once with the cart to the woods. Covey
followed, overtook him there, and said he would
teach him how to waste time and break gates. He
cut from a black gum-tree three young shoots, from
four to six feet long, such as are used for ox-goads.
Then he commanded the slave to take off his clothes.
No heed was given to the order ; Covey tore them off
himself. The tough goads were worn out, one by
one, and such sores were left on the back as kept
open, under the coarse shirt, for weeks. This was
the first instance of what happened every few days
for six months.

Douglass says it was then, if at any one time, more
than another, that he was " made to drink the bitterest
dregs of slavery." " A few months of this discipline
tamed me." . . . " I was broken in body, soul and spirit."
. . . " My natural elasticity was crushed ; my intellect
languished ; the disposition to read departed ; the
dark night of slavery closed in upon me ; and behold
a man transformed into a brute ! " . . . " I had neither
sufficient time in which to eat or sleep, except on
Sunday." . . . " I spent this in a sort of beast-like stupor,
between sleeping and waking under some large
tree." . . . " I was sometimes prompted to take my
life, and that of Covey, but was prevented by a com-
bination of hope and fear." . . . " The over-work,
and the brutal chastisement, combined with that ever-
gnawing and soul-devouring thought, ' I am a slave—
a slave for life—a slave with no rational ground to
hope for freedom,' rendered me a living embodiment
of mental and physical wretchedness."

On one of the hottest Friday afternoons in August Covey was thrashing out his wheat in barbaric fashion. Horses were treading it loose from the straw ; and Frederick was carrying the mixture of wheat, chaff and dirt to the fan. He was in a hurry, for he was to have time to go fishing, if the work was finished before sunset. About three o'clock he br٫ ٫e down, with no strength left, an extreme dizziness, and a violent headache. The fanning had to stop, for every hand was needed for the work. Covey found him lying by the fence, and, with a savage kick in the side, bade him rise. He tried to, but fell back. Another heavy kick brought him to his feet ; but as soon as he stooped to pick up the tub in which he had been carrying food for the fan, he fell to the ground, utterly helpless. Then Brother Covey took up the hickory club with which the wheat had been struck off level with the sides of the measure, and gave him such a wound on the head as made blood run freely, saying, " If you have got the headache, I'll cure you." He was still unable to rise, and was left bleeding by the fence.

His head was soon relieved by the flow of blood ; and he resolved to go and complain to Captain Auld. He started up while Covey was looking another way, and gained the woods. There he had to lie down, for his strength failed him. At last the bleeding ceased, and he made his way barefoot, through bogs and briars, to St. Michael's. It took him five hours to make the seven or eight miles ; and Auld insisted on his going back again to the good, religious man. He did so the next morning, and before the house he met Covey, with rope and cow-hide, ready for him. He had but just time to get through the corn into the woods. There he lay down exhausted, for he had lost much blood and eaten nothing since noon the day before. All day he lay unpursued, for it was hoped that hunger would bring him back. His recent experiences with members of his church made prayer seem useless. There he lay all day in pain and despair. During the night another slave came by, on his way to spend Sunday with his wife. The good couple fed and sheltered the sufferer, at the risk of being treated in the same way. Sandy, as his benefactor was named, advised him not to attempt an escape, which would then have been very difficult, but to trust to the magic power of a root, whose wearer ran no danger of being whipped by any white man. The incredulous listener was reminded that all his book learning had not protected him. Sunday morning found him with his pocket full of roots in front of Covey's house. He was kindly received, for the good man was about to go to church. While regaining his strength, he resolved upon a course worthy of his white as well as of his Indian blood. He knew that those slaves who could be whipped easiest were whipped oftenest; and he felt that he had listened too blindly to sermons in which non-resistance was enjoined as the peculiar virtue of the colored race. "My hands," he says, "were no longer tied by my religion." He had made up his mind to risk being sold South, or incurring the penalty of the State law, which provided that any slave who resisted his master should be hung, and then have his head cut off and set up, with the four quarters of his body, in prominent places.

Long before daylight the next morning he was called out and sent to feed the horses. As he was going up to the loft in the stable, Covey sneaked in behind and tried to slip a rope around his leg, in order to tie him up for a flogging. He fell heavily, but leaped up at once and sprang at his master's throat. There the strong black fingers kept their grasp until the nails drew blood. The white man tried to strike; but every blow was parried, though none was struck in return. He closed with the slave, but went down again and again upon the floor. "Are you going to resist, you scoundrel?" "Yes, sir," was the steady answer. Covey called his cousin to his assistance; but the white boy was at once doubled up with pain by the black boy's kick. "Are you going to keep this up?" "Yes, indeed, come what may. You have treated me like a brute the last six months, and I shall stand it no longer." Covey dragged him out of the stable to a stick of wood, with which he meant to knock him down. Just as he stooped to pick it up, he was seized by the black hands and flung out his full length into the cow-yard. Another slave now came up, and was commanded to take hold of the rebel. He at first pretended not to understand the order, and finally said, "My master hired me here to work, and not to help you whip Frederick." This man's owner would not let him be flogged unless he deserved it; and the two were left to fight it out. The only slave whom Covey owned was a woman who had been avowedly bought for breeding. She, too, was called upon for aid as she came in to milk the cows; and she, too, refused, though she knew she must suffer for it. For two hours the fight had gone on, and Covey had not been able to draw a single drop of blood, while blood had been drawn from him. He had not been able to whip the slave ; but at last he said, " Now, go to your work ; I should not have whipped you half so much, if you had not resisted." He never tried it again, although he had plenty of opportunity, and even provocation, during the next six months.

Douglass is right in calling this the turning point in his life as a slave. It made him a man instead of a timid boy, " a freeman, in fact, while I remained a slave in form." He was four years more in bondage, but he was never again whipped. It was several times attempted, but without success. Not the slightest punishment was inflicted for his resisting Covey. The latter probably kept his defeat as much of a secret as possible, lest his reputation as a slave-breaker should be forfeited. Captain Auld may have felt even then what he acknowledged forty years afterwards, on his death-bed, to his visitor, then Marshal Douglass, that he always thought him too smart to be a slave.

At all events he was hired out, for the two years after that with Brother Covey, 1835 and 1836, to a neighbor who seldom whipped his slaves, and always gave them plenty of time to sleep and eat, while the supply of food was never stinted. Mr. Freeland did not profess religion, but he was a much better master than the church-members just mentioned, or two ministers in Talbot County, about whom a good deal is said in " My Bondage and My Freedom." The author had reason to think that the religion of slave-holders often put their consciences to sleep. He did not, however, give up all idea of preaching some day himself, and he used, when every one else slept, to try to prepare for the pulpit by going out to the pigs and talking to them as " Dear Brethren." It was much more proper for him to say so to pigs than to white men, according to the laws of the land, and the opinions most revered throughout the United States. He was only a field-hand, and reading matter was more out of reach than in Baltimore. He did, however, manage to re-open his Sunday-school, and this time it escaped attack, although it numbered more than forty scholars. Many learned to read, either there or during the three evenings a week which were devoted to this work in winter ; and the teacher afterward met several of his former pupils as freemen.

This employment made the first year pass pleasantly, but early in 1836, the position of a slave, even in this mild form, began to seem intolerable to the young agitator ; and the ideas which he had learned from the " Columbian Orator," in Baltimore, were earnestly set forth to his companions. Two of the slaves who labored beside him were fully aroused by his passionate declamations on the rights of man and the glories of liberty. Two other young men on the plantation of his owner's father-in-law, Mr. Hamilton, joined them. All agreed to set at naught the teachings of the pulpit, and the dangers which threatened fugitives. The conspirators held frequent meetings, and kept up each other's zeal by songs with a secret meaning, like

" I am bound for the land of Canaan,
I don't expect to stay much longer here," etc.

According to the plan invented by our hero, they were going to take a large canoe, belonging to Mr. Hamilton, sail and paddle to the head of the bay, seventy miles off, and then make their way on foot to the North. The only free city known to them, even by name, was New York. The leader had written passes permitting the bearers to spend the Easter holidays in Baltimore, and they were getting ready to start on the Saturday evening previous. That morning, just as Frederick had been called in from the field for breakfast, he saw Mr. Hamilton gallop up to the house ; three other white men followed on horseback ; and after them walked two negroes whose hands were tied. He saw that he was betrayed and that his best plan was to submit quietly. One of Mr. Freeland's slaves followed his example, but the other fought bravely, though pistols were pointed against his heart. The scuffle gave the writer of the passes a chance to burn his own unobserved, and the others were eaten, by his advice, as the slaves were dragged along the road by the mounted constables. Mr. Freeland's mother had supplied the slaves whom he owned with food, while she scolded the " long-legged yellow devil," who had made them think of running away. They stopped during the tramp of fifteen miles at his master's store, and there, as the leader directed, they all protested that they had not the slightest intention of absconding, and asked indignantly what evidence there was against them. At last they reached Easton, the county seat, and were locked up in the jail. They could expect nothing better than to be sold to die in the rice swamps. Mr. Freeland and Mr. Hamilton had the slaves they owned released, however, after the holidays were over, and took them back. The ring-leader was left behind. Captain Auld would have let him work out the year with Mr. Freeland, but Hamilton declared that he would shoot the dangerous fellow if he appeared again in that neighborhood. He was the only slave there who could read and write. Large sums were offered by the negro-traders, but Auld declared that money would not tempt him to sell Frederick South. Finally he was sent to Baltimore to learn a trade, and promised that, if he would behave himself, he should be emancipated at twenty-five. He had resisted his master with success, he had taken the lead in a plot to run away, and his courage did not go without its reward.

Three years previous he had left Baltimore an unruly boy. He came back a strong man, resolved to protect himself against injury, and to use the first good opportunity for setting himself free. During the rest of 1836 he worked as apprentice in a large ship-yard, where he was at the beck and call of seventy-five carpenters. These white men, just before he entered the yard, had been led by fear of lower wages to refuse to let colored carpenters work there any longer ; and now they encouraged the white apprentices to pick quarrels with the new nigger. In one of these he would have lost his life if he had not succeeded in parrying a blow from an adze. Another time he flung the man who struck him into the dock. Whenever he was struck he struck back again, and thus he held his own for about eight months. At last, the man who had been ducked came at him with three other apprentices. One was in front, armed

with a brick, one on each side, and the fourth behind
with a heavy hand-spike. They closed in upon him.
He defended himself, but a blow from the hand-spike
stunned him and brought him to the ground. Then
all four fell upon him with their fists, while the carpenters shouted : "Kill the d——d nigger! He
struck a white man!" By and bye he came to himself and rose to his hands and knees. As he did so he
got a kick in the left eye which closed it completely.
Then they left him, but even then he would have run
after them with the hand-spike if the carpenters had
not interfered.

This scene deserves attention, on account of his
dauntless courage. The worst of it is, that he could
get no protection from the law. He had been put
once more under the charge of his master's brother,
Hugh Auld ; but when this gentleman applied for a
warrant, the magistrate refused to issue one, unless
white witnesses would come forward. Neither the
word of the colored man, nor the sight of his wounds,
was of the slightest importance. The laws of Maryland were for the protection of whites. All that Mr.
Auld could do for the slave was to take him, as soon
as his wounds had healed, into the yard where he was
foreman. There the apprentice became an expert
calker, and was able, before the end of 1837, to earn
a dollar and a half a day, the highest wages paid to
men of that trade in Baltimore. He was allowed to get
a job where he could, and to collect the money ; but
he had to hand over every cent he received. He saw
more plainly than before that slaves were not protected, but plundered.

His literary education had stood still while he was

away from Baltimore ; but now he met colored people who knew more than he did. Some of them were able to teach him geography and arithmetic. The young freedmen even permitted him to enter a club from which other slaves were excluded, " The East Baltimore Mutual Improvement Society ; " and he took a prominent part in its debates. He also, in all probability, spoke often in religious meetings ; and among his delighted hearers may be supposed to have been Anna Murray, a free woman of color, who afterward became his wife.

As his condition and prospects improved, his desire for freedom grew still stronger ; and he longed to have money enough of his own to be able to escape. In May, 1838, he persuaded Hugh Auld to let him hire his time. He had to buy his tools and clothes, pay his board, and hand over three dollars a week, whether work was good or bad. He succeeded in carrying out the bargain and in laying aside some money. One Saturday evening in August, instead of going to Mr. Auld with the sum due, he went off with a party of friends to camp-meeting, and did not return before Sunday night. The privilege of hiring out was taken away, in punishment ; and his indignation led him to spend the next week in idleness. On Saturday night there was a violent quarrel in consequence of his having no money to hand over ; but, fortunately for him, they did not get to blows. The next day he made up his mind to go to work early Monday morning, to make Master Hugh as well satisfied as possible with him during that week, and the two following, and then to run away.

His success will be related in the next chapter.

Thus far we have seen him become familiar with some of the best, as well as the worst, aspects of slavery. He had been a half-starved boy, running wild on a plantation, a petted house-servant, a field-hand, first under a master who fed him so poorly that he was obliged to steal, then under a professional negro-breaker, who over-worked him systematically, and whipped him cruelly, until he saved himself from more torture by making a resistance which might have brought him to the gallows. The result was his coming under a master who gave him plenty of food and rest, and never struck him. His attempt to escape, in company with other slaves, whom he had induced to join him, sent him back to Baltimore, where he was cruelly treated at first, but was soon able to learn a good trade and to support himself in almost complete liberty. He had worked his way upward by his own strength and courage, going through fight after fight, with his life in his hand. He had taught himself not only to read and write, but to speak effectively. He knew what to say about slavery, and how to say it. The principal thing which he needed to do in order to reach the platform was to break his chain.

CHAPTER II.

It was on Monday, September 3, 1838, that the great purpose, which had been cherished for more than a dozen years, amid many changes in place and fortune, was carried out with complete success. It was many years before the fugitive told how he escaped. He was often tempted to give this additional charm to his lectures and editorials, but he would not resort to this easy way of conquering those slanderers who said that he had never been a slave. He kept his lips firmly shut, partly because he meant to save those who had assisted him from punishment, and partly because he was determined to have this path to freedom remain open to his brothers and sisters still in bondage. He knew that if no accounts of the escape of a slave who let himself be nailed up in a box, and sent North by rail, had been published, there might have been a thousand "Box Browns" a year. Such secrets were often printed, and it was not the slave who read them, but the master. Fortunately there was, at least, one enemy of slavery who was wise enough to fight her with silence as well as speech. His secret was not told in print before 1872.

His plan was, in the first place, as already men-

32

tioned, to work for three weeks so diligently and profitably as to avert all suspicion. He succeeded so well that, on the second Saturday night, he paid over, as the result of that week's work, nine dollars to his master. The latter was so delighted that he actually presented him with the generous sum of twenty-five cents, bidding him make a good use of it. We shall see that he did. He had already saved up seventeen dollars, and by the end of the third week all his preparations were made. The laws of Maryland required every free negro to carry papers describing him accurately and to pay liberally for this protection. Slaves often escaped by borrowing papers from a friend, to whom the precious documents would be returned by mail. Whenever a colored man came with free papers to the railroad station to buy a ticket, he was always examined carefully enough to insure the detection of a runaway, unless the resemblance was very close. Our hero was not acquainted with any free negro who looked much like him ; but he found out that passengers who paid on the cars were not scrutinized so minutely as those who bought tickets, and also that sailors were treated with peculiar indulgence by the conductors. The dominant party was doing all it could to encourage the shipping interest, and rapidly reducing the tariff. The cry of " Free Trade and Sailors' Rights " meant in this instance " Free Labor and the Rights of the Slave."

Among his friends was a sailor who was of much darker hue than he was himself, but who owned a protection, setting forth his occupation, and bearing the sacred figure of the American eagle. This was borrowed ; sailors' clothes were purchased, and, on

Monday morning, the fugitive jumped on the train just as it started. His baggage had been put aboard by a friendly hackman. He was greatly troubled, for, as he wrote to his master, ten years later, "I was making a leap in the dark. The probabilities, so far as I could by reason determine them, were stoutly against the undertaking. The preliminaries and precautions I had adopted previously, all worked badly. I was like one going to war without weapons—ten chances of defeat to one of victory. One in whom I had confided, and one who had promised me assistance, appalled by fear at the trial hour, deserted me." "However, gloomy as was the prospect, thanks be to the Most High, who is ever the God of the oppressed, at the moment which was to determine my whole earthly career, His grace was sufficient : my mind was made up."

His anxiety increased in consequence of the harshness with which the conductor questioned other passengers in the negro car. The sailor, however, was addressed kindly and told, after a mere glance at the protection, that it was all right. Thus far he was safe ; but there were several people on the train who would have known him at once in any other clothes. A German blacksmith looked at him intently, and apparently recognized him, but said nothing. On the ferry boat, by which they crossed the Susquehanna, he found an old acquaintance employed, and was asked some dangerous questions. On they went, however, until they stopped to let the train from Philadelphia pass. At a window sat a man under whom the runaway had been at work but a few days before. He might easily have recognized him, and would certainly have had him arrested ; but fortunately he was looking another way. The passengers went on from Wilmington by steamer to Philadelphia, where one of them took the train for New York and arrived early on Tuesday. In less than twenty-four hours the slave had made himself a free man. It was but a few months since he had become twenty-one.

He was astonished at "the dazzling wonders of Broadway," and so full of joyous excitement that, as he wrote at once to a friend—we can guess what friend—in Baltimore, he felt as if he had escaped, like Daniel, from a den of lions. That very day, however, he met another fugitive, whom he had known in Baltimore as "Allender's Jake," and was told that they were both in deadly peril. The city was full of Southerners returning home. Many of the colored people could be bribed into betraying a runaway. All their boarding-houses were closely watched, and the new comer must not think of looking for work upon the wharves. In fact, the danger of recapture was even greater then in New York, than after the passage of the Fugitive Slave Bill. Every door seemed closed against the stranger. He had no home, no friends, no chance of work, and he was likely soon to be out of money, although his first night in New York was passed in the open air, where he slept amid piles of barrels. He felt all the more alarmed because he had never before taken the full responsibility of looking after himself.

At last he was obliged to tell his story to a sailor who looked good-natured, and he took him at once to his own house, and then to that of the Secretary of the New York Vigilance Committee, Mr. David Ruggles. Here he was sheltered for several days, during which time Anna Murray came on from Baltimore and became his wife. She could not have been married to him according to the laws of Maryland. He stated afterwards, in a letter to Captain Auld, that "Instead of finding my companion a burden, she was truly a help-mate."

The children of this marriage were Rosetta, born June 24, 1839; Lewis Henry, October 2, 1840; Frederick, March 3, 1842; Charles Remond, October 24, 1844; and Annie, March 22, 1849. The certificate, as given in his "Narrative," is dated September 15; but this was Saturday, which was the day on which he traveled to New Bedford and found workmen busy on the wharves. The wedding took place, I understand, on Friday, September 14.

The bridegroom had heard of New Bedford as a place where he might be able to work at his trade. Accordingly the newly-married couple set out thither, on the day of the ceremony, by steamer, and in conformity with the system then universally enforced against people of color in the United States, spent the night on the deck. A stage-coach took them from Newport to New Bedford, but they had no money to pay for breakfast or to the driver, and he took possession of their baggage, which included three music books. What a wedding journey!

The entire trip from Baltimore to New Bedford occupied less than two weeks. The fugitive had changed his name from Bailey, first to Stanley, and then, before his marriage, to Johnson, and he soon made a final change. He had been recommended to

a free colored man, named Nathan Johnson, who at
once redeemed the baggage, in which was a music
book, the " Seraph," which I saw in use just fifty
years afterward in the Douglass mansion, near Washington. At Johnson's house the fugitives were treated
with the utmost kindness. During breakfast, the
Sunday after reaching New Bedford, the host remarked that there were so many Johnsons in the
town as to make it difficult to tell them apart. On
this he was invited to choose a surname for his guest,
who insisted on still calling himself Frederick " to
preserve a sense of my identity." Nathan Johnson had
just been reading the " Lady of the Lake," and he at
once selected the name of the noble fugitive. We
shall see, hereafter, that the choice was singularly
apt.

Among the first lessons which Douglass learnt at
New Bedford, was the immense superiority of free to
slave labor. On the very day he arrived he saw five
or six men do more work on the wharves, with the
aid of an ox and a pulley, than had been done by
twenty or thirty in Baltimore. He also soon found
out the fallacy of two assertions, often made before
the war, namely, that the South was more prosperous
than the North, and that the negro was incapable of
supporting himself as a free citizen. New Bedford
was the richest community in the United States in
proportion to its population, which trebled between
1820 and 1840. In 1838 she sent out nearly two
hundred whalers, and the previous year had brought
in a hundred and sixty thousand barrels of oil.
Nathan Johnson and his wife earned their bread by
hard work ; but these two colored people had a neater

house, better food, more books and newspapers, and more general information than nine-tenths of the slaveholders in Talbot County. Many a fugitive was living more comfortably than the master from whom he had fled less than seven years before. The colored people were better treated in New Bedford than in any other place, Northern or Southern ; their children went to school with the whites ; and their determination to stand by each other made the capture of a fugitive impossible.

Our hero now felt so safe that, on Monday morning, he dressed himself for work, and went out to find it. Seeing a pile of coal in front of a house he got leave to shovel it into the cellar. This was his first work as a freeman, and it was for the minister who had just been installed over the Unitarian Society, Rev. Ephraim Peabody. Four years earlier he had written from New Orleans to Harriet Martineau : "All my sympathies, and to a very great extent, my judgment is with the Abolitionists—entirely so if Dr. Channing is one." His preaching did not fulfill this promise, either at New Bedford, or afterward, at King's Chapel, where his ideal was "not an agitator, nor a revolutionist, nor a professional reformer." He and Douglass had much to teach each other ; the fugitive did get help from the clergyman, and if the latter's official position had not stood between them, it is possible that Unitarianism would have made an illustrious convert, that the oppressed would have gained an influential champion, and that King's Chapel would have lost the chance to get a pastor who could offend nobody. It was Mrs. Peabody who gave leave to carry in the coal, and it was she who

put two silver half-dollars into a hand which clasped
the coins gladly, in the knowledge that no master
could take them away, but whatever was earned by
the laborer would remain his own.

His next job was to help load a sloop with oil.   He
soon got courage enough to try to work at his trade
of calker, and a place was offered him by an anti-
slavery man who was fitting out a whaler.   He had
no sooner set foot on the float, however, than all the
white calkers declared that they would leave the ship
unfinished, if he were allowed to strike a single blow
upon her.   It was a busy season, and the employer
could do no better for him than give him work as a
common laborer.   The same prejudice met him everywhere, and obliged him to content himself with earning only a dollar a day, whereas he was perfectly
competent to earn two.   In this respect he was even
worse treated than in Baltimore, where he was paid
a dollar and a half a day, as much as any white man,
for calking.   Later in the season he supported himself by sawing wood for the whalers, and he never
worked harder, even for Brother Covey.   On borrowing Mr. Johnson's saw, he found it needed a cord as a
brace ; so he went to a store and asked for a fip's
worth, but was at once told, rather sharply, that he
must have come from the South.   No harm came
from this blunder, however, except a fright.

His wife went out to service, and he was obliged to
do so during the first winter, when prices were unusually high.   While waiter in the family of Colonel
John H. Clifford, who was Governor of Massachusetts
in 1853, he once listened with great delight to the
conversation of Robert C. Winthrop, behind whose

chair he stood. He seems, however, to have found
waiting at table less pleasant than even sawing wood,
rolling oil casks, digging cellars, removing rubbish
from back yards, and scouring cabins. His preference
for steady work made him soon take a place in an oil
refinery, where he stayed as long as he was needed.
Then he found employment, with other colored men,
whom he esteemed highly, in fitting out whalers ;
and his last place in New Bedford was at Richmond's
brass foundry. Here he often worked every day and
two nights a week besides, his principal task being to
blow the bellows. This was afterward done by
steam ; but he kept working at it until he was promoted to blow one of the trumpets before whose
blast fell the walls of Jericho.

His zeal for religion had been much weakened by
what he saw of the white professors in Maryland ; but
now he felt that the Lord had brought him out of the
house of bondage, and he sought to unite with one of
the New Bedford churches. The Methodists, who
then worshiped in Elm Street, and afterward in
County Street, had, in 1838, a preacher who was so
attractive that Douglass determined to become a
member. He was not permitted, on account of his
color, to sit in the body of the house ; but he accepted
this proscription as a necessary deference to the
prejudices of the unconverted part of the congregation. He felt sure that the church members would
treat him as a man and a brother. "Surely," he said
to himself, "these Christian people have none of this
feeling against color. They, at least, have renounced
this unholy feeling. When none but the saints are
assembled they will certainly recognize us as children

of the same Father, and heirs of the same salvation on equal terms with themselves."

"Communion day came; the sermon was preached; the congregation departed; and I remained to see, as I thought, this holy sacrament celebrated in the spirit of its Great Founder. There were only about half a dozen colored people attached to the Elm Street Church at this time. After the congregation was dismissed these descended from the gallery and took a seat against the wall most distant from the altar. Brother B. was very animated, and sang very sweetly, 'Salvation, 'tis a joyful sound;' and soon he began to administer the sacrament. I was anxious to observe the bearing of the colored members; and the result was most humiliating. During the whole ceremony they looked like sheep without a shepherd. The white members went forward to the altar by the bench-full; and when it was evident that all the whites had been served with the bread and wine, Brother B., after a long pause, as if inquiring whether all the whites had been served, and fully assuring himself on that important point, then raised his voice to an unnatural pitch, and, looking to the corner where his black sheep seemed penned, beckoned with his hand, exclaiming, 'come forward, colored friends! come forward! You, too, have an interest in the blood of Christ. God is no respecter of persons. Come forward and take this holy sacrament to your comfort.' The colored members—poor, slavish souls—went forward as invited. I went out, and have never been in that church since."

Other churches were tried with the same result. When one of them was holding a revival, he ventured to try to sit on the broad aisle; but a deacon hastened to say, what was then often said by drivers of omnibuses, door-keepers at menageries and theaters, and officials on board of steamboats and railroad cars, "We don't allow niggers in here." After

many such rebuffs from the white ministers and deacons, he joined the African M. E. Zion Church, but
he soon left it, because the pastor was persuaded by
other clergymen to refuse, like them, to give out
notices of anti-slavery meetings. He remained, however, one of the colored Methodists, and occasionally
officiated as a lay preacher in the little school-house
on Second Street, where they worshiped.

During these early years at New Bedford, he saved
from drowning a boy, whom no one else ventured to
try to rescue ; a man named Sullivan had been also
saved at St. Michael's, after grappling with his pre-
server in a way which nearly proved fatal to them
both ; and a white boy, who broke through the thin
ice in a basin near Baltimore, owed his life to the
courage and presence of mind with which the black
boy, then only twelve, managed to reach him with an
oar.

The New Bedford Lyceum was not open at that
time to colored people, but they held many meetings
for discussion among themselves, and Douglass was
an eager listener, as well as an impressive speaker. He
had little time to read, but how well it was used may
be judged from his habit of nailing up a newspaper on
a post in the foundry, so that he could look at it
while he worked the heavy beam up and down to fill
the bellows. He made himself well acquainted with
Scott, Whittier, and other poets, while Combe's " Constitution of Man," taught him the supremacy of law
and order in nature, as well as the possibility of
attaining happiness here on earth by obedience to
natural laws. This book, he says, " relieved my path
of many shadows ;" but what he read most devoutly,

next to the Bible, was the "Liberator." Soon after
becoming a subscriber, he listened, on April 15, 1839,
to a lecture from Garrison, of whom he speaks thus:

"As I looked upon this man from the gallery of old Liberty
Hall, then otherwise deserted, dilapidated, and in ill-repute,
with its wood-work defaced, its doors off hinges, and its windows broken by stones and bad eggs, thrown to break up anti-
slavery meetings, the only place in town where such meetings
could be held, I saw that the hour and the man were well met
and well united. In him there was no contradiction between
the speech and the speaker, but absolute sympathy and one-
ness. The faces of millions of men might be searched without
finding one just like his; at least, it seemed so to me. In him
I saw the resurrection and the life of the dead and buried hopes
of my enslaved people. As I now remember, the style of Mr.
Garrison's speaking would not be called eloquent. There was
no fine flow of words, no dazzling sentences formed to tickle
the ear. His power was the power which belongs only to
character, conviction, and high moral purpose, and which cannot well be counterfeited."—(" Thoughts and Recollections of
the Anti-Slavery Conflict." A Lecture not yet printed.)

The express statement (in "Life and Times of
Frederick Douglass," pp. 242-3), about the first Abolitionist, that, "On this occasion he announced nearly
all his heresies," has been declared inconsistent with
his habits when he spoke as agent of the Massachusetts Anti-Slavery Society, which was then the case.
("William Lloyd Garrison: the Story of His Life.
Told by his Children." Vol. ii., p. 292, note.)

The columns of the "Liberator," however, were
full of arguments in favor of making no resistance to
evil, and it is possible that some allusion to this subject may have inadvertently been made in the lecture,

and eagerly taken up by an enthusiastic hearer, who did not see that he had demonstrated the falsity of the doctrine in his own victory over slavery, in the person of Covey. In this and other respects, Douglass was then an ardent Garrisonian. He "loved this paper and its editor ;" he took frequent occasion to attack slavery, not only in assemblages of colored pec₊ple, but in conversation with white laborers, and he promptly attended every anti-slavery meeting in New Bedford, his "heart burning at every true utterance against the slave system, and every rebuke of its friends and supporters."

Among other speakers whom he heard in Liberty Hall was Rev. Dr. Garnett, a man of pure African blood, afterwards Minister to Liberia. It is remarked that only a man who has felt the iron of slavery in his own soul, and has been accustomed to look on his own race as doomed and altogether wanting in great mental qualities " can well imagine my exultant feeling, while looking upon, and listening to, this brilliant contradiction to the degrading and disheartening theories which had been forced upon me by nearly all my previous history."

Such speakers were sorely needed in 1840. The Pennsylvania Abolition Society had been formed, books had been printed against slavery, and laws to check its increase had been passed before the Revolutionary War. Soon after that struggle, new societies were formed in Rhode Island, Connecticut, New York, New Jersey, Delaware, Maryland, and even Virginia. Vermont prohibited the wicked institution in 1777 ; and her example was followed throughout the North. A demand for immediate emancipation

was published in 1816, and another in 1824. Few
desired any but gradual measures, however ; and the
general character of the controversy was mild and
peaceable before 1830. Then began what Harriet
Martineau has called " The Martyr Age of the United
States." William Lloyd Garrison insisted zealously,
as one of the editors of a Baltimore newspaper, in
1829, on immediate and unconditional emancipation,
without expatriation. He showed that the Coloniza-
tion Society, while professedly friendly to the colored
race, was really an enemy ; and he frequently exposed
the horrors of the domestic slave trade, then flour-
ishing rankly in Baltimore. An attack on a merchant
in Massachusetts, who allowed his ship to be employed
in this traffic, caused Garrison to be imprisoned for
seven weeks, in the spring of 1830. He could get no
church that fall in Boston for his lectures, nor any
hall, except one belonging to a society of unbelievers,
who showed especial interest in his cause, and who
did believe in freedom of speech. The first number
of the "Liberator" was published on January 1,
1831 ; and before the close of that year, five thousand
dollars was offered by the State of Georgia as a reward for kidnapping the editor. Opposition only
made him more zealous and steadfast. To a fellow-
laborer, who urged him at this time to keep cool,
saying, "Why, you are all on fire !" he answered,
"Brother May, I have need to be all on fire, for I
have mountains of ice about me to melt."

And it must not be supposed that all the fire and
fury were on one side. Among the events of the
seven years between 1831 and 1839 were the following. A Connecticut lady was put into a prison cell,

which had been occupied by a murderer, because she was trying to educate colored girls; she and her pupils were molested in every possible way, and the school was finally broken up by attempts to burn and tear down her house. An academy, which was opened to colored people in New Hampshire, was dragged from its foundations by a hundred yoke of oxen, according to a vote in town-meeting, and set up as a laughing-stock upon the common. The formation of anti-slavery societies in New York and Philadelphia took place with great difficulty, amid dangerous mobs. The meeting of the American Society in New York, on July 4, was broken up by rioters, who held possession of the city for three days, and did much damage to churches, schools, and private residences; and that August a Philadelphia mob destroyed forty-four houses of colored people and murdered a black man, while another was drowned in trying to escape. One day, in the next year, October 21, 1835, there were three mobs, that in broad-cloth which put a rope around Garrison's waist, tore his clothes from his body, and might have injured him seriously, if a refuge had not been found in Boston jail; that headed by a member of Congress, which drove out of Utica, New York, a convention of some seven hundred delegates, engaged in the formation of a State anti-slavery society; and that which broke up a meeting in Montpelier, Vermont. The brother of the Connecticut lady just mentioned was then serving out a sentence of eight months in the Washington jail for having used anti-slavery newspapers as wrappers for botanical specimens; and a divinity student, who had committed a similar offence at Nashville, Tennessee,

was whipped with twenty lashes on his bare back.
And among the outrages of 1835 should also be mentioned the attempts of various Southern States to
have their example, in suppressing all discussion of
slavery, carried out, by law as well as by violence,
throughout the North. During the next year the
printing-press of J. G. Birney, soon to be a candidate
for the Presidency, was destroyed by a Cincinnati
mob ; a New England clergyman was sentenced to
three months of hard labor in the house of correction
for his lectures ; and despotic interference with the
mails was proposed in Congress. But these details
seem almost trivial when we think that a fugitive
slave was burned alive in St. Louis soon after, for
having stabbed the officers who took him prisoner ;
that a Presbyterian clergyman, who was trying to
save from destruction the printing office, where he
had denounced this and other fruits of slavery, was
shot dead in Illinois ; and that Pennsylvania Hall,
which had been built at a cost of $40,000, as a place
for freedom of speech about all reforms, was burned
by a mob, who also set on fire the "Shelter for
Colored Orphans."

All these persecutions took place before the arrival
of Mr. Douglass in New Bedford, where he must
have heard them often discussed ; and they show,
like his own treatment in churches and shipyards,
that the North was still with the South against his
race. All the anti-slavery philanthropists were but a
helpless minority, amid the violence of opposition,
which marshaled churches and newspapers, State and
city governments, police and militia, colleges and
courts of justice, fine ladies and business men,

laborers and rowdies, in fact, almost the entire population of the free States against them. The evils of
slavery were scarcely realized in the North ; the
pressure of family, denominational, political, and
commercial ties with the South, was very strong ;
fears that agitation would bring on civil war had
already been excited ; and many good and wise men
considered themselves bound by the Constitution of
the United States to refrain from any attacks on institutions whose preservation seemed guaranteed by
that great compact. Conservative people were especially alarmed at the irreverence with which the laws
and the Constitution were treated, as well as at the
encouragement of women to speak in public. The
latter fact was peculiarly important to the clergy, as
the former was to lawyers and business men.

Disunionism could not, strictly speaking, be fairly
charged against the Abolitionists before 1842 ; but
the Declaration of Sentiments, which had been
adopted nine years earlier by the American Anti-
Slavery Society, on organizing at Philadelphia, and
which had been drawn up by Garrison, with the
approval of Whittier and S. J. May, speaks thus of
the support given to slave-holders by people of the
free States, under the Constitution : " This relation
to slavery is criminal and full of danger ; it must be
broken up." Even from the beginning there was
strong temptation to overlook the many peculiarly
good features of our form of government, in the
earnestness of indignation against one black spot.
Mr. Garrison was led, by a desire to follow the
Gospels literally, into maintaining that physical force
ought never to be used in resisting evil, or accepted

as the foundation of government. He declared in the "Liberator" for 1837, that human governments are the results of disobedience to God, that they are to be preferred to anarchy just as is "the small-pox to the Asiatic cholera," and that "They are all anti-Christ. ("William Lloyd Garrison : the Story of His Life. Told by His Children." Vol. ii., pp. 150, 202.)

Whittier complained that "He fills his paper with no-governmentism," and Elizur Wright declared that "His plan of rescuing the slave by the destruction of human laws is fatally conflictive with ours." The discontent of the most patriotic Abolitionists was increased, as he founded, in 1838, a Non-Resistance Society, with the approval of Oliver Johnson, S. J. May, Edmund Quincy, H. C. Wright, Stephen S. Foster, Lydia Maria Child, Maria W. Chapman, Abby Kelley, and Lucretia Mott. The Declaration of Sentiments pledged its members not to vote or hold office, and it is expressly stated, that "We cannot acknowledge allegiance to any human government."

Such language, at a time when an anti-slavery meeting was sure to call out a mob, was more courageous than prudent. A clergyman or magistrate might seem to justify himself for declining to interfere by saying : "Men who disown allegiance to our government have no right to be protected against the righteous indignation which is called out by their disloyalty. They are to blame themselves for these mobs." We can all see now that these early Abolitionists were men and women of whom the world was not worthy ; but I cannot help regretting that they were not a little more under the guidance of worldly wisdom.

Mr. Garrison's anarchism, as it would now be called, was particularly important, because this was in all probability, as is expressly stated by a fellow-champion who is also one of the historians of the great conflict, William Goodell, what kept him from becoming " an early and zealous leader of the Liberty party." This organization, which developed first into the Free Soil and then into the Republican party, and finally abolished slavery, nominated a singularly good candidate for the presidency in 1840. Birney had been a prominent lawyer in Alabama, and had emancipated his slaves before he tried, first in Kentucky, and then in Ohio, to edit an anti-slavery paper which was destroyed three times by mobs ; and he was then serving as secretary of the American Anti-Slavery Society. The nomination was supported by Whittier, Sewall, Goodell, Gerrit Smith, Myron Holley, and other prominent Abolitionists, and it was made under the official direction of the State Anti-Slavery Society of New York. Most of the men who sympathized with the movement were determined to vote, and the only question was whether they should support Birney or one of the pro-slavery candidates, Van Buren and Harrison. The 'good of the cause demanded that the vote of the Liberty party should be made as large as possible, and I see a sad lack of ability either to appreciate a republican form of government, or to coöperate with those who differed with him even slightly, in Garrison's course. He followed up the nomination by expressing in the " Liberator " his surprise at " the folly, the presumption, the almost unequaled infatuation of the handful of Abolitionists." It rested largely with him to say

what gains should be made by this handful among
the two hundred thousand members of the anti-
slavery societies ; and Birney's failure to get much
more than seven thousand votes was largely due to
the action taken six weeks after his nomination by
the Garrisonians at the annual meeting of the
American Anti-Slavery Society in May, 1840, in New
York. Fearing to be outvoted, about four hundred
and fifty of them came from New England by a
special steamer, forming what their leader called in
the " Liberator " " a heart-stirring spectacle ! " About
a hundred others of his followers came by rail ; and,
as only about a thousand votes were cast, the convention was completely under his control. He used it to
pass resolutions, disapproving of the nomination of
Birney and another Abolitionist, " as inexpedient and
injurious to the cause," and declaring that " We
cannot advise our friends to waste their energies in
futile efforts to promote their election."

There is no pleasure in dwelling on the mistakes of
men like Garrison, and I hasten to speak of a point of
controversy where he was clearly in the right. One
reason why he and his adherents captured the convention was that they feared it might be packed
against them by men who wished to shut out all
women from the work. Lucretia Mott was not allowed to vote at the formation of the American Society, in 1833, but only to speak ; the two sexes had
to organize separate associations ; and it was not considered proper for women to advocate reforms in
print or in any place more public than a Quaker
meeting-house. Shortly before Garrison was mobbed
in Boston, he published, in the " Liberator," a letter of

sympathy from the daughter of a judge in the Supreme Court of South Carolina. Miss Angelina Grimké had abandoned her home and family in horror at the system in which she had been brought up, and in 1836 she felt it her duty to publish an "Appeal to Southern Women," which was publicly burned by the postmasters in South Carolina, while the Mayor of Charleston sent her word that she could not be suffered to go there on a visit to her mother. She was soon afterward invited to hold a series of women's meetings in New York parlors, but the audience increased so much that she made the unheard-of innovation of speaking in the session room of a Baptist church. Her next step was to address colored people of both sexes, and in June, 1837, at Lynn, she spoke for the first time to a mixed audience in which white men listened eagerly. Her sister Sarah assisted her ; both asserted their right to speak and publish ; and both were denounced by the Congregational ministers of Massachusetts in the " Pastoral Letter," best known through the poem which was called out in reply from Whittier. Even he, however, felt obliged to warn them privately against injuring the cause of the slave by bringing in a new question prematurely. " Carolina's high-souled daughters," as he calls them, knew better than any one else how to help the slave, and Angelina was soon seen standing in the Speaker's place in the Hall of Representatives in Boston, speaking to the members of the Legislature, while the seats were filled with the best and brightest people in the State. Her last appearance in public was in Pennsylvania Hall, before a mob who became quiet under the power of

her voice ; but twenty hours later the building was
set on fire. She had then been for three days a bride.

By this time there were fighting in the front rank
against slavery, not only Lucretia Mott and the
Grimké sisters, but Mrs. Lydia Maria Child, Miss
Abby Kelley, who has been sadly confounded with the
half-witted Abby Folsom, and that gifted lady whose
activity had caused her to be nick-named " Captain
Chapman." To recognize their services was simply
just, and it would have been a disgrace to the cause
if the American Society had failed, in May, 1839, to
enlarge its membership beyond the line of sex. The
motion was supported by Garrison, Phillips, Gerrit
Smith, C. C. Burleigh, and Oliver Johnson, but it had
only a hundred and eighty-one votes against a hundred and forty-one. A year later the question was
decided again in the same way, by giving Miss Kelley
a place on a committee ; and this time the vote was
five hundred and fifty-seven against four hundred
and fifty-one. The fact that each side had trebled its
strength favors the supposition that both had tried to
pack the convention.

The result of this action, and of the attack on the
Liberty candidates, was a secession in which clergymen were prominent. Rival societies were formed ;
and a new paper was started in opposition to the
" Liberator." This last manifestation was short-lived;
but it is estimated that about four-fifths of the men
who had been working with Garrison, now parted
company with him permanently. Most of the churches
which had hitherto been open to the Garrisonians
were now closed against them. Where they did
speak, their audiences were, for a time, unexpectedly

scanty ; and Stephen S. Foster was driven to adopt
the plan of speaking in church without leave, where
he had failed to obtain it. What he suffered in consequence will be told in the next chapter. It must
now be remarked that, previous to 1841, the Abolitionists had shown no hostility to the Church ; although
they had good reason to regret her supporting slavery against them. They were among the most saintly
of her children, and they still hoped to save her from
being misled by time-serving hirelings. If the Garrisonians erred at all in regard to the Gospel, it was
in following it too literally and zealously.   It is true,
that Garrison had called out some opposition by
views about the Sabbath, which do not now seem
irreligious ; but his main heresies were in regard to
the prejudices about color and sex.

No one of these new movements can be properly
understood, except by looking at it in connection with
many other recent and alarming innovations. The year
1840 stood nearer to 1890, in the readiness with which
all received opinions, even about clothing and food,
were called in question, than to 1820, when controversy was mainly inside of the old-fashioned limits.
Then Sidney Smith complained that " The Americans are a brave, industrious, and acute people ; but
they have hitherto given no indications of genius,
and made no approaches to the heroic, either in their
morality or in their character." . . . " During
the thirty or forty years of their independence, they
have done absolutely nothing for the sciences, for the
arts, for literature, or even for the statesman-like
studies of politics or political economy." . . . " In
the four quarters of the globe, who reads an American

book ? " Twenty years, from the time when these
words were written, sufficed to bring forward Emerson, Channing, Prescott, Bancroft, Poe, Hawthorne,
Cooper, Holmes, Longfellow, Whittier, and other
authors who were read in many lands. The thinker,
who rightly stands first on this list, as most original,
and who has made many readers feel as completely
emancipated as Douglass did on reaching New Bedford, said in his lecture on " Man, the Reformer," in
1841 : " In the history of the world, the doctrine of
reform never had such scope as at the present hour."
Former accusers of society " all respected something
—Church or State, literature or history, domestic
usages, the market town, the dinner table, coined
money. But now these and all things else hear the
trumpet and must rush to judgment—Christianity,
the laws, commerce, schools, the farm, the laboratory;
and not a kingdom, town, statute, rite, calling, man,
or woman, but it is threatened by the new spirit." In
another lecture of the same year he says, " The present age will be marked by its harvest of projects for
this reform of domestic, civil, literary, and ecclesiastical institutions. The leaders of the crusades against
war, negro slavery, intemperance, government based
on force, usages of trade, court and custom-house
oaths, and so on to the agitators on the system of
education and the laws of property, are the right successors of Luther, Knox, Robinson, Fox, Penn, Wesley,
and Whitefield."

Before these last words were spoken in public, the
band of agitators had been joined by a new member,
who had deeper experience than any of his brethren
of the wrongs which he helped to right. We shall see

him rapidly rise to his full height of culture and genius, bear his share of persecution, and master all the conditions of success in that great reform with which his name is forever associated, so thoroughly as to grow wiser than his original teacher, Garrison, and do good service in rolling up the anti-slavery votes from the seven thousand for Birney, in 1840, to the eighteen hundred thousand, in 1860, for Abraham Lincoln.

CHAPTER III.

THE CRUSADER.

At the beginning of August, 1841, an anti-slavery convention was held at New Bedford, where Douglass heard not only Garrison, but Parker Pillsbury, a Universalist clergyman named Bradburn, and other leading Abolitionists ; and he became so much interested that he determined to take a holiday, the first he had that summer, and go with his wife to attend the next series of meetings at Nantucket. He had already become somewhat noted as a speaker to colored people ; but he felt greatly embarrassed when, on the evening of Wednesday, August 11, as is recorded in the " Liberator," he was called out, for the first time in his life, to address a white audience. " My speech on this occasion," he says, " is about the only one I ever made of which I do not remember a single connected sentence. It was with the utmost difficulty that I could stand erect, or that I could command and articulate two words without hesitation and stammering. I trembled in every limb." He has since told me, that he did manage to thank the champions of his race for their devotion, and also to express his hearty sympathy with their methods. It was then too late in the evening to say more. The impression he made was so favorable, however, that

57

he was persuaded to open the last session of the
Nantucket convention the next morning, when, as is
related by Garrison, "After apologizing for his ignorance and reminding the audience, that slavery is a
poor school for the human intellect and heart, he
proceeded to narrate some of the facts in his own
history as a slave, and in the course of his speech gave
utterance to many noble thoughts and thrilling reflections." He could not safely tell his real name, or his
master's, or where he had lived in the South ; but
according to Parker Pillsbury, he succeeded in prov-
ing that he had been there by giving "a most side-
splitting specimen of a slave-holding minister's sermon," on the text, "Servants, obey in all things your
masters." A passage from this very effective parody
will be found in the next chapter, where Miss Holley
quotes it as she heard it, two years later, in Buffalo.

The meetings had begun tamely, but gradually
gained in fervor ; and now "The crowded congregation had been wrought up almost to enchantment, as
he turned over the terrible apocalypse of his experiences in slavery." Then Garrison arose ; and as
Douglass says, his speech "was one never to be forgotten by those who heard it. Those who had heard
him oftenest, and had known him longest, were
astonished. It was an effort of unequalled power,
sweeping down, like a very tornado, every opposing
barrier." Garrison says himself, "I think I never
hated slavery so intensely as at that moment." He
began by declaring that Patrick Henry never spoke
more eloquently in the cause of liberty. Then, according to Pillsbury, he asked, "Have we been listening to a thing, a piece of property, or to a man ?"

"A man! A man!" shouted full five hundred voices.
"And should such a man be held a slave in a republican and Christian land?" "No, no! Never, never!"
"Shall such a man ever be sent back to slavery from
the soil of old Massachusetts?" shouted Garrison,
with all his power of voice. "Almost the whole
assembly sprang with one accord to their feet, and
the walls and roof of the Athenæum seemed to shud-
der with the 'No, no!' loud and long continued in
the wild enthusiasm of the scene. As soon as Garrison could be heard, he caught up the acclaim, and
superadded: 'No! a thousand times no! Sooner
the lightnings of heaven blast Bunker Hill monument,
till not one stone shall be left standing upon another.'"
(Pillsbury, "Acts of the Anti-Slavery Apostles," pp.
325–8.)

Before Douglass returned to New Bedford, he
accepted an invitation from Mr. Collins, agent of the
Massachusetts Anti-Slavery Society, to enter into its
service as a lecturer, and go to and fro with him, telling his story wherever he could find an audience.
His salary was to be four hundred and fifty dollars a
year. He was very unwilling at first, not only
because he would be dangerously exposed to discovery and arrest, but because he distrusted his own
ability. The Abolitionists insisted on his enlisting in
their forlorn hope; "and I finally consented to go
out for three months, for I supposed I should have
got to the end of my story and my usefulness in that
length of time." He has been out before the public,
pleading for his race, almost fifty years, and he has
not yet got to the end of his usefulness.

The next place where he seems to have attracted

much notice was Hingham, where he spoke at the
Plymouth County convention, November 4. According to an article copied into the " Liberator," from
the " Hingham Patriot," he reminded those who saw
him of Spartacus, the rebel gladiator, as presented by
Forrest. " A man of his shrewdness, and his power,
both intellectual and physical, must be poor stuff,
thought we, to make a slave of. Any way, we would
not like to be his master." . . . . " He is very fluent
in the use of language, choice and appropriate language, too ; and talks as well, for all we could see, as
men who have spent all their lives over books." . . .
" His master valued him at $2,000. He told us that
he could distinguish a slave-holder or a slave by the
cast of his eye, the moment he saw one." He seems,
even then, to have done much more than tell his own
experience. He did, it is true, in favoring the presentation of petitions as a means of attracting notice,
relate how he learned himself who the " Bobolition-
ists " were, by hearing what they asked of Congress ;
but he went on to express his decided preference for
moral suasion over political action. " We ought to
do just what the slave-holders don't want us to do,
that is, use moral suasion." He called the pledge of
the North to return fugitives " the bulwark of
slavery ;" for it " discourages very many from making any attempt to gain their freedom." . . . " This is
the Union whose dissolution we want to accomplish ;
and he is no true Abolitionist who does not go against
this Union. The South cares not how much you talk
against slavery in the abstract. They will agree with
you, yet they will cling to it as for life ; and it is this
pledge, binding the North to the South, on which

they rely for its support." This is, of course, simply
what he had been taught by Garrison, Phillips, and
Collins. What was most original in his speeches at
this time was the zeal with which he lashed the
churches of the North for their alliance with those in
the South.

The most important work done by the Abolitionists
in 1841 was in Rhode Island. This State was still
under the charter of 1663, which had originally been
very liberal, but had now become plainly unjust.
The voters must not only be white, but must also be
holders, or eldest sons of holders, of real estate, so that
almost two-thirds of the men were disfranchised ; and
the majority of the Representatives were elected by a
portion of the State inhabited by only about one-
third of its citizens. Thus it was perfectly possible
for fifteen hundred men to get the control of a legislature which ruled over fifty thousand adults. About
seven hundred of the disfranchised men were colored.

A movement to enlarge the suffrage, and equalize
the representation, began in 1790, was renewed in
1829, and assumed formidable proportions in 1841.
The Legislature was willing to make some changes,
but not enough to satisfy the suffragists. These
Dorrites, as they were called, on account of being led
by Mr. T. W. Dorr, were mostly Democrats, and
were determined to have full justice done to the
white man at once. Those of them who wished to
do something for the colored man also were over-
ruled by the others, and persuaded to make a compromise. A new constitution was proposed in
November, 1841, allowing all white men to vote, but
postponing the question of enfranchising colored

people for decision afterwards; and all who would thus be entitled to the ballot were invited to show themselves at the polls on December 27, 28, or 29.

There were men in Rhode Island who were determined that the negro should have his just part in whatever reform was accomplished. A series of conventions was arranged for December, and among the companions of Douglass was one of whom he says " No man thrilled me more on the slavery question than Parker Pillsbury." There, too, were Abby Kelley and Stephen S. Foster, whose conscience was never at peace unless he was stirring up a mob. He was now carrying out his own favorite plan, of rebuking lukewarm ministers and congregations in the midst of what they called public worship, with such success that even he was satisfied. Again and again he was dragged out by deacons and class-leaders. His collar was torn off by excited Quakers in Lynn, and he had been put in prison several times before he was ejected, in September, 1842, from the City Hall in Portland, with only one tail left on his long coat. How he spoke to opponents may be imagined from this fact. A number of Methodist ministers were led, partly by sympathy and partly by curiosity, into one of the anti-slavery conventions in Boston. Foster recognized their peculiar costume, and began his speech thus: "Is there a single member of the Methodist Episcopal Church within the sound of my voice, who dares deny that he is a villain?" His three companions in Rhode Island were not so fond of church-work; but the violence of the mob was increased by prejudice against the color of Douglass and the sex of Miss Kelley. I cannot but feel indignant, even now, when I think of the foul words and rotten eggs that were hurled at her of whom Lowell wrote thus :

> " A Judith there, turned Quakeress,
> Sits Abby in her simple dress.
>
> *   *   *   *   *   *   *
>
> No nobler gift of heart or brain,
> No life more white from spot or stain,
> Was e'er on Freedom's altar laid
> Than hers—the simple Quaker maid."

Convention after convention was mobbed, but still the friends of equal suffrage went on pointing out the black spot in the Dorr constitution. Its supporters were indignant, and its opponents rejoiced to see the suffragists at war among themselves. Of the last of these conventions, and one of the noisiest, that held in Providence, while the vote was being taken on the merits of the new plan, we have the following description, from the pen of Mr. N. P. Rogers, who was making the " Herald of Freedom," published at Concord, New Hampshire, a noble ally of the " Liberator " :

" Friday evening was chiefly occupied by colored speakers. The fugitive Douglass was up when we entered. This is an extraordinary man. He was cut out for a hero. In a rising for liberty, he would have been a Toussaint or a Hamilton. He has the ' heart to conceive, the head to contrive, and the hand to execute.' A commanding person—over six feet, we should say, in height, and of most manly proportions. His head would strike a phrenologist amid a sea of them in Exeter Hall, and his voice would ring like a trumpet in the field. Let the South congratulate herself that he is a fugitive. It would not have been safe for her, if he had remained about the plantations a year or two longer. Douglass is his fugitive name. He did not wear

it in slavery. We don't know why he assumed it, or who bestowed it on him—but there seems fitness in it, to his commanding figure and heroic port. As a speaker he has few
equals. It is not declamation—but oratory, power of debate. He watches the tide of discussion with the eye of the
veteran, and dashes into it at once with all the tact of the forum
or the bar. He has wit, argument, sarcasm, pathos—all that
first-rate men show in their master efforts. His voice is highly
melodious and rich, and his enunciation quite elegant ; and yet
he has been but two or three years out of the house of bondage.
We noticed that he had strikingly improved since we had heard
him at Dover in September. We say thus much of him, for he
is esteemed by our multitude as of an inferior race. We should
like to see him before any New England legislature or bar, and
let him feel the freedom of the anti-slavery meeting, and see
what would become of his inferiority. Yet, he is a thing, in
American estimate. He is the chattel of some pale-faced
tyrant. How his owner would cower and shiver to hear him
thunder in an anti-slavery hall. How he would shrink away,
with his infernal whip, from his flaming eye when kindled with
anti-slavery emotion. And the brotherhood of thieves, the
posse comitatus of divines, we wish a hecatomb or two of the
proudest and flintiest of them, were obliged to hear him thunder for human liberty, and lay the enslavement of his people at
their doors. They would tremble like Belshazzar. Poor Way-
land, we wish he could have been pegged to a seat in the Frank-
lin Hall the evening the colored friends spoke. His ' limitations '
would have abandoned him like the ' baseless fabric of a vision.'
Sanderson, of New Bedford, Cole, of Boston, and Stanley,
of North Carolina, followed Douglass. They all displayed excellent ability." . . . " These are the inferior race, these young
black men, who, ten years ago, would have been denied en-
trance into such an assembly of whites, except as waiters or
fiddlers. Their attempts at speaking would have been met with
jeers of astonishment. It would have amazed the superior race
as the ass's speech did Balaam. Now they mingle with
applause in the debates with Garrison, and Foster, and Phillips,

Southern slavery—' hold thine own '—when the kindred of your victims are thus kindling Northern enthusiasm on the platform of liberty and free debate."

A series of events in 1842, which attracted much attention at the time, justified fully the course pursued by the Abolitionists against the Dorrites. These latter attempted, merely as agents of the popular will, and without any sanction from the laws of the land, to substitute the new constitution for the old one, and make their leader Governor. President Tyler was appealed to by the lawful Governor, and promised him the support of the nation. Dorr tried to seize upon the administration by force ; but most of the leading citizens, including his father and brother, took up arms against him ; his most influential supporters deserted him; the cannons which he attempted to discharge with his own hands against the state troops, were found to be primed with wet paper ; and he was soon obliged to disband his adherents. The law and order party, who were nicknamed Algerines, on account of their severity, made their victory permanent, by enacting, before the end of 1842, the constitution which was in force until very recently, and which has admitted black men to vote on the same terms as white, the property qualification being reduced so far as to allow any citizen to vote who would pay a tax of one dollar, and who had resided two years in the State.

These details are important, because this experience, of the advantage of acting in harmony with our national spirit of respect for the laws and for the magistrates elected under them, may have done something to prepare Douglass for breaking with the

Garrisonian disunionists, as he ultimately did. At this time, however, he was completely carried away by his admiration for the enthusiasts, who gave their lives to the emancipation of his race, and who were free from that prejudice against any association with colored people, which was then almost universal at the North. He was surprised and delighted at the friendly welcome they gave him when he came to Boston in January, 1842. The first house in the city, where he was welcomed as a guest, was that of one of the few members of the Liberty party, Dr. Henry I. Bowditch, who was, he says, " the first of his color who ever treated me as if I were a man." This organization was not, however, handled very tenderly in the speech which he delivered before the Massachusetts Society in the Melodeon, on Wednesday, January 26. On Thursday evening he helped Garrison, Phillips, Rogers, and Abby Kelley take advantage of the convention's having been invited to occupy the Representatives' Hall, in the State House, to pass a resolution declaring " That Massachusetts is degraded and dishonored by her connection with Southern slavery; that this connection is not only dishonorable, but in the highest degree criminal; and that it must be broken up, at whatever sacrifice or hazard." If the meaning of these words was not plain enough, it was made so twenty-four hours afterward.

The next evening, Friday, January 28, an audience of four thousand people was collected in Faneuil Hall, to demand the abolition of slavery in the District of Columbia. Garrison presided; and, among the resolutions which were adopted, was one declaring that " The American Union is such only in form, but not in substance, a hollow mockery instead of a glorious reality." This action was taken with the hearty support of both Phillips and Douglass. The latter enlivened the proceedings by giving his very funny imitation of the way in which slave-holding clergymen would exhort servants to obey their masters. His mimicry of the Southern preacher's whine was irresistibly comical.

This sermon was often delivered by him in county conventions and other local meetings. His conscience was clear in the use of this weapon; for he was convinced, to quote a resolution which he introduced at Worcester, January 6, 1842, that, "The sectarian organizations of this country, called churches, are, in supporting slavery, upholding a system of theft, adultery, and murder; and it is the duty of Abolitionists to expose their true character before the public." His own attempts to get a chance to plead for his race in the pulpit were often unsuccessful; and he tells me that "When I asked for a church and the minister said, 'Brother Douglass, I don't know about this. I must ask the Lord. Let us pray,' I always knew I should not get it." He used to say in his early lectures, that he had offered many prayers for freedom; but he did not get it, until he prayed with his legs. His dissatisfaction with the clergy even led him to sing the parody on a familiar hymn, about being saved from a burning hell, and dwelling with Immanuel "in heavenly union."

> " Come, saints and sinners, hear me tell,
> How pious priests whip Jack and Nell,
> And women buy, and children sell,
> And preach all sinners down to hell,
> And sing of heavenly union.

" They'll bleat and baa, dona like goats
Gorge down black sheep, and strain at motes,
Array their backs in fine black coats,
Then seize their niggers by the throats,
    And choke for heavenly union.

" They'll church you, if you sip a dram,
And damn you, if you steal a lamb,
Yet rob old Tony, Doll, and Sam,
Of human rights, and bread and ham,
    Kidnappers' heavenly union.

" They'll loudly talk of Christ's reward,
And bind his image with a cord,
And scold, and swing the lash abhorred,
And sell their brother in the Lord,
    To hand-cuffed heavenly union.

" They'll read and sing a sacred song,
And make a prayer both loud and long,
And teach the right, and do the wrong,
Hailing the brother, sister throng,
    With words of heavenly union.

*   *   *   *   *   *   *

" They'll raise tobacco, corn, and rye,
And drive, and thieve, and cheat and lie,
And lay up treasure in the sky,
By making switch and cowskin fly,
    In hope of heavenly union.

" They'll crack old Tony on the skull,
And preach and roar like Basham bull,
Or braying ass, of mischief full,
Then seize old Jacob by the wool,
    And pull for heavenly union.

" A roaring, ranting, sleek man-thief,
Who lived on mutton, veal, and beef,
Yet never would afford relief,
To needy, sable sons of grief,
    Was big with heavenly union.

"' Love not the world,' the preacher said,
And winked his eye, and shook his head.
He seized on Tom, and Dick, and Ned,
Cut short their meat, and clothes, and bread,
    Yet still loved heavenly union.

" Another preacher, whining, spoke,
Of one whose heart for sinners broke.
He tied old Nanny to an oak,
And drew the blood at every stroke,
    And prayed, for heavenly union.

" Two others ope'd their iron jaws,
And waved their children-stealing paws.
There sat their children in gewgaws !
By stinting negroes' backs and maws,
    They kept up heavenly union."

The " Liberator," of February 25, contains this little paragraph : " Will Frederick Douglass inform the general agent of his whereabouts ? " During the next three months he seems to have spoken almost every night in Massachusetts. His attacks on clerical conservatism, and on the color prejudice, were heard with delight ; but the attempts made by him and his associates to pledge their hearers to disunion, did not by any means meet with invariable success. He was indebted to the members of the Hopedale Community for a chance to speak at Milford, after having

been denied a hearing.   They told him, " We will go
there with you to-night, and you shall have forty of us
to hear you at all events."   That night the Milford people not only allowed him to speak to them in the town
hall, but kept as still as mice ; and there never afterward was any difficulty about his getting a hearing
there.   Among other places in Massachusetts where
he spoke, early in 1842, were Salem, Andover, and
Lexington.

When the American Society held its annual May
convention in New York, Douglass, Phillips, and
Abby Kelley tried to carry a resolution to the effect
that " The cause of human rights imperatively
demands the dissolution of the American Union."
They failed, although two hundred and fifty Garrisonians had come in a body from New England.
Garrison himself had thought it better, on account of
the open opposition of the managers of this society,
to send only a letter.   During the anti-slavery convention, which now formed one of the May meetings
in Boston, a fortnight after those in New York,
Phillips brought forward a resolution, calling the
Union "a rope of sand."   Abolitionism was now
rapidly becoming synonymous with disunionism in
Massachusetts, although there were still many thoroughly loyal and sagacious friends of the slave, like
Whittier, who now, according to an opinion expressed
by the editor of the " Liberator," on August 12, had
become " incapable of doing anything important for
the cause." . . . " Politics will complete his ruin ! "

Probably it was dislike of disunionism which
brought down a shower of stones and brickbats on
that same day in August, at Nantucket, upon Mr.

Douglass and his companions. Forty-eight hours before he had exposed the short-comings of the clergy in his most effective manner ; his mimicry is said to have been very amusing ; and there were probably friends of the Church in the mob. The year between his two visits to the island had made him a terror to all not in the anti-slavery ranks. Even then he was as irresistible in making men swear as in making them laugh. One thing also he could do better than any other of the anti-slavery orators, even Phillips. He could make people cry ; and he seldom spoke long before he could see " the white flags wave." He had by this time ceased to confine himself to telling his experience, and mimicking sermons and hymns. He now exposed the essential wickedness of slavery, as well as the guilt of the North in conniving at it, with such power and skill that his hearers found it hard to believe that he had grown up outside of the influence of schools and books. Mr. Collins began to fear that he would no longer be taken for a fugitive slave ; and he was advised not to speak such good English, but to use as much as he could of the plantation accent.

Soon after revisiting Nantucket, he followed Collins and Abby Kelley into the region where he was afterward to spend twenty of his most useful years. He spoke for the first time at Rochester, N. Y., on August 30. It was, I think, on his first visit to Western New York, that this little incident occurred at Victor, where he spoke on September 6. He was constantly annoyed in hotels, steamboats, and railway cars by the prejudice against his color, and never let a chance slip of rebuking it. He was now invited to

eat by himself, at a little table set out in one corner
of the dining-room, and at once asked the landlord
what he meant by it. "Why, you see, Mr. Douglass," was the reply, "I want to give you something
a little better than the rest." The joke was so good
that he could only say that he did not wish to have
any distinction made for his benefit, and eat his
dinner in peace. He tried at this time to speak in
Lima, but was told that the people there would not
let him. Instead of trying, like Foster, to make
them listen, he merely said : " The Lord can abolish
slavery without the aid of Lima."

The first place to which he was sent in New Hampshire was Concord. No hall or church could be
obtained then, in 1842, for an anti-slavery meeting, so
he took his stand, one Sunday afternoon, at the corner where a little court ran out from one of the principal streets, and collected an audience by appealing
to the sympathies of people on their way to church.

Among other New Hampshire towns which he
visited that summer was Pittsfield, where an offer to
entertain a speaker against slavery had been made by
a subscriber to the " Liberator," named Hilles. This
man's principles did not stand the sight of his visitor's
color, and he could not eat at the same table with his
guest. They did unite in family worship, but the
next morning Mr. Hilles drove off to church, with
two vacant seats in his phæton, leaving the lecturer
to walk two miles to the hall. He found no one
there to introduce him, but spoke an hour or two,
and then paused to give his hearers time to lunch.
No one offered him a morsel, not even Mrs. Hilles,
who was in the audience. One o'clock came and he

made his second speech that Sunday. By the time he had spoken he was very hungry. This time the people dispersed as soon as he had finished. He went to the tavern and offered to pay for a meal, but was told that "We don't entertain niggers." He went away hungry, and chilly also, for an east wind had sprung up, and rain was falling. He saw people looking at him from their comfortable homes as if he were a stray bear. At last he went into the grave-yard, where he "felt some relief in contemplating the resting-place of the dead, where there was an end to all distinctions between rich and poor, white and colored, high and low."

He was thinking of a Great Reformer, who had not "where to lay his head," when a gentleman came up and asked his name. "You do not seem to have any place to stay while in town. Well, I am not an Abolitionist, I'm a Democrat, but I'm a man. Come with me and I'll take care of you." Douglass accepted with thanks, but was surprised to find, before they reached the house, that this was the same Democratic Senator who had recently had a clergyman arrested in the pulpit for attacking slavery, and imprisoned. As soon as his children saw them enter they ran away, screaming "Mother, mother, there is a nigger in the house;" and it was all the father could do to quiet them. The mother, too, was evidently much disturbed; and only the kind assurances of Mr. Norris kept his guest from going back to the cemetery. When the storm had subsided he ventured to tell the lady that he had taken cold, and asked for a little sugar and water. The mother's heart was touched. She brought him what he wanted with her own hands, and after that he found himself fully welcome at his adversary's fireside. He spoke at five, and for the fourth and last time at seven. After that there was quite a contest between Mrs. Norris and Mrs. Hilles, as to which should entertain him over night. He decided to go back to his former quarters, and Mr. Hilles eagerly offered to drive him, saying, "I kind of missed you this morning." The next day Douglass was carried on to a neighboring town in the very carriage where he had not been permitted to ride twenty-four hours before ; and its owner told him that he felt it more of an honor to do this for him than for the President of the United States.

His most effective theme thus far had been the unfaithfulness of the clergy ; but he and the other Abolitionists were fortunate enough, before the close of 1842, to find an issue on which they could all unite and have the best men in the North with them. A fugitive from Virginia, named Latimer, was arrested without a warrant, at his master's request, under a false charge of theft, by men who pretended to act under the laws of Massachusetts, and was confined in the same jail where Garrison had found a refuge. Not only the enemies of slavery but other friends of liberty were indignant. On Sunday, October 30, all the clergymen who officiated in Boston were requested to pray for the prisoner, and also to read a notice of a mass-meeting to be held that evening in Faneuil Hall. Among the twenty-four clergymen who complied, in part at least, may be mentioned the honored names of Father Taylor, Baron Stow, Clarke, Dr. Lowell, Sargent, Waterston, Neale, and Brownson. Among the twenty who would not, were such eminent ecclesiastics as Huntingdon, Lothrop, Gannett, Whittemore, Blagden, and Nehemiah Adams.

Letters of cordial sympathy were read at Faneuil Hall that night, from Bancroft and John Quincy Adams, and Judge Sewall took the chair; and all the Boston ministers appear to have had followers in the audience. When Mr. Charles L. Remond, a colored man who had been brought up at the North and was doing a good work for his race, stepped forward to address the meeting, his voice was drowned by shouts of "Sell the nigger." Even the rioters were willing to listen to Wendell Phillips, though he said : "I know I am speaking to the white slaves of the North." Hisses followed, but he went on, "Yes, you dare to hiss me, of course. But you dare not break the chain which binds you to the car of slavery." The uproar after he concluded was so great, that Douglass is said to have stood before the audience for twenty minutes, making passionate gestures, but not succeeding in uttering a single audible word. Mrs. Folsom was in the hall, and was called for, as usual, by the rioters ; but this time she was saner than they, and would say nothing. Colored women who sat in the gallery, under the national emblem of Liberty, were stripped of their shawls and bonnets, and the whole scene was one which only sympathy with slave-holders could have produced in Boston on Sunday night. It is pleasant to read an account of a much more successful meeting a week later, in the same cause.

On November 8, Mr. Douglass wrote from Lynn to the "Liberator : "

"DEAR FRIEND GARRISON : The date of this letter finds me quite unwell. I have for a week past been laboring, in company with Bro. Charles Remond, in New Bedford, with especial reference to the case of our outraged brother, George Latimer, and speaking almost day and night, in public and private. . . . On Sunday we held three meetings in the Town Hall. . . . In the morning we had quite a large meeting, at the opening of which I occupied about an hour on the question whether a man is better than a sheep. . . . Long before the drawling, lazy church bells commenced sounding their deathly notes that afternoon, mighty crowds were making their way to the Town Hall. They needed no bells to remind them of their duty to bleeding humanity. . . . As I gazed upon them my soul leaped for joy. . . . The splendid hall was brilliantly lighted in the evening, and crowded with an earnest, listening audience. . . . A large number had to stand during the meeting, which lasted about three hours ; where the standing part of the audience were at the commencement of the meeting, there they were at the conclusion of it. . . . Prejudice against color was not there. . . . We were all on a level ; every one took a seat just where he chose ; there was neither man's side nor woman's side ; white pew nor black pew ; but all seats were free, and all sides free. . . . I again took the stand, and called the attention of the meeting to the case of Bro. George Latimer, which proved the finishing stroke of my present public work. On taking my seat I was seized with a violent pain in my breast, which continued till morning, and with occasional raising of blood. . . . It is a struggle of life and death with us just now. No sword that can be used, be it never so rusty, should lay in its scabbard. Slavery, our enemy, has landed in our very midst, and commenced its bloody work. . . . I can sympathize with George Latimer, having myself been cast into a miserable jail, on suspicion of my intending to do what he has said to have done, viz., appropriating my own body to my own use. My heart is full ; and had I my voice, I should be doing all that I am capable of for Latimer's redemption. I can do but little in any department ; but if one department is more the place for me than another, that one is before the people. I can't write to much advantage, having never had a day's schooling in my life; nor have I ventured to give publicity to any of my scribbling before; nor would I now, but for my peculiar circumstances.

"Your grateful friend,

"FREDERICK DOUGLASS."

It is a great pity that this misfortune marred his day of triumph. He had entered New Bedford a penniless fugitive, fit only for the most menial tasks. He left it a popular orator, a leader of the people in the noblest cause. He had made all his arrangements for removing to Lynn with his family, which now included three little children, and he succeeded in carrying out his plan on Monday or Tuesday. His recovery was so complete that he was able to sing the parody on slave-holding clergymen, at Essex, the last Sunday of the month. The day previous he had attempted in vain to amend a resolution proposed there by one of the leading Abolitionists, James N. Buffum. His resolution was passed, as follows: "Resolved, That no person ought to be considered a Christian unless he is a practical Abolitionist." The amendment proposed was to insert the words "who is acquainted with the principles of anti-slavery."

Latimer had, by this time, been purchased by Dr. H. I. Bowditch and other friends of the slave for four hundred dollars. He got his freedom; his master got the money; and the Abolitionists got an unusual amount of popular sympathy. Early next year they presented, at the State House, where Hon. Charles Francis Adams acted in their behalf, a petition with more than sixty thousand signatures, asking that

fugitives from slavery should never again be arrested
by town or city officials, nor held as prisoners in the
jails of this commonwealth ; and also that the Constitution of the United States should be so amended
as "shall forever separate the people of Massachusetts from all connection with slavery." The legislature made it a penal offence for any magistrate or
executive officer of the State to help arrest fugitives,
and forbade use of the jails for confining them. The
excitement sprang throughout New England and
into Western New York. The opposition to the
Fugitive Slave Bill did not cease until it was repealed;
and this was certainly one of the wisest parts of the
great anti-slavery movement. Nothing which its
advocates could say was heard so willingly by the
people, as the call to protect men and women already
at the North, from being dragged back into bondage.
All discussion of theories was tame in comparison
with appeals for individuals seen to be oppressed.

The Latimer meetings continued to be held during
the early months of 1843 ; and among the most enthusiastic speakers was Douglass. He was also a supporter of the resolution, passed on January 27, by the
State Society in Faneuil Hall, declaring that "The
compact between the North and the South is a cove-
nant with death and an agreement with hell," and that
" It should be immediately dissolved." On March 6,
he lectured in Amory Hall, Boston, on "Slavery as
actually existing in the South." Among the other
speakers in this course were Phillips, Pierpont, and
Garrison.

Fear that a new field might be opened for slavery,
by the annexation of Texas, was among the causes

which made the annual meeting of the American Society in New York, on May 9, 1843, larger than any
that had ever been held before, with the single exception of 1840. Then there was a bitter contest between
New York and New England. Now there was perfect unanimity; and most of the delegates came from
the West. Some of the friends traveled in wagons
from Pennsylvania and Illinois, holding meetings
along the road. One of the vehicles thus used was
named the "Liberator," and did good service that
same summer at conventions in Ohio and Indiana.
Douglass, on the second day, spoke thus: "Such
have been my habits of life as to instil into my heart
a disposition I can never quite shake off, to cower
before the white man. But one thing I can do. I
can represent here the slave, the human chattel." He
then introduced a resolution, stating that "The anti-
slavery movement is the only earthly hope of the
American slave." "Instead of being regarded as a
powerful aid to abolition," he continued, "it is far
too generally viewed as retarding that event. But
this is a grievous error, I know; for I speak from
experience." . . . "Prior to this movement, Sir,
the slave in chains had no hope of deliverance. But
when he heard of it, hope sprung up in his mind."
. . . "I knew, I felt that truth was above error,
that right was above wrong, that principle was above
prejudice, and that I should one day be free." . . .
"There is no hope for the slave in Church or State.
But this Society is above either Church or State. It
is moving both daily, more and more."

The resolution was seconded by Abby Kelley, whom
John Neal, who was one of the audience, describes as

"a pleasant Quakerish woman, with a white shawl on, the smoothest possible hair, the smoothest possible voice, and no very great superabundance of action." A more sympathetic observer praises her "fine person, clear blue eye, delicate complexion, fair hair, and lady-like hands." "Mr. Douglass," said she, "is free and can speak for himself; but his sisters are still in the hands of the outragers; and it is therefore fit that a woman should stand here by his side."

CHAPTER IV.

WHAT Shakespeare says of his Douglas, (" Henry IV.," Part I, Act V, Scene I), was perfectly true of our hero, as soon as he got over the embarrassment, caused by being suddenly brought into association with gentlemen and ladies whom he revered even more for their character than for their culture and race. He had not resided long in Lynn before he vindicated his rights, by main force, against the Eastern Railroad. This corporation had been denounced, week after week, in the "Traveller's Directory" in the " Liberator," for "an odious distinction on account of color, and a bullying propensity to carry it out." The passengers had fight after fight with conductors and brakemen, before the battle of which this account is given by a writer, who also describes the chief combatant :

" Mr. Douglass lived in Lynn about this time. He was not then the polished orator that he has since become, but even at that early date he gave promise of the grand part he was to play in the conflict which was to end in the destruction of the system that had so long cursed his race. He was more than six feet in height ; and his majestic form, as he rose to speak, straight as an arrow, muscular, yet lithe and graceful, his flashing eye, and more than all, his voice, that rivaled Webster's in its richness, and in the depth and sonorousness of its cadences, made up such an ideal of an orator as the listeners never forgot. And they never forgot his burning words, his pathos, nor the rich play of his humor. He had just escaped from the ' house of bondage ' ; and as he recited his experience as a slave, his sufferings as he grew old enough to realize the bitterness of his lot, his alternate hope and despair as he attempted to lift the veil of the future—his eyes would now flash with defiance, and now grow dim with emotions he could not control ; and the roll of his splendid voice, as he hurled his denunciations against the infamous system, would pass to the minor key, whose notes trembled on his tongue. Then, with inimitible mimicry, he would give a droll recital of some ludicrous scene in his experience as a slave, or with bitter sarcasm he would tell a tale of insult offered by some upstart who fancied he held his title to manhood by the whiteness of his skin ; and then again, with flashing eye, he would hurl his indignation at ' wickedness in high places,' against men who, under the pretended sanction of religion, defended the ' infernal institution,' whose horrors had filled his days with dread, and his night dreams with terror. An incident, which the writer heard him relate in his peculiar manner, half amusing and half indignant at the outrage he had suffered, occurred about this time. Its recital will sound strangely some years hence. These were the days when ' negro cars ' were on our railroads. Mr. Douglass and his friend, James N. Buffum, having purchased their tickets, entered one of the cars, not taking special pains to get into the negro car. It was on the Eastern Railroad, and they were bound for Newburyport. The conductor came along and, spying Mr. Douglass, asked him what he was in that car for. Mr. Douglass replied in substance, that he wanted to go to a certain place, and thought that the most direct way. The conductor ordered Mr. Douglass to leave. Mr. Douglass assured the conductor that he was satisfied with his seat, and excused himself from accepting the invitation. The conductor called to his aid two or three brakemen, who proceeded to make a demonstration, that looked as though Mr.

Douglass was to be taken from the car, without gaining the consent of his will or the aid of his limbs. It was amusing to hear Mr. Douglass relate this part of the scene. 'When they took hold of me,' said Mr. Douglass, with a broad grin, 'I felt my hands instinctively clutch the arms of the seat where I sat, and I seemed to be very firmly attached to the place.' But two or three stout brakemen were too much for young Douglass, though he had the grip of a giant ; or rather, they were too strong to deal with the kind of car furniture then in use. Douglass left the car, and left behind him an empty space in one end of it where seats had been."—(Johnson's "Sketches of Lynn," pp. 230–232.)

The amount of damage was to great that the superintendent refused, during two or three days, to allow any trains to stop for passengers at Lynn, while the people took part with their townsman. Some of them remonstrated with the official against his " Jim Crow Car," but he replied that they ought not to object to it, so long as the churches had negro pews. The only other railroad in the State which made this distinction was that on which Wendell Phillips rebuked the prejudice, in a way described as follows, in " Thoughts and Recollections of the Anti-Slavery Conflict," a lecture not yet published, by Frederick Douglass :

" I knew him, after delivering his famous lecture on ' The Lost Arts ' in New Bedford, Mass., more than forty years ago, enjoying the hospitality of the wealthiest citizens of that opulent city, and moving in its most refined society, to alight at the railroad station from a splendid carriage, walk deliberately down the platform, past the long line of elegantly cushioned and richly ornamented coaches, till he came to a little box next the engine, exposed to dust, sparks, and smoke, and there take his seat for Boston, because that miserable little box—then known as the Jim Crow Car—was exclusively set apart for negroes."

Douglass kept on fighting against this indignity, until it was abolished. After that he was, he says, a gainer by the color prejudice ; for it usually gave him the whole of a seat. He did, however, at first, feel annoyed at being shunned ; and he mentions gratefully, ("Bondage and Freedom," p. 403,) how Governor Briggs once asked for the vacant place, and behaved so courteously that no seat was more sought after in that car. Another time, he found only a single place left empty on a crowded train, and asked the man who sat next to it, to let him come in.

" My fellow-passenger gave me a look, made up of reproach and indignation, and asked me why I should come to that particular seat. I assured him, in the gentlest manner, that, of all others, this was the seat for me. Finding that I was actually about to sit down, he sang out, ' Oh, stop, stop ! and let me get out.' Suiting the action to the word, up the agitated man got, and sauntered to the other end of the car, and was compelled to stand for most of the way thereafter. Half-way to New Bedford, or more, Colonel Clifford, recognizing me, left his seat, and not having seen me before since I ceased to wait on him (in everything except hard arguments against his pro-slavery position), apparently forgetful of his rank, manifested in greeting me something of the feeling of an old friend. This demonstration was not lost on the gentleman whose dignity I had an hour before most seriously offended. Colonel Clifford was known to be about the most aristocratic gentleman in Bristol County ; and it was evidently thought I must be somebody, else I should not have been thus noticed by a person so distinguished. Sure enough, after Colonel Clifford left me, I found myself surrounded by friends ; and among the

number my offended friend stood nearest, and with an apology
for his rudeness, which I could not resist, although it was one
of the lamest ever offered."

About this time Mr. Douglass, on finding no church
open to him at Concord, New Hampshire, told his
audience, in the dirty Town Hall, that he was not a
fugitive from slavery, but still a fugitive in slavery,
and that it was because their religion sanctified the
system. This was on Sunday afternoon ; and that
evening, according to Mr. Rogers, after relating his
sufferings and struggles, "in a somewhat suppressed
and hesitating way, interesting all the while for its
facts, but dullish in manner, he closed his slave narrative, and gradually let out the outraged humanity
that was laboring in him, in indignant and terrible
speech. It was not what you could describe as oratory or eloquence. It was sterner, darker, deeper
than these. It was the volcanic outbreak of human
nature, long pent up in slavery and at last bursting its
imprisonment. It was the storm of insurrection ; and
I could not but think, as he stalked to and fro on the
platform, roused up like the Numidian lion, how that
terrible voice of his would ring through the pine
glades of the South, in the day of her visitation." . . .
"There was great oratory in his speech, but more of
dignity and earnestness than what we call eloquence.
He was not up as a speaker, performing. He was an
insurgent slave, taking hold on the rights of speech,
and charging on his tyrants the bondage of his race.
One of our editors ventured to cross his path by a
rash remark. He had better have run upon a lion.
It was fearful, but magnificent, to see how magnani-
mously and lion-like the royal fellow tore him to

pieces, and left his untouched fragments scattered around him."

The members of the New England Anti-Slavery Convention, which came together in Boston, May 30, 1843, were greatly encouraged by the strong opposition made in the legislature to the "Jim Crow Car," by the permission of intermarriage, by the passage in Vermont, as well as in Massachusetts, of laws to protect fugitives, and by the large attendance from the West in New York two weeks previous. It was agreed that one hundred conventions should be held in various States ; and the ablest of the speakers engaged was Douglass, who "never entered upon any work with more heart and hope."

The first meetings, held that July in Vermont, were thinly attended ; and the students of the Congregationalist College, at Middlebury, covered the town with placards, describing him as an escaped convict from the State prison, and doing equal justice to his companions. Thence they went to Western New York, where these disunionists were naturally regarded with some suspicion by the leaders of the Liberty party, who were re-organizing for the presidential campaign of 1844, with a vigor which crushed the hopes of one of their most formidable opponents, Henry Clay, and insured a much needed and highly beneficial reduction of the tariff. At their headquarters, Syracuse, no church or hall could at first be had by the Garrisonians. Some of them could think of nothing better than shaking off the dust from their feet against the wicked city ; but the Douglass was not to be defeated thus. On the morning appointed for opening the mass-meeting, July 31, he took his stand under a little tree, in the corner of the park, and began with an audience of five people. There were five hundred at the close of the afternoon meeting ; and they had the use of an abandoned church for the remainder of the convention, which continued three days longer.

Before it closed, there broke loose, from an unexpected quarter, a storm which might easily have wrecked Garrisonianism. Mr. John A. Collins, who engaged Douglass at Nantucket, two years before, to work for the Massachusetts society, was its general agent for five years, and had shown great energy, especially in packing conventions. How little he shared that single-hearted sincerity, which was the secret of the success of the Abolitionists, is shown by several incidents. In 1842 he complained to the county convention at Littleton, of a tavern-keeper, who charged twice the usual sum for taking care of his horse, saying that "this was cheap enough for Abolition beggars." The convention voted that the publican was "a public imposition ; " and he got a verdict for a hundred and fifty dollars in damages, as is related in the "Liberator" for that year, page 72. Collins had been a divinity student, and used to open meetings with prayer ; but, either this or the previous summer, he had been invited to say grace and had turned over the duty to Douglass, who went through it with an embarrassment which was much increased by the pinches which were administered under the table. As soon as they were alone together, the "field-hand" remonstrated with his superior, who said, with a laugh, "If your religion cannot stand a pinch, it is not worth much." "Mr. Collins," was the reply, "you took me off of the wharf in New Bedford ;

and I had rather go back there than help a hypo-
crite."

Collins had suggested the hundred conventions ;
but, according to the report of the State society for
1844, " his ill-health did not permit him to partake of
the labors." The fact is that he was trying to ride two
horses, or, perhaps, it would be more correct to say
that he had been carried off his feet by the tide of
socialism, which was sweeping over the land. Communities had been founded in 1842 at Brook Farm,
Hopedale, and Northampton ; and the next year produced some fifteen or twenty new phalanxes and
associations, more or less under the influence of
Fourierism. This doctrine was regularly promul-
gated in the " New York Tribune," and among its
adherents were Greeley, Parke Godwin, Dana, Rip-
ley, Curtis, Dwight, Hawthorne, Parker, Margaret
Fuller, Lowell, and Whittier. The general plan had
some of the attractive features of that recently made
familiar by Mr. Bellamy. All the evils of poverty,
over-work, luxury, idleness, and competition were to
vanish before a system which should make us all
equally well off, and unite a maximum of culture and
comfort with a minimum of constraint. A new community of this sort was the real object for which
Collins was working in 1843. He came with some
other Socialists to Syracuse, and asked the Abolitionists to turn their convention into a No Property
one. If this little game had succeeded, it would have
been kept up at subsequent meetings. How the
influence of the Garrisonians would have suffered
from such a close alliance with communism may be
imagined from this fact. The basis on which

Collins founded his community, that same month at
Skaneateles, near Syracuse, was a declaration, that
when married people "have outlived their affections,
and cannot longer contribute to each other's happiness, the sooner the separation takes place the better;" that "There is to be no individual property,
but all goods shall be in common;" that "All forms
of worship should cease;" that "All religions of
every age and nation have their origin in the same
great falsehood, viz., God's special providence;" and
that "We regard the Sabbath as other days, the
clergy as an imposition, and the Bible as no authority."
(See Noyes' "History of American Socialism.")

This feature of the Skaneateles scheme was not
known when Collins tried to capture the Syracuse
convention; but the man who had made it a success,
instead of an utter failure, had his heart full of love
for the slave, and he protested that the building and
the money, which had been given for this cause,
could not honestly be used for any other. This argument carried everything before it at Syracuse; communism got no assistance from anti-slavery conventions; and Collins not only resigned his place as
general agent of the M. A. S. S., but declined any
salary for 1843.

His old associates say nothing of the reason why he
left them, in their report for 1844, and speak of him
much more kindly than if he had gone into the
Liberty party. Douglass was promptly and sharply
reprimanded for insubordination by "Captain Chapman," but he is still confident that he was in the
right, and events have justified him fully. Glowing
reports of the New Dispensation were sent out from

Skaneateles; but as soon as they had gathered in their first harvest, they began to throw out hints that they would not be offended by the gift of potatoes, or apples, or cabbages. The difficulty, fatal sooner or later to all such undertakings, of getting work enough out of the members, was aggravated by the unwillingness of Collins, who was still a non-resistant, to save the community from the burden of any lazy vagabond, who chose to quarter himself upon it. Debts increased; quarrels arose; the communists separated before they had been three years together; and Collins went back, as was said of him, "to God and the Whig party." His desire to go to Congress made him deny that he had been an Abolitionist, and even say that he did not know men who had received him as a guest, while he was general agent, and who sought to renew their friendship in California. Abolitionism, meantime, has changed the whole condition of things in this country, while socialism has contributed nothing of much importance to history, except the ruin of the second French republic.

In order not to seem to treat superficially and flippantly of schemes which are still enthusiastically advocated by many of the noblest men and women in this country as well as in Europe, I venture to present some further considerations, in substantial conformity with the present views of Mr. Douglass. We all know that our existing system, of free labor in keen competition, has many lamentable defects. The weak, clumsy, and ignorant suffer pitiably; the rich oppress the poor; competition produces fraud; and the wealth thus gained is often wasted viciously. But it must

not be forgotten that these and similar evils are growing less, although they are too closely connected, I
fear, with the fundamental conditions of human
existence to disappear entirely. Nothing seems to
me plainer than that this competitive system has
succeeded much better than any other, not only in
increasing the general wealth, to the benefit of even
the poorest, but in developing individual energy,
intelligence, industry, economy, foresight, perseverance, and self-control. These and other good
qualities flourish much more bountifully in the man
who knows that he must have them in order to be
respectable and prosperous, than they would if he
knew his utter lack of these virtues would not prevent
his enjoying as much comfort as his neighbors. In
order to understand the real value of this system, we
must also remember that there is only one other
which has ever proved capable of even sustaining
itself on any large scale, or for any considerable
time. It is often said that the only successful communities have been religious ones ; but even the
Puritans could not make communism succeed at
Plymouth ; and no amount of religion would have
made Brook Farm prosper permanently. What success has been attained by religious communities, like
the Shakers, has been owing to the willingness of
the members, not only to live very cheaply, but to
yield the most submissive obedience to superiors who
keep them at work. Comparatively little work has
ever been done, except in free competition or else
under compulsion. No authority has ever made men
work as well as they can do in competition, a fact
of which Douglass became fully aware, when he

exchanged Baltimore for New Bedford ; but ascet-
icism enables the laborers to live so cheaply as to
make up for the loss of energy and ambition. Thus the
ancient monks were able to turn deserts into gardens.
One secret of their success, and that of the Shakers,
was that all the members began by obeying willingly,
even gladly ; and most of them continued perfectly
docile. If all the laborers, however, in a whole
nation, were brought under a system of compulsory
labor, some of them would be sure to dislike it ; and
very severe punishments would have to be employed.
This was sometimes necessary in the monasteries ;
and any general system of compulsory labor would
necessarily resemble slavery in its cruelties, as well as
in its privations. The only alternative, besides our
competitive system, is one which has too much in
common with negro slavery. The only system of
labor which a lover of liberty can favor consistently,
is the one which we have already established among
us. We ought to do all we can to lessen its defects ;
but to abandon it would be not only " looking backward," but going backward.

From Syracuse the Garrisonians came to Rochester,
where the Liberty men received them hospitably.
Then Douglass went to Buffalo with Bradburn, who
refused to stop, because no better place had been engaged than a deserted room, without doors or windows, formerly used as a post-office, and nobody came
to the convention except a few hackmen, of various
colors, who sat there, whip in hand. Such was the
audience before which Bradburn deserted his companion and went off to Cleveland. But the spirit of
Douglass rose to the occasion ; and so did his voice.

It pealed forth from that old building, like a trumpet, through the streets, and called in the passers-by. Every meeting increased his audience; ere long he was invited into a church; this soon became too small; and he had to speak in the park, where there were four or five thousand hearers. The audience in the old post-office was so fully in keeping with the place, that he "was delighted to see there, one day, a young lady, who brought no escort but a little girl, and who was so beautiful as to look, in that rough crowd, like an angel of light." He did not expect to see her there again; but she came every time. He asked her name; and found she was the daughter of Myron Holley, one of the founders of the Liberty party. Her father had been reduced to earning his living by carrying round milk; but he still retained such dignity, that a little girl, who was a visitor at the house of a Rochester clergyman, once ran into the parlor to say, "God did bring in milk." His daughter has done good service as an Abolitionist lecturer, and is still working, as a teacher, among the freedmen. A letter of recollections, which she has kindly contributed, opens thus:

"In the early autumn of 1843, at an anti-slavery meeting in Buffalo, I first had the happiness to hear Frederick Douglass make a speech. He was then a young man, only in the faint dawn of his splendid day. It was a poor little meeting—the odds and ends of the city—not a soul there I had ever seen. I had never heard a fugitive slave speak, and was immensely interested to hear him. He rose, and I soon perceived he was all alive. His soul poured out with rare pathos and power. Among other things, he told how a slave-holder would preach to an audience of slaves and take the text: ' *Servants, be obe-*

dient to your masters,' and then proceed to say, ' The Lord in
His Providence sent pious souls over to Africa—dark, heathen,
benighted Africa—to bring you into this Christian land, where
you can sit beneath the droppings of the sanctuary and hear
about Jesus! The Lord has so established things that only
through the channel of obedience can happiness flow. For instance, Sam, the other day, was sent out by his master to do a
piece of work that would occupy about two hours and a half.
At the expiration of that time, Sam's master went out ; and, lo !
and behold ! there lay Sam's hoe in one place, and Sam in another, fast asleep ! The master remembered the words of
Scripture : ' He that knoweth his master's will, and doeth it
not, shall be beaten with many stripes.' So Sam was taken up
and whipped, so that he was disabled from doing any work for
the short space of three weeks and a half. ' For only through
the channel of obedience can happiness flow ! ' "

Soon after the convention which opened among the
hackmen in Buffalo, another was held there by the
colored people ; and then Douglass carried his audience with him in opposition to Dr. Garnett, who
wished to have the slaves advised to rise and slay
their masters. His pacific course did not prevent an
attempt to lynch him at Manayunk, near Philadelphia,
on his return from a meeting of the Abolitionists of
Pennsylvania at Norristown. The danger was known
in season ; and the train dashed through without
stopping, in spite of an attempt to wreck it.

We next find him in Ohio as one of the speakers
at the mass-meeting, held by the State Society in
Oakland, Clinton County, where several thousand
Abolitionists were gathered together, after having in
some cases traveled hundreds of miles. It may have
been on this occasion, and it was at all events in this
State, that an Irishman, who was in the audience, said

to another, "And what do ye think of that for a
naygur?" "Be aisy," was the answer. "He's only
half a naygur." "And if a half a naygur can spake
like that, what could a whole one do?" His companions on the platform found that when he was
among the first speakers, the interest ended too soon;
but when he was not, it did not begin until he did.

Before leaving Ohio, they separated into two parties, with different routes. He was not in that which
rode through Indiana in the "Liberator;" but he
had the honor of being hospitably entertained by
Hon. J. R. Giddings, as well as of having other members of Congress take part in greeting him at Richmond, Indiana, with a shower of pro-slavery eggs.
At Pendleton, in that State, things looked so black
on the first day, September 15, that they had reason
to be glad of the rain, which drove them away from
their platform in the woods. That night, the citizens
adopted resolutions insisting on the rights of free
discussion. Scarcely had the meetings begun, however, when a column of rowdies, armed with pistols
and clubs, marched in, two by two, one of the leaders
wearing a coon-skin cap, to show that he was a Whig;
while the other was supposed to be a Democrat of the
old school, from his dirty, ragged shirt, and no coat.
One of them asked the Abolitionists, why they did
not go South to speak ; and they politely invited him
to mount the platform. He made so poor an appearance on it, however, that his friends began to tear it
down. Others were about to attack Douglass ; but
the lady who had received him as a guest, Mrs. Re-
becca Fussell, wife of a physician in the town, held up
her baby before him ; and he was left unharmed for

a while. A little boy ran up, however, crying, " They
are killing Mr. White ! " Douglass thought it was a
friend who had come with him from the East. All
his principles of non-resistance vanished. He seized
a stick, and plunged, as eager as any knight, into the
fray. He soon found that his friend was in no danger;
but another Mr. White had been knocked down, and
had lost several teeth ; his club was wrested from
him and he had to retreat. He was pursued, and
struck down with a blow that broke his right hand.
A second blow was aimed at his head, and might have
been fatal, if his friend, White, had not saved him, at
the cost of being knocked down himself and badly
wounded in the head. Douglass was able to lecture
next day, however ; but he never went back to non-
resistance. Bradburn's first words to him were,
" Where's your consistency ? Why did you fight ? "
" Where's yours ? " was the answer. " Why didn't you
fight ? "

It was, I think, at another place in Indiana, that
Bradburn received warning, just as he was about to
begin a meeting in company with Douglass, that the
latter was going to be taken out of the hall to be
tarred and feathered. Bradburn quietly looked
about, and found, in the rear of the platform a little
door, opening on a passage which led out into a back
street. Scarcely had he made this discovery when
the mob began to mount the platform and order the
Abolitionists to disperse. He whispered a word or
two to Douglass and then went forward to meet the
rioters. " What can I do for you, gentlemen ? " said
Bradburn, with the utmost politeness. " We don't
want nothing of you," was the reply.   " We want

that nigger of yours." "Beg your pardon, gentlemen, but I am very deaf," as was really the case.
"Please speak a little louder." "We want Fred
Douglass," shouted the mob ; "and we are going to
have him. We mean to take his jacket off." "What
do you say, please," said Bradburn, with his hand to
his ear ; and so it went on, until it was found that
Douglass had escaped.

Another incident of this campaign was, that White
and Douglass once happened to be invited to pass
the night with a farmer, who had only one bed-room
for all his household, and only one spare bed. When
it was time to go to rest, there was a good deal of
anxious whispering, until the dark guest said :
" Friend White, having got entirely rid of my prejudice against color, I think, as a proof of it, I must
allow you to sleep with me to-night."

The last convention of 1843 was held on December
4, in Philadelphia, to commemorate the foundation,
ten years before, of the American Anti-Slavery
Society, and Douglass was among the speakers,
although he was told, as he passed through Gettys-
burg, that he was in danger of being kidnapped, and
had better not go out of doors except at night. He
also held a debate with Mrs. Ernestine L. Rose, who
had done good work for abolitionism, as well as for
the enfranchisement of her own sex. She now
asserted the superior importance of socialism, and
Douglass said nothing against it, but simply insisted
on the claims of the slave to be considered first.

The next year gave disunionism a complete victory, first in January and then in May, at the three
annual conventions in Boston and New York.

At the annual meeting of the M. A. S. S., in 1844, Douglass opposed a resolution, which was passed in Faneuil Hall, January 24, declaring that the American Church "Is not the Church of Christ, but the synagogue of Satan." During subsequent sessions, Ex-president Adams, then almost eighty, was censured for not doing more against slavery, which he was then resolutely opposing to the best of his judgment in Congress. The Liberty party was voted pro-slavery. Birney, who had been nominated for the Presidency once more, in opposition to both Whigs and Democrats, was declared to have "conspired to betray the anti-slavery cause into the hands of its most insidious foes," and to be "a man not deserving of the approval or support of any genuine Abolitionist ; " and on January 27 the publication was ordered of a "Protest of the Massachusetts Anti-Slavery Society against the Constitution of the United States and the Union." This was written by Foster, whose influence was now said to be greater than even Garrison's ; and among the characteristic sentences are these : "We now publicly adjure our allegiance : " "Henceforth let Repeal be our watchword."

The best thing done at this convention was to agree to hold a hundred others, that winter and spring, in various towns of Massachusetts. One of these meetings was held at Townsend, where Douglass, as he says in a letter written for the "Liberator," on March 6, noticed in the old church, then belonging to the town, as they came together, a hole in the wall about twelve feet long, beside the pulpit. He asked what it was, and was told that this had formerly been "the niggers' seat," but had gone out of use. The sexton showed him how to climb up there by a ladder, but it made him giddy to look down. Then the Hutchinsons took possession, and sang there through the meeting.

At Sudbury there was a strong opposition from the enemies of temperance, who had just carried the town-meeting, and who are thus described :

"Such a set of rum-faces, rum-noses, rum-heads, I think I never saw congregated in town-meeting anywhere. It was impossible to get us a meeting in this place. The clergy here bear almost entire sway. They decide for the people what they shall hear, and what they shall not hear. Each of the ministers devoted a good part of last Sunday to warning their congregations against attending our meetings. The consequence is that a mob is threatened, if we should attempt to hold our meeting according to notice. We should not, however, be intimidated by that, if we could get the people out. But this we cannot do, and must therefore pass this place by, at least for the present. It was not a little amusing to see the harmony and perfect agreement of the Rabbis and rummies of the place, in their opposition to our meeting."

In Grafton our hero was allowed to decide for himself whether there should be a meeting. "I was alone," he says, "and there was neither house, hall, nor church in which I could speak to the people. But, determined to speak, I went to the hotel and borrowed a dinner-bell, with which in hand I passed through the principal streets, ringing the bell and crying out, 'Notice! Frederick Douglass, recently a slave, will lecture on American slavery, on Grafton Common, this evening at seven o'clock. This brought out a large audience, but after that evening the largest church in town was open to me." He had afterward to take the same course at Manchester, New Hampshire, and with similar results.

On Thursday, May 10, at New York, the A. A. S. S. adopted, by a vote of three to one, a resolution declaring that " Secession from the present United States government is the duty of every abolitionist." Mr. White, who had saved the life of Douglass in Indiana, protested in vain, as did Mr. Child, who then gave up editing the " National Anti-Slavery Standard," on which his gifted wife, too, had labored. On the last day of this month, the New England convention, in Boston, voted to agitate for a dissolution of the Union. In the list of two hundred and fifty names in the affirmative, that of Douglass stands tenth ; and there were but twenty-four in the negative. That Friday evening a disunion banner was publicly presented by C. C. Burleigh, in behalf of this convention to Garrison, as President of the A. A. S. S. On one side was the new motto, " No Union with Slaveholders," and on the other a slave lay prostrate and trampled down by the American eagle, who was wrapped in the national flag, on which was the word " Protection," and had under one wing the Capitol with a slave-sale in front, while under the other was a church with a negro under the lash. The ground was red, and highest of all the emblems was the eye of God. The audience was so excited by this scene, as well as by the attacks made on the Church, that the convention ended that night in a row.

Neither a resolution condemning the Church, nor one repudiating the Union, could be carried by Douglass, Burleigh, and Remond, in the meeting, held on June 12, in the Universalist church, now a

Catholic one, in Concord. But few of the residents would go to the Court House, and the Unitarians would not suffer their bell to be rung, except for two or three unauthorized strokes, when Emerson lectured, on August 1, on "The History of Emancipation in the British West Indies." Little reference seems to have been made by him to the condition of the slaves in the United States ; but his treatment of the subject announced was so lofty, that when the audience, mostly from abroad, met for a collation afterward, they said to each other, "Can you eat? I cannot." Douglass was among the listeners that morning, and also among the speakers in the afternoon. The next day he took part with Pierpont and James Freeman Clark, in a great mass-meeting, appointed for the first, but postponed on account of the weather, at Hingham, where the disunion banner was carried through gaily decorated streets in a long procession, amid the ringing of the bells. He is described by a lady who saw him this summer, and often afterwards, as showing as much culture from the very first as ever after, and as displaying in his conversation rare integrity of character, as well as great activity of intellect. She also says that he made no gestures, unless excited ; and that he was not only very fond of horses, but perfectly able to pick out a good one.

That same month Douglass revisited Norristown ; and on August 17, he spoke on a table in the State House yard in Philadelphia. During the autumn we hear of him at various cities in New Hampshire, Maine, Massachusetts, and Rhode Island. There was now great excitement on account of the prospect that Texas would soon be annexed, as actually happened in

1845 ; and Douglass took part with Phillips, Garrison, and Remond in the protest made by the M. A. S. S., in Representatives' Hall, on Friday evening, January 26, against throwing open this new field to slavery.

He had abstained, hitherto, from telling the public where he had been a slave, or what was his original name. These precautions seemed necessary for his safety ; but they were not favorable to his reputation for veracity. People began to think that he had never been a slave. They said he did not talk, or look, or act like one ; and his failure to give particulars was sadly against him. His education, too, was not to be reconciled with the ignorance in which slaves were said to live. As he walked down the aisles of a church, after a lecture, he used to hear people say, " He's never been a slave, I'll warrant you." Douglass has never been so little of a man as to stand any doubt of his honor. He preferred to run the risk of recapture, and tell all about himself to the world, except the way he escaped. When he declared his intention at New Bedford, there was a general murmur through the audience of " He had better not." This Phillips mentioned in a lecture that March, and exclaimed, " God dash the Commonwealth of Massachusetts into a thousand pieces, till there shall not remain a fragment on which an honest man can stand and not dare to tell his name." He added that " Frederick ——, to our disgrace, we know not what to call him " . . . " has won a colorless reputation in these parts." Soon after saying this, he wrote him thus, " I shall read your book with trembling for you. Some years ago, when you were beginning to tell me your real name and birthplace, you may remember I stopped you, and preferred to remain ignorant of all. With the exception of a vague description, so I continued till the other day, when you read me your memoirs. I hardly knew at the time, whether to thank you or not for the sight of them, when I reflected that it was still dangerous in Massachusetts for honest men to tell their names." . . . " In all the broad lands which the Constitution of the United States overshadows, there is no single spot, however narrow or desolate, where a fugitive slave can plant himself and say, ' I am safe.' The whole armory of Northern law has no shield for you. I am free to say that, in your place, I should throw the manuscript into the fire."

This letter was printed, with the " Narrative of the Life of Frederick Douglass, an American Slave, Written by himself ; " in a bound volume of a hundred and forty pages, which was published at the Anti-Slavery office in Boston, and sold for fifty cents. The little book also contains a portrait of the author and a letter describing his first appearance at Nantucket, from Garrison, who also says that, " His success in combating prejudice, in gaining proselytes, in agitating the public mind, has far surpassed the most sanguine expectations that were raised at the commencement of his brilliant career." Scarcely anything is said about this career in the " Narrative," which, so far as it goes, is substantially the same as the autobiographical accounts published in 1855 and 1882. The earliest of the three memoirs was merely expanded to form the second ; and that was contracted again to make part of the third. The principal peculiarities of the " Narrative " are the portrait, the introductory letters from Garrison and Phillips, and the appendix, containing not only the parody of the slave-holders' hymn, but this explanation of rebukes often administered :

"I find, since reading over the foregoing 'Narrative,' that I have, in several instances, spoken in such a tone and manner respecting religion, as may possibly lead those unacquainted with my religious views to suppose me an opponent of all religion. To remove the liability of such misapprehension, I deem it proper to append the following brief explanation. What I have said respecting and against religion, I mean strictly to apply to the slave-holding religion of this land, and with no possible reference to Christianity proper ; for, between the Christianity of this land, and the Christianity of Christ, I recognize the widest possible difference, so wide, that to receive the one as good, pure and holy, is of necessity to reject the other as bad, corrupt, and wicked. To be the friend of the one is of necessity to be the enemy of the other. I love the pure, peaceable, and impartial Christianity of Christ; I therefore hate the corrupt, slave-holding, woman-whipping, cradle-plundering, partial and hypocritical Christianity of this land. Indeed, I can see no reason, but the most deceitful one, for calling the religion of this land Christianity. I look upon it as the climax of all misnomers, the boldest of all frauds, and the grossest of all libels. Never was there a clearer case of 'stealing the livery of the court of Heaven to serve the devil in.' I am filled with unutterable loathing when I contemplate the religious pomp and show, together with the horrible inconsistencies, which everywhere surround me. We have men-stealers for ministers, woman-whippers for missionaries, and cradle-plunderers for church members. The man who wields the blood-clotted cowskin during the week, fills the pulpit on Sunday, and claims to be a minister of the meek and lowly Jesus. He who sells my sister for purposes of prostitution, stands forth as the pious advocate of purity. The man who robs me of my earnings at the end of each week, meets me as a class-leader on Sunday morning, to show me the way of life and the path of salvation. He who proclaims it a religious duty to read the Bible, denies me the right of learning to read the name of the God who made me. He who is the religious advocate of marriage, robs whole millions of its sacred influence, and leaves them to the ravages of whole-sale pollution. The warm defender of the sacredness of the family relation, is the same that scatters whole families, sunder-ing husbands and wives, parents and children, sisters and brothers, leaving the hut vacant, and the hearth desolate. We see the thief preaching against theft, and the adulterer against adultery. We have men sold to build churches, women sold to support the gospel, and babes sold to purchase Bibles for the poor heathen—all for the glory of God and the good of souls. The slave-auctioneer's bell and the church-going bell chime in with each other; and the bitter cries of the heart-broken slave are drowned in the religious shouts of his pious master. Revi-vals of religion and revivals in the slave-trade go hand in hand together. The slave-prison and the church stand near each other. The clanking of fetters and the rattling of chains in the prison, and the pious psalm and solemn prayer in the church may be heard at the same time. The dealers in the bodies and souls of men erect their stand in the presence of the pulpit; and they mutually help each other. The dealer gives his blood-stained gold to support the pulpit; and the pulpit in return covers his infernal business with the garb of Christianity. Here we have religion and robbery the allies of each other, devils dressed in angels' robes, and hell presenting the semblance of paradise."

The words of Jesus against the Pharisees are then quoted with the comment:

" Dark and terrible as is this picture, I hold it to be strictly true of the overwhelming mass of professed Christians in America. They strain at a gnat and swallow a camel. Could anything be more true of our churches? They would be shocked at the proposition of fellowshiping a sheep-stealer; and at the same time they hug to their communion a man-stealer, and brand me with being an infidel, if I find fault with them for it." . . . " They love the heathen on the other side of the globe. They can pray for him, pay money to have the Bible put into his hands, and missionaries to instruct him ; while they despise and totally neglect the heathen at their own doors. Such is very briefly my view of the religion of this land ; and, to avoid any misunderstanding, growing out of the use of general terms, I mean by the religion of this land, that which is revealed in the words, deeds, and actions of those bodies, North and South, calling themselves Christian churches, and yet in union with slave-holders. It is against religion, as presented by these bodies, that I have felt it my duty to testify."

The same week that this little book was published, we find its author, on May 8, 1845, repeating the Covey episode in full in the Broadway Tabernacle, at the convention of the A. A. S. S., to prove that slavery was necessarily cruel. Various portions were copied by friendly newspapers with high praise. The "Tribune," for instance, says that, "Considered merely as a narrative, we never read one more simple, true, coherent and warm with genuine feeling. It is an excellent piece of writing, and on that score to be prized as a specimen of the powers of the black race." The " Liberator " says, on May 28, two weeks after announcing the publication, that " The edition is passing off rapidly." The demand was so brisk that the author had to carry copies into the churches, where he lectured, and go with them through the aisles. Four more editions were called for within twelve months, besides two at Dublin and another at Leeds of five thousand copies. There is also, I think, a German or Dutch translation, and certainly a French one, made by Miss Parkes, who contributed an excellent preface, but left out the introductory letters and part of the appendix. This last version, which is a reasonably faithful one, except that the proper names are sometimes misspelled, was published by Pagnerre, Paris, in 1848.

At the N. E. Convention in Boston, May 27, 1845, a resolution was proposed by Wendell Phillips, and passed as follows :

" *Resolved*, That we joyfully welcome to our ranks the new anti-slavery lecturer, the ' Narrative of the Life of Frederick Douglass, Written by himself ;' that we commend it with confidence to all who believe the slaves of the South to be either well treated, or happy, or ignorant of their right to freedom, or in need of preparation to make them fit for freedom ; and that we urge upon the friends of the cause the duty of circulating it among all classes."

At a subsequent session, presided over by Remond, Robert Owen, the great philanthropist, who had been advocating for nearly thirty years a socialistic scheme, whose basis much resembled that adopted at Skaneateles, tried to prove that there was worse slavery in England than at the South. But the members of the convention were perfectly aware that, as Douglass had said in one of the sessions, twelve months before, " The hungry Englishman is a freeman ; while the slave is not only hungry but a slave. The difference is said to be, that the Briton says to his victim, ' Work for me, or you shall starve,' while the American says to the slave, ' Work, or you shall be whipped.' But I know something of this matter at home ; and I have found that we say, 'Whip' and 'Starve' too." He did not, however, strike another such blow this year, when the good old man was within his sword's length, but reserved his full strength for Bradburn. The latter had gone over to the Liberty party and now spoke with great ability and bitterness against his former associates, protesting against any money being given to people who were so violent and abusive. Then Douglass carried the war into Africa, by saying to Bradburn, "I heard you myself, not two years ago, at Pittsburgh, denounce the very party which you have since joined, as a set of unprincipled scoundrels. I heard you." "So did I!" "And I!" shouted others. A spectator describes the scene as one of the most exciting he ever witnessed. Another account says, "There was the high-born and high-minded representative of the African race, into whose hands (if he is the man I think and trust he is) God seems to have given a mission as lofty and inspiring as that entrusted to any one man of our generation, Frederick Douglass, to whom I look more than to any other, as the herald of his people's redemption." This was written by a clergyman, who thought that his cloth was too roughly handled. Pillsbury and Phillips finally charged Christianity with being less humane to the slave than Moslemism ; and the convention broke up in a disgraceful row.

This I mention partly because Rogers had now carried the No Government doctrine so far as to hate every kind of organization. He blamed the Abolitionists for not letting poor crazy Mrs. Folsom say all she chose ; and he now seemed glad of the mob, and said, in the "Herald of Freedom," "In such a contest between Platform and People, I am glad to see Platform defeated." His head seems to have been much less clear than when he wrote the descriptions of Douglass already quoted, and corrected the saying of Garrison, that slavery was a sin because the slave was the image of God. "Nay," said Rogers, "Slavery is sin, because the slave is the reality of Man." His paper had come, early in 1841, under the control, so far as receipts and expenses were concerned, of the New Hampshire Anti-Slavery Society ; and he had himself announced in an editorial, calling for continued support, that "Every subscription aids the society." In 1844 the "Herald" collapsed, and he tried to revive it in complete independence of the N. H. A. S. S. Some of the members objected, others stood by him, and the dispute was referred to a committee, which included Garrison, Phillips, and others of his best friends, and which decided unanimously against him. He refused to submit, and there was a sad quarrel early in June, 1845, at the meeting of the N. H. A. S. S. in Concord. Phillips spoke for the Society so strongly that there was no reply, and Garrison charged Rogers with dishonesty. His partisans became too excited to listen for more than a moment to any criticism ; and Douglass, who admitted the innocence of his motives, insisted so earnestly on being allowed to blame his course, that Rogers charged him with falling into "the vein of a plantation slave, with the overseer's whip put into his hand." He also said, "I deny here that Douglass, or anybody else, has the right of speech-making," or delivering "a long, uninterrupted, and uninterruptible harangue."

That July Douglass made another trip to Western

New York. The Liberty party organ in Utica speaks
thus of his visit :

" This fugitive from oppression lectured in this city last
Tuesday evening.   There are not Garrisonian Abolitionists
enough in this city to get him up a meeting, and he was
indebted to ourself for the one he held.   Pity that so noble a
specimen of a man should have been spoiled by the miserable
fallacies of the Garrisonian philosophy.   We knew Frederick
held those peculiarities, but we hoped he was not so set upon
the project of abolishing the Liberty party and the Union, as to
make these objects the prime end of his mission.   In this,
however, we were mistaken.   He labored an hour and a half to
bring contempt upon the position, the consistency, and the
morality of the very persons by whose courtesy he had obtained
a hearing in this city.   We regret this exceedingly."

Another incident of this journey is that, while he
was going on a canal-boat from Palmyra to Rochester,
he was told that he must not sit down to breakfast
with the other passengers, but might with the
" hands."   " No," said he, "They have just as much
right as your passengers to be free from the disgrace
of my company."   His color had often shut him out,
even in December, from the cabin of the steamboat.
On one such occasion Phillips refused to leave him,
but passed the night with him on deck.   Another
time one of the officers took pity on him, and asked
him if he were not an Indian.   The Douglass would
not stretch the truth to get into comfortable quarters,
but answered, " No.   Only a d——d nigger."
We have seen him fighting against brakemen in
Massachusetts and armed rioters in Indiana, arguing
against Socialists, Anarchists, and Liberty party men,
addressing sometimes half-a-dozen hackmen, and

sometimes, as at Hingham, six or eight thousand intelligent sympathizers. For seven years he had been in constant danger of arrest, and the peril was very serious after he chose to publish the name and address of his master. We shall next meet him in safer and smoother paths. This change of scene will fortunately make it unnecessary to dwell on the errors of the men and women whose services to our nation are really beyond all praise, but whose mistakes must be kept in mind, to understand why our black knight was finally obliged to ride against them also, with lance in rest.

CHAPTER V.

BEYOND THE COLOR-LINE.

THE Fugitive Slave Law was not so severe in 1845, as it became five years later; and recent legislation forbade State officials in Massachusetts to assist a kidnapper. He could, however, easily get support enough from the national courts, and also from public sentiment, to secure his prey; and the publication of the "Narrative" made it very rash for its author to remain even for three months, as he actually did, in the United States. Great Britain offered perfect security, and also new opportunities of education, as well as the possibility of obtaining liberal aid. For these reasons he took the Cunard steamer "Cambria," for Liverpool, on Saturday, August 16, 1845, in company with one of his best friends at Lynn, where he still resided, James N. Buffum. His color shut him out from the first cabin; but his book was eagerly read there. Mr. Buffum, the Hutchinsons, and other passengers visited him often and invited him not only to their cabin, but to the saloon-deck. All parts of the steamer soon became almost equally free to him. But, "I preferred to live within my privileges and keep upon my own premises. I found this quite as much in accordance with good policy as with my own feelings. The effect was, that, with the majority of

112

the passengers, all color distinctions were flung to the winds ; and I found myself treated with every mark of respect." (" Bondage and Freedom," p. 367.)

There were, however, so many Southerners on board, as to produce a curious mixture of " anti-slavery singing and pro-slavery grumbling." The system was subjected to continual discussion, so that, as he wrote to the " Liberator," from Dublin, on September 1:

" If suppressed in the saloon, it broke out in the steerage ; and if it ceased in the steerage, it was renewed in the saloon ; and if surpressed in both, it broke out with redoubled energy high up on the saloon-deck, in the free ocean air. I was happy. Everything went on nobly. At last, the evening previous to our arrival in Liverpool, the slave-holders, convinced that reason, morality, common humanity, and Christianity were all against them, abandoned their post in debate, and resorted to their old and natural mode of defending their morality by brute force." . . . " Things went on as usual, till between five and six o'clock in the afternoon of Wednesday, when I received an invitation from the captain to deliver an address upon the saloon-deck. I signified my willingness to do so ; and he at once ordered the bell to be rung and the meeting cried. This was the signal for a general excitement. Some swore I should not speak ; and others said I should. Bloody threats were made against me, if I attempted it. At the hour appointed I went upon the deck, where I was expected to speak. There was much noise going on among the passengers, evidently intended to make it impossible for me to proceed. At length, our Hutchinson friends broke forth in one of their unrivalled songs, which, like the angel of old, closed the lions' mouths, so that, for a time, silence prevailed. The captain now introduced me ; and after expressing my gratitude to a kind Providence that had brought us safely across the sea, I proceeded to portray the condition of my brethren in bonds. I had not uttered five words, when a Mr. H., from Connecticut, called out in a loud voice, ' That's a lie!' I went on, taking no notice of him, though he was murmuring nearly all the while, backed up by a man from New Jersey. I continued, till I said something which seemed to cut to the quick; when out bawled H., 'That's a lie!' and seemed anxious to strike me. I then said to the audience, that I would explain the reason of his conduct. The colored man in our country was treated as a being without rights. 'That's a lie!' said H. I then told the audience, that as almost everything I said was pronounced lies, I would endeavor to substantiate them by reading a few extracts from slave-laws. The slavocrats, finding that they were now to be fully exposed, rushed up about me, with hands clenched, and swore I should not speak. They were ashamed to have American laws read before an English audience. The captain said he had tried to please all his passengers; a part of them had expressed a desire to hear me lecture; and those who did not wish to hear me might go to some other part of the ship. He then returned and requested me to proceed." [Another account is that he said, " Give it to them, Douglass, like bricks!"] " I again commenced, but was again interrupted, more violently than before. One slave-holder shook his fist in my face and said, 'Oh, I wish I had you in Cuba.' 'Ah,' said another, 'I wish I had him in Savannah. We would use him up.' Said another, 'I will be one of a party to throw him overboard.' A noble-spirited, Irish gentleman assured the man, that two could play at that game; and, in the end, he might be thrown overboard himself. The clamor went on, waxing hotter and hotter, till it was quite impossible for me to proceed. I was stopped; but the cause went on. The clamor was only silenced by the captain, who told the mobocrats that he would have them put in irons; and he actually sent for them, and doubtless would have made use of them."

Nothing shows more clearly the inability of the friends of slavery even to listen to facts, than this curious incident, the original account of which has been copied with scarcely any omissions.

The next morning, Thursday, August 28, 1845, they landed at Liverpool, and the pro-slavery champions soon had their visit to Eaton Hall spoiled; for the hated negro was actually admitted at the same time with them, and treated equally well. They said all they could about him in the newspapers, and thus greatly increased his popularity.

Three days after disembarking we find him in Ireland. The potato-rot, which was to destroy, but little more than a year later, a quarter of a million lives, and make three million paupers, had already shown itself, and the condition of the people had long been pitiable. Popular education, poor-laws, and other practical remedies had been introduced by the government, but public attention was absorbed by a wild agitation for repealing the Union with the country which was soon to feed the whole island. O'Connell's imprisonment for sedition kept alive his popularity until the end of 1845, when it was discovered, not only that his schemes were hopelessly visionary, but that he had long been one of the most iniquitous landlords in Ireland. There was a caricature of him in "Punch," as the real potato-blight. Douglass was just in time to get the full benefit of the cordial relations between Irish and American disunionists. The "Liberator," as O'Connell was called, had denounced slavery nobly. Garrison had been among his open admirers, and vast sums had come over from the United States. No wonder that "the black O'Connell," as he was soon named, was able to write to Boston, from Dublin, on September 16:

"Our success here is even greater than I had anticipated. We have held four glorious anti-slavery meetings, two in the

Royal Exchange, and two in the Friends' meeting-house, all crowded to overflowing. I am to lecture to-morrow evening in the Music Hall. It will hold three thousand persons, and is let for about fifty dollars a night. But its generons proprietor has kindly agreed to let me have it free of charge. I have attended several temperance meetings, and given several temperance addresses. One of the most pleasing features of my visit, thus far, has been a total absence of all prejudice against me, on account of my color. I find myself not treated as a color, but as a man; not as a thing, but as a child of the common Father of us all."

Thirteen days later he writes that he has heard O'Connell condemn slavery at a great Repeal meeting in Dublin, has been introduced to him on the platform, and has then said to the multitude, " I have stopped in this country for a month to see the ' Liberator,' and when I heard of his approach in the streets to-day, I rushed forward to catch a sight of him who had befriended the poor negro."

Next he went to Cork, where a public breakfast was given him, and the Mayor took the chair the first evening he spoke. Would the Mayor of any city in the United States, in 1845, have gone into an Abolitionist meeting, unless he wanted to have it dispersed? A soirée was given by Father Mathew, on October 21, to Douglass and Buffum ; and the dark guest writes that he was " so entirely charmed by the goodness of this truly good man, that I besought him to administer the pledge to me. He complied with promptness, and gave me a beautiful silver pledge. I now reckon myself with delight the fifth of the last five of Father Mathew's 5,487,495 temperance children." He was invited soon after to a reception in

St. Patrick's Temperance Hall, where a song of welcome, especially composed for the occasion, was sung,
and all the company joined in the chorus.   In his
speech that night, he uttered this great truth : " All
true reforms are kindred."   He went on to say of
those who spoke of the Irish as slaves, a word still
grossly misapplied by agitators, that

> " They do not sufficiently distinguish between certain forms
> of oppression and slavery.   Slavery is not what takes away any
> one right or property in man ; it takes away man himself, and
> makes him the property of his fellow.   It is what unmans man,
> takes him from himself, dooms him as a degraded thing, ranks
> him with the bridled horse and muzzled ox, makes him a
> chattel personal, a marketable commodity, to be swayed by the
> caprice and sold at the will of his master."

So important is this distinction that I will here
quote from a speech of his, made at Rochester, New
York, December 1, 1850, as follows :

> " It is often said by the opponents of the anti-slavery cause,
> that the condition of the people of Ireland is more deplorable
> than that of the American slaves.   Far be it from me to under-
> rate the suffering of the Irish people.   They have long been
> oppressed ; and the same heart that prompts me to plead the
> cause of the American bondmen, makes it impossible for me not
> to sympathize with the oppressed of all lands.   Yet, I must say,
> that there is no analogy between the two cases.   The Irishman
> is poor, but he is not a slave. He may be in rags, but he is not a
> slave.   He is still the master of his own body, and can say with
> the poet :
>> " The hand of Douglas is his own.
>> " The world is all before him, where to choose ; "
> " and poor as may be my opinion of the British Parliament, I
> cannot believe that it will ever sink to such a depth of infamy as

to pass a law for the re-capture of fugitive Irishmen! The shame and scandal of kidnapping will long remain wholly monopolized by the American Congress. The Irishman has not only the liberty to emigrate from his country, but he has liberty at home. He can write, and speak, and co-operate for the attainment of his rights and the redress of his wrongs. The multitude can assemble upon all the green hills and fertile plains of the Emerald Isle ; they can pour out their grievances, and proclaim their wants without molestation ; and the press, that 'swift-winged messenger,' can bear the tidings of their doings to the extreme bounds of the civilized world. They have their 'Conciliation Hall,' on the banks of the Liffy, their reform clubs and their newspapers; they pass resolutions, send forth addresses, and enjoy the right of petition. But how is it with the American slave ? Where may he assemble ? Where is his Conciliation Hall ? Where are his newspapers ? Where is his right of petition ? Where is his freedom of speech ? His liberty of the press ? And his right of locomotion ? He is said to be happy ; happy men can speak. But ask the slave what is his condition—what his state of mind—what he thinks of enslavement ? and you had as well address your inquiries to the silent dead. There comes no voice from the enslaved. We are left to gather his feelings by imagining what ours would be, were our souls in his soul's stead. If there were no other fact descriptive of slavery, than that the slave is dumb, this alone would be sufficient to mark the slave system as a grand aggregation of human horrors."

After a very successful tour through southern Ireland, Douglass went to Belfast, where, on January 6, 1846, a public breakfast was given to him, with a member of Parliament in the chair. On this occasion he was presented, in behalf of the local branch of the British and Foreign Anti-Slavery Society, with a Bible, "splendidly bound in gold." In receiving it, he said : " I accept thankfully this Bible ; and while it shall have the best place in my house, I trust also to give its precepts a place in my heart." After refering to his having been led, by hearing the first chapter of Job, to wish to know how to read, he said :

" Twenty years ago while lying, not unlike a dog, at the feet of my mistress, I was roused from the sweet sleep of childhood, to hear the narrative of Job. A few years afterward found me searching for the Scriptures in the muddy street gutters, and rescuing its pages from the filth." . . . " A few years later I escaped from my chains, gained partial freedom, and became an advocate for the emancipation of my race. During this advocacy, a suspicion obtains that I am not what I profess to be, to silence which it is necessary to write out my experience in slavery, and give the names of my enslavers. This endangers my liberty. Persecuted, hunted, outraged, in America, I have come to England, and behold the change ! The chattel becomes a man. I breathe, and I am free. Instead of culling the Scriptures from the mud, they come to me dressed in polished gold, as the free and unsolicited gift of devoted hearts."

A few days before he wrote thus to the " Liberator : "

" I can truly say I have spent some of the happiest months of my life since landing in this country. I seem to have undergone a transformation. I live a new life. The warm and generous coöperation extended to me by the friends of my despised race ; the prompt and liberal manner with which the press has rendered me its aid ; the glorious enthusiasm with which thousands have flocked to hear the cruel wrongs of my down-trodden and long-enslaved fellow-countrymen portrayed ; the deep sympathy for the slave, and the strong abhorrence of the slave-holder, everywhere evinced ; the cordiality with which members and ministers of various religious bodies, and of various shades of religious opinion, have embraced me and lent me their aid ; the kind hospitality constantly proffered to

me by persons in the highest rank in society ; the spirit of freedom that seems to animate all with whom I come in contact,
and the entire absence of anything that looked like prejudice
against me, on account of the color of my skin, contrasted so
strongly with my long and bitter experience in the United
States, that I look with wonder and amazement on the transi-
tion. In the southern part of the United States I was a slave,
thought of and spoken of as property ; in the Northern States a
fugitive slave, liable to be hunted at any moment, like a felon,
and to be hurled into the terrible jaws of slavery—doomed by
an inveterate prejudice against color to insult and outrage on
every hand (Massachusetts out of the question)—denied the
privileges and courtesies common to others in the use of the
most humble means of conveyance—shut out from the cabins
on steamboats—refused admission to respectable hotels—cari-
catured, scorned, scoffed, mocked, and maltreated with
impunity by any one (no matter how black his heart), so he
has a white skin. But now behold the change ! Eleven days
and a half gone, and I have crossed three thousand miles of
the perilous deep. Instead of a democratic government, I am
under a monarchical government. Instead of the bright, blue
sky of America, I am covered with the soft, grey fog of the
Emerald Isle. I breathe ; and lo ! the chattel becomes a man.
I gaze around in vain for one who will question my equal
humanity, claim me as his slave, or offer me an insult. I
employ a cab—I am seated beside white people—I reach the
hotel—I enter the same door—I am shown into the same parlor—I dine at the same table—and no one is offended. No
delicate nose grows deformed in my presence. I find no difficulty here in obtaining admission into any place of worship,
instruction, or amusement, on equal terms with people as white
as any I ever saw in the United States. I meet nothing to
remind me of my complexion. I find myself regarded and
treated at every turn with the kindness and deference paid to
white people."

So pleasant, in fact, was this part of Mr. Douglass'

life that he recently selected it as the subject of his
address, on being invited to speak to a literary club
in Washington.

On January 10, 1846, the two travelers left Ireland,
where Douglass had given "upward of fifty lectures
in four months;" and an even more promising field
of labor was entered at once in Scotland. The Free
Church had been created by the heroism of the four
hundred Presbyterian clergymen, who resigned, on
May 23, 1843, their pulpits and salaries, a loss of a
hundred thousand pounds a year, rather than support any longer a system by which pastors were
appointed by wealthy laymen, without the consent of
the parishioners. The way in which this body was
formed gave high authority to all its utterances, and
it was shocking to see Dr. Chalmers condemn exclusion of slave-holders from church fellowship, while the
deputies who were sent to the United States, to raise
funds, carefully avoided showing any sympathy with
Abolitionists. They thus managed to collect about
three thousand pounds, and a large part of this sum
came from South Carolina, where a white man had
recently been sentenced to death for trying to help
the woman he loved to escape from slavery. O'Connell had refused to accept contributions from the
Southern States, saying, "I do not want your blood-
stained money." Earnest appeals to do likewise were
made by the women of Glasgow, and other friends of
the slave, to the Free Church, as early as 1844, but
the ministers were much too shrewd. The question
was of great importance, because it involved that of
the duty of the churches to teach morality; as well
as because the most effective way of turning public

opinion against slavery was to disfellowship slave-
holders. And this course was far less objectionable
than that of trying to withdraw from political relations. The latter have given the opportunity of
emancipation, while the only way in which the
churches could exert any authority was through
excommunication. The religious relations with
slavery were, of course, the only ones which ought to
have been discussed in Great Britain, where there
were no political ones, except those necessary for the
world's peace.

Decidedly too much, however, was said in favor of
disunionism by Henry C. Wright, in southern Scotland, early in 1846; and Buffum, who went through
the North and West with Douglass, used to repeat so
often a story about the hatred which he was able to
call out in Scotland against the Declaration of Independence, that I am not altogether sorry to hear it
said that his roguish companion once cut him out, by
going over all his points before he could repeat them.
At all events, Douglass himself kept true to the real
issue, as may be judged from a speech made on February 10, at Arbroath, where he was charged with
being in the pay of some rival sect. "So far," he
says, "as the charge is brought against me, I pronounce
it an unblushing falsehood." . . . "I am not here
alone, I have with me the learned, wise and reverend
heads of the church. But with or without their sanction, I should stand just where I do now, maintaining
to the last that man-stealing is incompatible with
Christianity; that slave-holding and true religion
are at war with each other, and that a Free Church
should have no fellowship with a slave church." . . .

"The Free Church in vindicating their fellowship of slave-holders, have acted upon the damning heresy, that a man may be a Christian, whatever may be his practice, so his creed is right. So he pays tithes of mint, anise and cummin, he may be a Christian, though he totally neglect judgment and mercy. It is this heresy that now holds in chains three million of men, women and children in the United States. The slave-holder's conscience is put at ease by those ministers and churches."

In this town the indignation was so great that people who came, one Sunday morning to worship in the Free Church, found that its walls had been decorated during the night with these words, painted in black letters, and not to be effaced, "The Slave's Blood," while around were red spots to represent gore. Other churches bore in bloody characters, "Send back the Slave Money." Posters were put on all the walls, wherever he spoke, and even on the pavements, repeating the words, "Send back the Money." In fact the war-cry got so familiar to him that he cut it in the turf, when he visited Arthur's Seat in Edinburgh ; and he still remembers a song, with a chorus running somewhat thus :

> "Where gat ye the bawbies, Tammy ?
> I dinna think they're canny," etc.

He was soon able to report that "Old Scotland boils like a pot." One of the best meetings was that in Glasgow, on April 21, when he complained that "Not only did the Free Church Deputation not preach the Gospel, or say a word in behalf of the slave, but they took care to preach such doctrines as would be palatable, as would be agreeably received, and as would

bring them the slave-holder's money." Mr. George
Thompson, a member of Parliament, whose presence
in Boston had done much to excite the mob in 1835,
and whose eloquence was still terrible, made that
night a very effective speech, in which he exclaimed,
"Oh, that a thousand pounds should out-weigh
the chains of three million slaves!" He also
brought up the fact that one of the clergymen who
was now foremost in holding fast the price of blood,
Dr. Cunningham, had formerly, at his suggestion,
reprinted a little book called "A Picture of American
Slavery," and put upon the title-page these lines :

> " Is there not some chosen curse,
>   Some hidden thunder in the stores of heaven,
>   Red with uncommon wrath, to blast the man
>   Who gains his fortune from the blood of souls ? "

A few days before these speeches were delivered,
Douglass wrote a letter to the "Tribune," which was
printed not only there, but in the "Liberator," and
which contains these words :

"I am called by way of reproach, a runaway slave,
as if it were a crime, an unpardonable crime, for a man
to take his inalienable rights." ·He also mentions
having been denounced by the "New York Express,"
as "a glib-tongued scoundrel," and says he is used to
such epithets ; and their force is lost on him ; for he
was reared where they were in the most common use.
"They form a large and very important portion of the
vocabulary of characters known in the South as
'plantation negro drivers.' A slave-holding gentleman would scorn to use them."

The friends of slavery had been so unwilling to see

any truth in the "Narrative," that its author was glad to have it substantially confirmed by an unfriendly witness. A Southerner, named Thompson, who had known him at St. Michael's, published, early in 1846, a letter which is reprinted in the "Liberator," page 29. He had evidently done his best to collect testimony; but it touched only two points in the statements of Douglass, namely that Thomas Auld had given him "a number of severe whippings," and had kept his slaves on very short allowance. In a letter quoted by Thompson, Auld says, "I can put my hand upon my Bible, and with a clear conscience swear, that I never struck him in my life, nor caused any person else to do it. I never allowanced one of my slaves." His neighbors speak of him as a kind master, who "has invariably emancipated his slaves, when they arrived at the age of twenty-five." He complains that Douglass does not mention, in the "Narrative," that this promise had been made him. A neighbor, who had boarded with him, says, "I speak from personal knowledge when I say that Fred and all his servants were treated well. Indeed, I never knew him to strike, much less abuse them. I knew Fred well; we were boys together in the same family." It is certainly in Auld's favor, that he had not sold his slave to the Georgia traders, when he first tried to escape, but sent him to learn a trade in Baltimore; that he never pursued him at the North; and that he felt so much aggrieved, on account of having been misrepresented that he forbade his son-in-law to talk with him, in 1859. They did, however, have a long conversation, in which the young man insisted, that Auld was really kind-hearted and a

good master. " I replied," says Douglass, " that there
must be two sides to the relation of master and slave,
and what seemed kind and just to the one was the
opposite to the other." On Auld's death-bed, in 1878,
he was reconciled to Douglass, who admitted that he
had been mistaken in charging him, in a letter written to him in England, and published in " Bondage
and Freedom," with turning out his grandmother to
perish as an outcast, whereas he had saved her from
this fate. Mr. D. added that " I regard both of us as
victims of a system." (" Life and Times," pp. 437 and
491.) Each of the two later autobiographies speaks
more favorably than the earliest of Captain Auld ;
but the statements to which he objected are repeated ;
and the author declared, in 1846, that he had nothing
to take back. It seems to me plain, that he did suffer
hunger, though perhaps not from any fault of his
master ; and that he was punished for stealing food ;
as his statements on these points are not only too
minute, but too much against himself, to be rejected.
He also published, at this time a circumstantial
statement, that Thomas Auld once beat him with a
coach whip until he was weary, and in the presence
of a white man whom he names, because a carriage
lamp had been lost through no fault of the victim.

The " Liberator " was soon able to publish a letter
from a man who knew the country where Douglass
was a slave. " I am fully prepared," he says, " to
bear a decided testimony to the truth of all his assertions with regard to the discipline upon the plantations of Maryland, as well as his descriptions of
cruelty and murder." It is to be particularly noticed
that Thompson, the American, makes no attempt to

refute what is said of Covey, and other wicked neighbors, but merely says they had a good reputation with other slave-holders. So we may take the worst charges brought by Douglass against slavery as substantially correct. He may have failed, as we should undoubtedly do, to see all the good points of a man who dared to treat him as property ; but he had a perfect right to say to Thompson :

" You have completely tripped up the heels of your pro-slavery friends, and laid them flat at my feet. You have done a piece of anti-slavery work which no anti-slavery man could do." . . . " I am now publishing a second edition of my 'Narrative,' in this country, having already disposed of the first. I will insert your article, with my reply, as an appendix."

He adds, with reference to the timid way, in which he used to pass him at St. Michaels :

" If I should meet you now, amid the free hills of old Scotland, where the ancient ' black Douglas' once met his foes, I presume I might summon sufficient fortitude to look you in the face ; and were you to attempt to make a slave of me, it is possible you might find me almost as disagreeable a subject as was the Douglas to whom I have just referred."

How much our black knight has of what was best in ancient chivalry, was shown while he was traveling through the Highlands. It was a rainy day, and he was one of the passengers who filled the inside of the coach. By and bye a lady asked for a seat, but there was none vacant except on the outside. Ther the Douglass gave her his own place, and climbed up himself to sit in the rain. He did this as a matter of course, and was surprised to find the sturdy Britons look at him as a second Don Quixote. It was not their way of treating women.

While unsuccessful agitations were going on in Scotland and Ireland, a great reform, destined to bless all mankind, was finished triumphantly in England. Ever since the beginning of the century the members of the working-classes had suffered pitiably ; and their distress had been aggravated by the tariff, which was laid on so many articles as to form an almost complete list of the world's products. Most oppressive of all was the duty on wheat, which was imposed for the enrichment of the owners of land, mostly members of the wealthiest class, and which kept bread at starvation prices. There were also heavy taxes on all manufactured articles, as well as on raw materials ; and the natural result was that the factories could not turn out goods cheaply enough to send much to foreign markets. Thus there was so little demand for skilled labor as to keep wages low, while prices remained cruelly high. It is now many years since there has been such destitution as in 1841, when there were twenty thousand people in Leeds who did not earn on the average a shilling a week, while nearly one-fifth of the population of Nottingham was on the parish. Fortunately, the manufacturers were intelligent enough to see the real cause of the people's sufferings, and generous enough to imperil their own immediate interest for the nation's permanent good. As early as 1838 they united with Cobden and Bright in the Anti-Corn Law League, so called, it may be observed, with an especial view to attacking the duties on wheat, which, with other kinds of grain, is known as " corn " in England. The Free-traders were fiercely opposed, not only by the Conservatives, but by the Chartists, who wished to make everything

else give way to their own visionary schemes ; but
the cause of practical reform was carried steadily
onward.   Important reductions were made in 1842
and 1844 ; and, on June 26, 1846, the Corn Laws were
repealed, and all the other protective parts of the
tariff abandoned.   The League dissolved soon after,
and "Punch" published a cartoon, in which it was
represented as the magic staff, now broken by Pros-
pero because its work was done.   In another picture
the British Lion was seen, fattened on free trade into
a strong resemblance to a prize pig at a cattle show.
And, as the present condition of England has been
badly misrepresented, for the purpose either of
hindering a much needed reform, or else of fostering
a fresh crop of visionary projects, it is well to mention
a few significant facts.   The average income of families in the working-class has doubled since 1840, as
has recently been shown in the "New York World,"
by calculations based on the British legacy and suc-
cession returns, while the cost of most of the neces-
saries of life has been reduced to about one-half of
the old prices.   There was twice as much money
deposited in the savings banks, in proportion to the
population, in 1878 as in 1841 ; and the ability of the
poor to purchase luxuries has increased so much as
to make the average consumption of sugar five times
as great in 1887 as in 1840, while that of eggs and
butter has more than doubled   The number of
paupers in England and Wales fell, as is easily com-
puted from the "Encyclopædia Britannica," during
the thirty years succeeding the abolition of pro-
tectionism, from one in seventeen of the population
to one in thirty, and there were less than one-half as

many able-bodied adults on the parish, on a given day in 1878, as in 1849. Great Britain, meantime, has become the leading manufacturer for all nations, and has had no occasion to abandon the principles which triumphed in 1846.

The men who then insisted that legislation should not be for the protection of the few, but of the many, were consistent enough to hate slavery and honor the Abolitionists. Garrison was in favor of " free trade and free intercommunication the world over ; " and his adherents agreed, for once, with both Liberty party men and Democrats, in supporting that reduction of our tariff which was made this very year, with the best possible results to all our industries. England looked back with pride to the recent emancipation in the West Indies ; and there was no such excuse as in Scotland for tolerating slave-holding. All these circumstances combined to make the eleven months which Douglass spent there one long ovation. An invitation to speak at the annual meeting of the British and Foreign Anti-Slavery Society, on Monday, May 18, brought him that day to London. The next night he spoke to a Peace convention ; Wednesday, to one for extending the suffrage to all Englishmen ; Thursday, on temperance ; and Friday, at a reception, the date of which is printed May 12, in " Bondage and Freedom," whereas it should be May 22. The speech, which he made that night, contains this passage :

"I have to inform you that the religion of the Southern States, at this time, is the great supporter, the great sanctioner of the bloody atrocities to which I have referred. While America is printing tracts and Bibles, sending missionaries abroad to convert the heathen ; expending her money in various ways for the promotion of the Gospel in foreign lands, the slave not only lies forgotten, uncared for, but is trampled under foot by the very Church of the land. What have we in America ? Why, we have slavery made part of the religion of the land. Yes, the pulpit there stands up as the great defender of this cursed institution, as it is called. Ministers of religion come forward and torture the hallowed pages of inspired wisdom to sanction the bloody deed. They stand forth as the foremost, the strongest defenders of this ' institution.' As a proof of this, I need not do more than state the general fact that slavery has existed under the droppings of the sanctuary of the South for the last two hundred years, and there has not been any war between the religion and the slavery of the South. Whips, chains, gags, and thumb-screws have all lain under the droppings of the sanctuary, and instead of rusting from off the limbs of the bondsmen, these droppings have served to preserve them in all their strength. Instead of preaching the Gospel against this tyranny and wrong, ministers of religion have sought, by all and every means, to throw in the background whatever in the Bible could be construed into opposition to slavery, and to bring forward that which they could torture into its support. This I conceive to be the darkest feature of slavery, and the most difficult to attack, because it is identified with religion, and exposes those who denounce it to the charge of infidelity. Yes, those with whom I have been laboring, namely, the old organization anti-slavery society of America, have been again and again stigmatized as infidels, and for what reason ? Why, solely in consequence of the faithfulness of their attacks upon the slave-holding religion of the Southern States, and the Northern religion that sympathizes with it. I have found it difficult to speak on this matter without persons coming forward and saying, ' Douglass, are you not afraid of injuring the cause of Christ ? You do not desire to do so, we know ; but are you not undermining religion ? ' This has been said to me again and again, even since I came to this country ; but I cannot be induced to leave off

these exposures. I love the religion of our blessed Saviour. I
love that religion that comes from above, in the ' wisdom of
God, which is first pure, then peaceable, gentle, and easy to be
entreated, full of mercy and good fruits, without partiality, and
without hypocrisy.' I love that religion that sends its votaries
to bind up the wounds of him that has fallen among thieves.
I love that religion that makes it the duty of its disciples to
visit the fatherless and the widow in their affliction. I love
that religion that is based upon the glorious principle of love
to God and love to man ; which makes its followers do unto
others as they themselves would be done by. If you demand
liberty to yourself, it says, grant it to your neighbors. If you
claim the right to think for yourself, it says, allow your
neighbors the same right. If you claim to act for yourself,
it says, allow your neighbors the same right. It is because I
love this religion that I hate the slave-holding, the woman-
whipping, the mind-darkening, the soul-destroying religion that
exists in the Southern States of America. It is because I
regard the one as good, and pure, and holy, that I cannot but
regard the other as bad, corrupt, and wicked. Loving the one,
I must hate the other ; holding to the one, I must reject the
other."

At the Peace convention, three days earlier, he
said :

" You may think it somewhat singular that I, a slave, an
American slave, should stand forth at this time as an advocate
of peace between two countries situated as this and the United
States are, when it is universally believed that a war between
them would result in the emancipation of three millions of my
brethren, who are now held in the most cruel bonds in that
country. I believe this would be the result ; but such is my
regard for the principle of peace, such is my deep, firm conviction that nothing can be attained for liberty universally by war,
that were I to be asked the question whether I would have my
emancipation by the shedding of one single drop of blood, my
answer would be in the negative."

This was all the nobler, because he undoubtedly knew then, as is mentioned in a letter written before the end of this week, that Hugh Auld, who now claimed him as property, had publicly threatened to arrest him as soon as he returned to the United States, and send him, for the vindication of the family honor, into slavery in those regions where it is most cruel. An attempt was made at the reception on Friday evening to induce him to remain in England ; and money was subscribed for bringing over his family. Reports soon reached Boston that he would never return ; but he wrote back in July from Belfast that " No inducement could be offered strong enough to make me quit my hold upon America as my home. Whether a slave or a freeman, America is my home ; and there I mean to spend and be spent in the cause of my outraged fellow-countrymen."

Garrison had already been invited by George Thompson to come over and assist in reorganizing the enemies of slavery in Great Britain. The night before he left, he said at a reception given him by the colored people of Boston, in their church in Belknap Street, that among his reasons for going was this : " I want to see Douglass ; and is he not in truth a man ? What a grand mistake his master made when he thought he was a chattel ! " Both champions were soon obliged to draw the sword against their own countrymen in London. At the opening session of the World's Temperance convention, August 4, Garrison rebuked a Boston clergyman for defending slavery, but was pronounced out of order, and stayed away afterward. Douglass was invited to speak on the night of the 7th, and called attention to a fact which had not been mentioned by the delegates from America. They had said a great deal in praise of their temperance societies ; but there were three millions of Americans who could not join them. Slaves could not meet by themselves for any purpose ; and the attempt of the free colored people to form societies of their own, had called out a mob in Philadelphia on August 1, 1842, when their procession was broken up by showers of stones and brickbats ; their teetotal banners were trampled in the dust ; one of their churches was burned to the ground ; and their best temperance hall was demolished. The British hearers were indignant at the outrage, and the Americans at the orator. He said afterward that " There was one Doctor of Divinity there, the ugliest man I ever saw in my life, who almost tore the skirt of my coat off, so vehement was he in his friendly attempts to induce me to yield the floor." The audience was with him by a large majority, and he was urged to go on ; but next morning the Rev. Dr. Cox wrote to the New York papers to denounce " the colored Abolition agitator and ultraist," who had ruined a moral scene which " was superb and glorious," by lugging in abolitionism, and " is supposed to have been well paid for the abomination." Douglass promptly denied this last charge ; and accepted the description " as a compliment." All he said was fully justified by " the deep depression of the colored people in America, and the treatment uniformly adopted by white temperance societies toward them." " The temperance cause," he added, "is dear to me. I love it for myself, and for the black man as well as for the white man. I have labored both in England

and America to promote the cause, and am ready still
to labor ; I should grieve to think of any act of mine,
which would inflict the slightest ruin upon the cause ;
but I am satisfied that no such injury was inflicted."

This correspondence did much to make Douglass
favorably known in Europe, and so did another controversy of his with the same clergyman. The Evangelical Alliance was organized on August 19, by about
a thousand delegates, representing fifty orthodox
sects, and coming from many lands. No slave-holders
had been invited ; and the question of fellowshiping
them brought up a discussion, in which almost all the
Americans, including Dr. Beecher, sided with Dr.
Cox. What he said, and how he was answered elsewhere, are stated by Douglass in his last speech in
London, thus :

" Dr. Cox said at the recent meeting of the Evangelical Alliance, ' I knew a brother in the South, a dear brother, to whom I
spoke on this subject, and I told him what a great sin I thought
it was for him to hold slaves ; but he said to me, " Brother, I
feel it as much as you do ; but what can I do? Here are my
slaves, take them. You may have them. You may take them
out of the State, if you please," said he. I could not ; so I left
them ; and what would you do, brethren of Manchester and
Liverpool, if you were placed in such difficult circumstances ? '
There is no truth in this at all ; let me tell you what has been a
standing article in anti-slavery journals for the last ten years.
As soon as the noble Gerrit Smith and others heard of this difficulty, under which the slave-holders represented that they
labored, what did they do ? They inserted advertisements in all
the respectable papers in America, stating that there were ten
thousand dollars at the service of any poor slave-holders who
might not have the means of removing their slaves. Now,
every slave-holder must have seen that, for they find no difficulty

in seeing money ; they must have seen this ; but was there ever a demand for a single red copper of all those ten thousand dollars ? Never, never ! "

He also pointed out the fact that there were many States, where slaves could be emancipated and not sent away ; and in reply to the bugbear, set up in the Alliance, of negro pauperism, he said :

" I do not know that I ever saw a black pauper. In Philadelphia they not only support their own poor by their own benevolent societies, but actually pay five hundred dollars *per annum* for the support of the white paupers of that city. We do not have black paupers. We leave pauperism to be taken care of by white people. I mean no disrespect to my audience ; for I have no prejudice against color."

Armed with facts like these, he made what Garrison calls " a very effective speech," and was " warmly applauded." At the meeting held on September 14, in Exeter Hall, for denouncing the cowardice of the Alliance, by the Anti-Slavery League, which had but just been formed, Mr. Garrison was so bitter as to call out much opposition and disturbance ; but Thompson succeeded in carrying the meeting with him ; and Douglass brought it to a triumphant close. The clergyman who edited a London paper, the "Christian Witness," says: "The speeches of Mr. Thompson and Mr. Douglass were all that could have been desired. Both were worthy of the occasion." He complains, however, that Garrison " seems to have made the science of offense a special study, and has, we think, attained to very great proficiency." The increasing heterodoxy of his views, about the Bible and the Sabbath especially, helped to create an unpopularity, which Douglass labored loyally and constantly to diminish. In one of his latest speeches, this year, he says, "I love the Abolitionists of England ; but they ask of me too much, when they desire me to step from the side of Garrison." He remarks, at present that he was one of the most amiable of men, to those who agreed with him, and makes the comparison between him and Thompson, that the latter was more of an orator than of a man, whereas Garrison was more of a man than an orator.

Douglass was now a lion in London, on account of the eloquence of his speeches against the Free Church and the Alliance, although we cannot, in view of the work done by the latter body against persecution, even recently, say, as his admirers then did, that he "shattered it to atoms." He was hospitably entertained, at the same time as Andersen, by the Howitts, who "were among the kindliest people I ever met." He went with Garrison and Thompson to breakfast at Sir John Bowring's, and also to call on the aged Abolitionist, Clarkson, then near his end. The Chartist leader, Lovett, speaks of "a very delightful evening," when "Our friend, Douglass, who had a fine voice, sang a number of negro melodies, Mr. Garrison sang several anti-slavery pieces, and our grave friend, H. C. Wright, sang an old Indian war-song." Douglass also met Lord Brougham and Douglas Jerrold, but he was too much in request for the platform to be able to meet many of the literary celebrities, though he must have heard a great deal about them, especially Carlyle, Macaulay, Thackeray, Dickens, and Tennyson. One curious result of this visit was that a gentleman, who had come over from one of our Southern States, was told by an Englishman, who was showing him his pictures and statues, "I want particularly to have you look at my bust of your countryman, Mr. Douglass." "With the utmost pleasure," was the reply. "Senator Douglas is one of our most distinguished men." But the bust was in black marble.

A more practically useful form was given to the admiration for our colored orator, by Mrs. Ellen Richardson, who now collected money enough to purchase his freedom of Hugh Auld. Garrison was among the contributors, and also one of the defenders of this act of generosity, which many Abolitionists condemned as a sanction of slavery. Henry C. Wright, for instance, wrote a most earnest letter, advising his friend never to make any use of his free papers. Douglass replied that it was just as proper for him to protect himself by them, as for Mr. Wright to protect himself, while traveling on the Continent, by so far acknowledging the claims of the despots as to take out a passport. He added :

"I am free to say that, had I possessed one hundred and fifty pounds, I would have seen Hugh Auld kicking before I would have given it to him. I would have waited till the emergency came, and only given the money when nothing else would do. But my friends thought it best to provide against the contingency. They acted on their own responsibility, and I am not disturbed about the result. But having acted on a true principle, I do not feel free to disavow their proceedings."

He also said, as the purchase continued to be blamed, "I expected that would be the case, and I deem no man the less my friend, for not being pleased with it." The controversy seems to have been finally extinguished by a lady, who wrote to the editor of the " Liberator " :

"Let me beg of you never to publish another word in your paper about the ransom of Douglass. I am quite ashamed that our American Abolitionists should expose their narrowness in expressing so many regrets at their loss of slave property in Douglass. They seem to feel that he was their property and not his own man."

After the August meetings in London, where the Slave-holder's Sermon was occasionally repeated to a delighted audience, we find the two champions from America at Sunderland, Birmingham, Wrexham (in Wales), Manchester, Glasgow, Dundee, and Edinburgh. In the last city Douglass was able to thank George Combe for what he had learned from the " Constitution of Man ; " and he also had the pleasure of taking part in the presentation of a silver tea-set, and a purse of gold, on October 21, to the agitator, who on that day, eleven years before, had been dragged about by a Boston mob. On November 4, he led the cheering, when his leader set out for America, where he had fresh experience of the iniquity of custom-houses. The letter in which Lowell describes the Anti-Slavery Bazaar—among whose treasures were an unusual number of gifts from British friends, for instance, the pupils of the Bristol Blind Asylum, who had become deeply interested in the black knight—contains these lines :

> " There's Garrison, his features very
> Benign for an incendiary.
> Beaming forth sunshine through his glasses
> On the surrounding lads and lasses.

(No bee could blither be or brisker,)
A Pickwick somehow turned John Ziska,
His bump of firmness swelling up,
Like a rye cup-cake from its cup.
And there, too, was his English tea-set,
Which in his ear a kind of flea set,
His Uncle Samuel, for its beauty,
Demanding sixty dollars duty.
'T was natural Sam should serve his trunk ill,
For G., you know, has cut his uncle."

Douglass remained to work in Great Britain, and
one of the most active of the Scotch Abolitionists
writes that " He is greeted with rapturous applause
wherever he goes, and cannot be spared, but must be
here at least till next summer."   On the last night of
1846, he said, at Newcastle, that there were three
million decided Abolitionists in the Union, while at
least forty periodicals advocated the negro's cause.
We find that on February 9, 1847, he "appeared
thoroughly worn out," and that sixteen days later, at
Sheffield, " Frederick was too ill from long continued
exertion to do himself justice ; but, for the cause in
which he so nobly labors, he pleaded powerfully."
In the meantime, one of the most deeply respected
of the English Abolitionists, Elizabeth Pease, wrote
thus :

" Much had I longed to see this remarkable man, and
highly raised were my expectations, but they were more than
realized. A living contradiction is he, truly, to that base
opinion, which is so abhorrent to every humane and Christian feeling, that the blacks are an inferior race."

He spoke every night in March, but was obliged,
during the last week, to decline more than thirty

invitations to lecture, for it was known that he was about to leave. At a farewell soiree, given in London, on March 30, William Howitt said :

"He has appeared in this country before the most accomplished audiences, who were surprised, not only at his talent, but at his extraordinary information. And all I can say is, I hope America will continue to send us such men as Frederick Douglass, and slavery will soon be abolished."

The orator himself began by insisting that not only the Constitution of the United States, but the American churches deserved all that had been said against them, by a man whose "name is unjustly coupled with opprobrium in this country." . . . "My beloved, my esteemed, and almost venerated friend, William Lloyd Garrison, who is hated and despised in this country, because he has fearlessly, on both sides of the Atlantic, unmasked their hypocrisy, branded their impiety in the language that it deserves." The execration in which Garrison was held had somewhat hindered his own recognition; but he had had sympathy here and coöperation there ; and the number of unfriendly Abolitionists was really insignificant. After an account, already quoted, of his passage at arms with Dr. Cox, he went on to speak of his purchase, and remarked : "By the bye, I want to tell the audience one thing, and that is, that I have just as much right to sell Hugh Auld as he had to sell me, and if any of you are disposed to make a purchase to-night, just say the word."

The conclusion of this speech is as follows :

"Let me say one word to you on parting, for this is probably the last time I will have an opportunity of speaking to a London audience. I came here a slave; I came here degraded; I came here under a load of odium heaped upon my race by the American press, by the American pulpit, by the American people; I have gone through this land; and I have steadily increased the amount of attention bestowed upon this question by the British people. Wherever I have gone I have been treated with the utmost kindness, with the utmost deference, with the utmost attention. I have reason to love England. Truly liberty in England is better than slavery in America; freedom at Hyde Park corner is better than slavery in front of the American Capitol. I have known then, these last nineteen months, what it was for the first time in my life to enjoy freedom. Just before leaving Boston for this country I was not allowed to ride in a public conveyance; I was kicked from an omnibus. I was driven from the lower floor of a church because I had dared to enter there, forgetting my complexion, remembering that I was a man, and thinking I had an interest in the Gospel there proclaimed. In my passage to this country I was driven out of the cabin of the steamboat, out of all respectable parts of the ship, onto the floor of the deck, among the cattle— not allowed to take any place among human beings as a man and a brother. I was not allowed to go into a menagerie or a theater, if I wanted to go, nor to a museum, nor to an Athenæum, nor into a picture gallery, if I wished to do so. I was not allowed any of these privileges; I was mobbed; I was beaten; I was driven, dragged out, insulted, outraged in all directions; every white man, no matter how black his heart, could insult me with impunity.

"I came to this land—how great the change! The moment I stepped upon the soil at Liverpool, I saw people as white as I ever saw in the United States, as noble in their exterior; and, instead of seeing the curled lip of scorn, the fire of hate kindled in the eye of the Englishman, all was respect and kindness. [Cheers.] I looked around in vain for the insult; I looked, for I hardly believed my eyes; I searched to see if I could see in an Englishman any look of disapprobation of me on account of my complexion—not one. [Loud cheers.] I have traveled in all parts of the country, in Ireland, in Scotland, and in England and Wales; I have traveled on highways, byways, railways, and steamboats; and in none of these instances have I met anything I could torture into an expression of disrespect of me on account of my complexion. [Loud cheers.] I have visited your Colosseum, your Museum, your gallery of paintings; I even had the pleasure of going into your House of Commons, and, still more, into the House of Lords, and hearing what I never heard before, and what I had long wished to hear, the eloquence of Lord Brougham. [Cheers.] In none of these places did I ever hear one word of scorn. I have felt, however much Americans may affect to despise and scorn the negro, that Englishmen —the best of Englishmen—do not hesitate to give the right hand of manly fellowship to such as I am. [Much cheering.]

" When I return to the United States, I will try to impress them with these facts, and to shame them into a sense of decency upon this subject. Why, sir, the Americans do not know that I am a man ; they think the negro is something between the man and the monkey. The very dogs here, sir, know that I am a man. I was at a public meeting at Bromley, the other day, and while I was speaking, a great Newfoundland dog came and put his paws on the platform, and gazed at me with such interest, that I could tell by the very expression of his eye, that he recognized humanity. [General laughter.] I came here a slave; but I go back free. I came here despised: I go back with a reputation. I am sure if the Americans will believe one tithe of all that has been said in this country respecting me, they will certainly admit that I am better than I was. Though in better circumstances than I came, yet I go back to toil, not to have ease and comfort. Since I came to this land I have had every inducement to stop here. The kindness of my friends in the North has been unbounded; they have proffered me every inducement to bring my family over to this country; they have gone so far as to offer to give money that they might be brought to this land ; and I should settle down here in a different position from that which I should occupy in the United States ; but I prefer to live a life of activity : I prefer to go home, to go back to America. I glory in the conflict, that I may also glory in the victory. I go back, turning away from comfort, and ease, and respectability which I might maintain here: I go back for the sake of my brethren. [Cheers.] I go back to suffer with them, to toil with them, for that emancipation which is yet to be achieved by the power of truth over the basest selfishness. [Great cheering.] I go back gladly, I leave this country for the United States on the fourth of April, which is near at hand. I feel not merely satisfied, but highly gratified, with my visit to this country. I will tell my colored brethren how Englishmen feel for them. It will be something to give them patience under their sorrows, and hope of a future emancipation. I shall try to have daguerreotyped upon my heart this sea of up-turned faces. I will tell them this; it will strengthen them in their suffering and in their toils; and I am sure in this I have your sympathy as well as their blessing. Pardon me, my friends, for the disconnected manner in which I have addressed you, but I have spoken out of the fulness of my heart; as the words came up, so they have been uttered; not altogether, perhaps, so delicately, and systematically, and refinedly as they might have been, but still you must take them as they are. They are the free outgushings of my heart, overborne with grateful emotion for the kindness I have received in this country, from the day I arrived here to the present moment. With deepest gratitude, farewell!"

The day after this speech a letter was written in Scotland, summing up his work there thus:

"He has divided the Free Church against itself on account of slavery. He has gained the admiration and esteem of all the friends of the slave in this country. He has always kept an open platform, yet none of the Rabbis have been found gallant enough to break a lance with him. He completely exploded their miserable attempts to reconcile slavery with Christianity."

His last speech in Great Britain was made on

Thursday, April 1, at Bristol, where he said, "This night, ten years ago, at least the night before Good Friday, I passed in the woods, planning with four of my friends an escape, which proved unsuccessful." A new disappointment was waiting for him.

He had bought his ticket four weeks before, and engaged a berth in the first cabin, on the express understanding that he was to be treated as well, in every respect, as the other passengers. When he reached Liverpool, the day before the steamer left, he was told that his berth would be occupied by some one else, and he would have to keep away from the other passengers. The reason assigned was his having lectured against slavery on this same vessel, nearly two years before. In fact, the agent, who came from one of the Southern States, declared soon after, in print, that he would have acted just so "if he had been the whitest man in the world." He at once wrote a protest, in which he said, "I have traveled in this country nineteen months, and have always enjoyed equal rights with other passengers; and it was not until I turned my face toward America, that I met with anything like proscription on account of my color." His friends at once printed this letter on slips, which were sent to all the British papers. More than a hundred of them published it at once, and there were very severe editorials against the Cunard Company in the London "Times," and a score of other leading journals. Douglas Jerrold, for instance, was indignant at the insult to "the man of color, whose eloquence has stirred the English hearts of tens of thousands;" and it was only American newspapers which approved of such treatment of the "negro impostor." A letter was published in England, purporting to be from a Virginian, named Burrop, a proprietor in the steamship company, and head-manager, and declaring that the exclusion was made on the color line, heavy losses having been sustained in consequence of acting otherwise. But these statements were pronounced entirely untrue by Mr. Cunard, who also said that he had never heard of Burrop, and would take care that nothing of the sort should happen again.

John Bright and his sisters made the last night which their friend passed in England cheerful, and the conversation lasted until morning. It was Easter Sunday, April 4, when he went on board the "Cambria." The other passengers, especially the ladies, looked at him with contempt, and he said to the Britons, who came to see him off, "I feel, friends, and I cannot help it, that in leaving this country I am going from home to a land of oppression and slavery—a land of man-stealers." Captain Judkins, who had stood by him on the voyage out, was still in command, and he was treated with the utmost politeness and kindness by every one. His room was the same that had been occupied shortly before by the Governor-General of Canada, and was large enough for a dozen people to sit in ; but he was treated as a prisoner of state, obliged to eat by himself, and not even permitted to attend the religious services. He felt deeply the humiliation, but " This I thought was American slave-holding religion under British colors, and I felt myself no great loser at being excluded from its benefits."

His sixteen days of solitary confinement must have

been consoled by the recollection of what were by far
the brightest scenes in his life, before he reached
fifty. He had made a great discovery, whose importance is not even yet recognized fully. He had proved
that the color-prejudice is not a universal characteristic of the white race, too widely diffused and deeply
seated to stand much chance of being eradicated, but
merely a local idiosyncrasy, destined to become obso-
lete, like the peculiar dialect in which the " Biglow
Papers " were at this time written. It is necessary in
" the survival of the fittest," that all national peculiarities of speech, dress, food, amusement, or opinion, not
limited by climate, should ultimately either become
universal and cosmopolitan, or else disappear entirely.
The color-prejudice is only an Americanism, and
never can be anything more. It may linger long
among the uncultivated ; but its days are numbered.
To prove this was worth a great deal to the anti-
slavery cause ; but otherwise the British sympathy
called out by Douglass and Garrison was not, I think,
of much value, especially as the money was never sent
back from Scotland. Ireland was more responsive ;
but the example of O'Connell and Father Mathew
does not seem to have had the slightest influence on
their admirers who emigrated to America. We shall
find George Thompson treated all the worse in
Boston in 1850, because he was an ambassador from
most of the respectable men and women in England.
The fathers of the men who now seem to think that
the principles of civil service reform and free trade are
false and dangerous here, because they have been
found true and beneficial in Great Britain, hated " the
nigger," Douglass, all the more bitterly after they saw

him honored by the Britishers. I doubt if a single
hunker would have been converted by hearing that
the "Liberator" had got a hundred thousand subscribers in England ; and the amount of national aid
which came across the water to Boston does not seem
to have been very great. I find no record of any
other contributions so large as that which purchased
freedom for Douglass, and that which, as we shall
see, soon enabled him to publish a newspaper, whose
name furnishes a title for our next chapter.

CHAPTER VI.

THE "NORTH STAR."

WHEN Douglass returned to the United States, April 20, 1847, he brought with him the news that the lady who had made him legally free, Mrs. Ellen Richardson, of Newcastle, had just opened a subscription for a newspaper, which he should edit in the interest of colored people. He had at first made several objections. His friends in Boston might not like it; the average American would be prejudiced against any enterprise started by British capital; he did not himself like a sedentary life; and money was more needed in Ireland, just then, than in America. All these objections were outweighed, however, by the zeal of his English friends, and the subscription was likely to be a success. The time was propitious for several reasons. His victories abroad enabled him to return in triumph. The war which had been undertaken against Mexico, for the extension of slavery, had now assumed a character of such atrocity as to justify the opening against it of a new battery, especially as Lowell and Whittier were furnishing abundance of ammunition. And the discontinuance of the " Herald of Freedom," in 1846, had left a gap which ought to be speedily filled.

The prisoner on the "Cambria" had consoled himself

by visions of what he was about to do for his race, when he could use his pen as well as his voice, and reach constantly all who sympathized with him, instead of only scattered portions intermittently. He was sadly perplexed and disappointed at finding Garrison and the other Boston Abolitionists insist that he was better fitted for speaking than writi.g; that editing a paper would interfere with his usefulness as a lecturer; and that there was no room for another anti-slavery journal. The field seemed, in fact, pretty full, as three new ones had been started that very year by the colored people, who are said to have got out as many as a hundred before 1855. The first on the list is dated as early as 1827 ; and twenty years later I find that the " Ram's Horn " was in full blast ; the " Mystery " was awaiting its solution or dissolution ; the " National Watchman " was going its rounds busily ; the " Disfranchised American " was on the war path; and the " Northern Star and Colored Farmer " was shining under the direction of the black pastor of a white congregation, Rev. S. R. Ward, who evidently believed that every farmer should hitch his wagon to a star. The " Elevator," however, was not running ; the " Struggler " had either ceased or not begun to struggle; and the " Palladium of Liberty " had, I fear, been captured by the enemy, in company with the " Demosthenian Shield." But at all events, there were now so many rivals to the proposed paper, and there had been so many failures in this quarter, that the enterprise naturally seemed perilous. How far Garrison was influenced by determination that there should be order in the ranks, it is hard to say. The fact which he brought forward in July, that he once had four hundred colored subscribers in New York City, and as many in Philadelphia, and now had not half-a-dozen in either place, was really a much more favorable indication than he represented it to be for Douglass ; and I hardly think Garrison had a right to say that " It is quite impracticable to combine the editor with the lecturer, without either causing the paper to be more or less neglected, or the sphere of lecturing to be seriously circumscribed." He had himself been so successful in making his lecturing and his editing help each other, that it is a great pity that he did not promptly and cordially urge his young friend and disciple to go and do likewise. He declared in the " Liberator," before the money had been sent over, that he considered "such a present inexpedient ; " and two days later, June 27, Douglass wrote a letter for publication, in which he said, " I have, with some reluctance, given up the idea of publishing a paper for the present." Four weeks later, in consequence of suggestions that he had been unduly influenced, he stated that he had acted " wholly on my own responsibility ; " but it was mainly due to Garrison that the publication of the " North Star " was delayed nearly a year ; and it finally had to appear without his approbation.

Our Douglass has so noble a nature that no opposition could damp his zeal for his race. The " Boston Post " mentioned, in May, that " The Abolitionists, headed by Mr. William Lloyd Garrison, and tailed by Mr. Frederick Douglass, the fugitive slave, are in full blast at the Broadway Tabernacle." It is further stated of Douglass that he " elaborates very eloquently and fearfully; " that he is " a good deal of a demagogue in black," and also that he " was armed to the teeth, and was in fact a walking San Juan de Ulloa." There was an attempt to silence him by force. But he did not hesitate to support Garrison's resolution against a proposal to give the Bible to the slaves, who ought first to have a chance to learn how to read it ; and he declared that " The only thing that links me to this land is my family, and the painful consciousness that here there are three million of my fellow-creatures, groaning beneath the iron rod of the worst despotism that could be devised, even in Pandemonium." He then took up the charge that he had irritated the American people and said, " I admit that we have irritated them. They deserve to be irritated." . . . " The conscience of the American public needs this irritation ; and I would blister it all over from center to circumference." The New York " Sun " complained that he had acted as ungratefully toward the country which protected him, as if he had accepted a gentleman's hospitality and abused the fare ; but he wrote from Lynn, on May 18, a letter for the " Ram's Horn," in which he suggests to the editor of the " Sun " that

" A cook-shop (a thing which I am surprised he should ever forget) bears a far greater resemblance to the government of this country than that of a gentleman's house and hospitality. Let 'Cook-shop' represent 'Country'—' Bill of Fare,' ' Bill of Rights,' and the ' Chief Cook,' ' Commander-in-Chief.' Enters editor of ' Sun ' with a keen appetite. He reads the bill of fare. It contains the names of many palatable dishes. He asks the cook for soup ; he gets dish-water. For salmon, he gets a serpent ; for beef, he gets bull-frogs ; for ducks, he gets dogs ; for salt, he gets sand ; for pepper, he gets powder ; and for vinegar, he gets gall." . . . " This is just the treatment which the colored people receive in this country at the hand of this government. Its Bill of Rights is in practice toward us a bill of wrongs. Its self-evident truths are self-evident lies." . . . " The great Constitution itself is nothing more than a compromise with man-stealers, and a cunningly devised complication of false-hoods, calculated to deceive foreign nations into a belief that this is a free country ; at the same time that it pledges the whole civil, naval, and military power of the nation to keep three millions of people in the most abject slavery. He says I abuse a country under whose government I am safely residing and securely protected. I am neither safely residing nor securely protected in this country. I am living under a government which authorized Hugh Auld to steal seven hundred and fifty dollars from me, and told me if I did not submit, if I resisted the robber, I should be put to death. This is the protection given to me and every other colored man from the South ; and nobody knows this better than the editor of the ' Sun.' And this piece of robbery the ' Sun ' calls ' the rights of the master,' and says that the English people recognized those rights by giving me money with which to purchase my freedom. The ' Sun ' complains that I defend the right of invoking England for the overthrow of American slavery. Why not receive aid from England to overthrow American slavery, as well as for Americans to send bread to England to feed the hungry ? Answer me that ! "

Another New York paper, very felicitously entitled the " Subterranean," was provoked by his having " reiterated his slanders in an obscure gathering of fanatics in this city," into calling him a " semi-baboon," and " a most repulsive-looking darkey."

When the New England Convention met at Boston in Anniversary Week, he was elected president, but was kept away by a " severe indisposition." On June 17, he gave an account of his visit to England, at Fall River; and on July 3 and 4, he took part at Plymouth in a discussion about a resolution, finally laid on the table, and meant to incite the slaves to insurrection. In August and September he took a journey, of which he does not speak in his autobiographies ; but his companion, Mr. Garrison, has left a full account in letters, from which I take these extracts. ("William Lloyd Garrison : the Story of his Life. Told by his Children." Vol. iii., pp. 189–205) :

" August 7.

" Our three days' meeting at Norristown closed last evening, and a famous time we have had of it. Every day two or three hundred of our friends from Philadelphia came up in the cars, and the meetings were uniformly crowded by an array of men and women who, for thorough-going anti-slavery spirit and solidity of character, are not surpassed by any in the world. Douglass arrived on the second day, and was justly the ' lion ' of the occasion ; though a considerable number participated in the discussions, our friend Lucretia Mott speaking with excellent propriety and effect. Thomas Earle was present to annoy us, as usual. Our meetings were not molested in any manner, excepting one evening, when Douglass and I held a meeting after dark, when a few panes of glass were broken by some rowdy boys while D. was speaking. It was a grand meeting, nevertheless, and the house crowded with a noble auditory to the end. The meetings will have a powerful effect in the prosecution of our cause for the coming year. It was worth a trip from Boston to Norristown merely to *look* at those who assembled on the occasion."

" HARRISBURG, August 9, 1847.

" On Saturday morning, Douglass and I bade farewell to our kind friends in Philadelphia, and took the cars for this place —a distance of 106 miles. Before we started, an incident occurred which evinced something of that venomous pro-slavery spirit which pervades the public sentiment in proportion as you approach the borders of the slave States. There is no distinction made at Philadelphia in the cars on account of complexion, though colored persons usually sit near the doors. Douglass took a seat in one of the back cars before I arrived, and, while quietly looking out at the window, was suddenly accosted in a slave-driving tone, and ordered to 'get out of that seat,' by a man who had a lady with him, and who might have claimed the right to eject any other passenger for his accommodation with as much propriety. Douglass quietly replied, that if he would make his demand in the form of a gentlemanly request, he would readily vacate his seat. His lordly commander at once laid violent hands upon him, and dragged him out. Douglass submitted to this outrage unresistingly, but told his assailant that he behaved like a bully, and therefore precluded him (D.) from meeting him with his own weapons. The only response of the other was that he would knock D.'s teeth down his throat if he repeated the charge. The name of this man was soon ascertained to be John A. Fisher, of Harrisburg, a lawyer, and the only palliation (if it be one) that I hear offered for his conduct is, that he was undoubtedly under the influence of intoxicating liquor. This was a foretaste of the violence to be experienced on our attempting to lecture here, and which I anticipated even before I left Boston.

"The Court House had been obtained for us for Saturday and Sunday evenings. Hitherto, nearly all the anti-slavery lecturers have failed to gather any considerable number together; but, on this occasion, we had the room filled, some of the most respectable citizens being present. At an early period of the evening, before the services commenced, it was evident that mischief was brewing, and an explosion would ultimately follow. I first addressed the meeting, and was listened to, not only without molestation, but with marked attention and respect, though my remarks were stringent, and my accusations severe. As soon, however, as Douglass rose to speak, the spirit of rowdyism began to show itself outside of the building, around the door and windows. It was the first time that a 'nigger' had attempted to address the people of Harrisburg in public, and it was regarded by the

mob as an act of unparalleled audacity. They knew nothing
at all of Douglass, except that he was a 'nigger.' They came
equipped with rotten eggs and brickbats, fire-crackers, and
other missiles, and made use of them somewhat freely—
breaking panes of glass, and soiling the clothes of some who
were struck by the eggs. One of these bespattered my head
and back somewhat freely. Of course, there was a great
deal of yelling and shouting, and of violent exclamation—
such as, 'Out with the damned nigger,' etc., etc. The
audience at first manifested considerable alarm, but I was
enabled to obtain a silent hearing for a few moments, when
I told the meeting that if this was a specimen of Harrisburg
decorum and love of liberty, instead of wasting our breath
upon the place, we should turn our back upon it, shaking off
the dust of our feet," etc., etc.

"PITTSBURGH, August 12, 1847.

" I endeavored to complete a letter for you at Harrisburg,
before leaving for this place, on Monday morning, but was able
to write only a portion of one before it was time to be at the
depot. In my perplexity, not knowing what else to do, I
requested a colored friend to finish my letter, explaining to you
the reason why he did so, and put it into the post-office. He
promised to do so, and I hope was faithful to his promise. As
I left off just as I was giving you the particulars of the rowdy-
ish outbreak at our meeting at H., I requested Mr. Brown to
mention that no attempt was made to molest me, and that
Douglass escaped without any serious injury, although he was
struck in the back by a stone, and a brickbat just grazed his
head. All the venom of the rowdies seemed to be directed
against him, as they were profoundly ignorant of his character.
. . . On Sunday forenoon and afternoon we addressed our
colored friends in their meeting-house at H., at which a number
of white ones were also present. The meetings were crowded,
and a most happy time we had indeed. Not the slightest
molestation was offered.

" On Monday we left Harrisburg in the cars for Chambersburg, a distance of fifty-four miles. On arriving, to our serious regret, we found that the ticket which Douglass obtained at H. for Pittsburgh, enabled him to go directly through in the 2 o'clock stage, while I should be compelled to wait until 8 o'clock (it proved to be 11 o'clock) in the evening. This was annoying and unpleasant in the extreme. Douglass had a hard time of it, after we parted. The route over the Alleghany Mountains, although a very beautiful and sublime one, is a very slow and difficult one, and with a crowded stage, in a melting hot day, is quite overpowering. It seemed to me almost interminable—almost equal to a trip across the Atlantic. Douglass was not allowed to sit at the eating table on the way, and for two days and nights scarcely tasted a morsel of food. O, what brutality! Only think of it, and then of the splendid reception given to him in all parts of Great Britain! On his arriving at Pittsburgh, however, a different reception awaited him, which was also intended for me. A committee of twenty white and colored friends, with a colored band of music, who had sat up all night till three o'clock in the morning, met him to welcome him to the place, and to discourse eloquent music to him. Of course, they were greatly disappointed at my not coming at that time.

" I arrived toward evening, entirely exhausted, but soon recovered myself by a good warm bath. A meeting had been held in the afternoon in the Temperance Hall, which was ably addressed by Douglass. In the evening we held one together in the same place, crowded to overflowing.—[August 13.] Yesterday, Friday, [Thursday], we held three large meetings, two of them in the open air, and concluded last night with the greatest enthusiasm. I have seen nothing like to it on this side of the Atlantic. The place seems to be electrified, and the hearts of many are leaping for joy."

On Wednesday, August 18, they took part in the mass-meeting of the Western Anti-Slavery Society, at New Lyme, a village in the Northeastern corner of Ohio. The great Oberlin tent, " capable of holding four thousand persons," had been put up ; many prominent members of the Liberty party were on the ground ; and

"Notwithstanding the unpropitious state of the weather, at an early hour vehicles of various descriptions began to pour into the place in great numbers. We held two meetings in the ten, on the first day, which were attended by a large concourse among them some of the choicest friends of our cause in the land—ay, and the choicest women, too. Messrs. Giddings and Tilden, members of Congress, who have nobly battled for freedom in that body, were also present. After the organization of the meeting, a poetical welcome to Douglass, Foster, and myself, written by Benjamin S. Jones, was sung with exquisite taste and feeling by a choir, causing many eyes to be moistened with tears. I then addressed the great multitude at considerable length, and was followed by Douglass in a capital speech. In the afternoon we again occupied the most of the time. The interest manifested, from beginning to end, was of the most gratifying character, and all seemed refreshed and greatly pleased. As the night approached, there appeared to be some symtoms of rowdyism, and it became necessary for some of our friends to watch all night, lest the tent should be damaged.

"Yesterday, all day, our meetings were still more thronged— four thousand persons being on the ground. The disunion question was the principal topic of discussion, the speakers being Douglass, Foster, and myself, in favor of disunion, and Mr. Giddings against it. Mr. G. exhibited the utmost kindness and generosity toward us, and alluded to me in very handsome terms, as also to Douglass; but his arguments were very specious; and I think we had with us the understanding and conscience of an overwhelming majority of those who listened to the debate. As a large proportion of the Abolitionists in this section of the country belong to the Liberty party, we have had to bring them to the same test of judgment as the Whigs and the Democrats, for supporting a pro-slavery Constitution ; but they are generally very candid, and incomparably more kind and friendly to us than those of their party at the East.

" To-day (Friday), we shall close this cheering anniversary; after which, Douglass and I must ride forty miles to attend another convention at Painesville, which commences to-morrow morning at 10 o'clock; at the conclusion of which we must take another long jaunt, to hold meetings on Sunday at Munson. Our friends here have so multiplied the meetings that not an hour is left us for rest. They are unmerciful to us, and how we are to fulfill all the engagements made, without utterly breaking down, I do not know. Douglass is not able to speak at any length without becoming very hoarse, and, in some cases, losing the ability to make himself heard.

" Up to the last hour" [says a later letter to Mrs. Garrison] " the audience was immense. We adjourned at half-past two o'clock P. M., and were then busily engaged for some time in shaking hands and bidding farewell to a host of friends. When the dense mass moved off in their long array of vehicles, dispersing in every direction to their several homes, some a distance of ten, others of twenty, others of forty, others of eighty, and others of a hundred miles, it was a wonderful spectacle. One man (colored) rode three hundred miles on horseback to be at the meeting."

On they went to Painesville, where " Frederick's voice was much impaired, and he had to have a bad tooth extracted during the meeting." Then they came on Sunday, August 22, to Munson, where

" We saw the great Oberlin tent in a distant field; but no village was to be seen, and only here and there a solitary log cabin. ' Strange,' said I to myself, ' that our friends should pitch their tent in such a place. From whence are we to get our audience ? ' But, on going to the spot, I found a large company already assembled, and in a short time the vast tent was densely filled, even to overflowing; so that the multitude was greater than we had even at New Lyme. It was a grand

and imposing spectacle.   Poor Frederick was still unwell, and
could only say a few words in the forenoon ; and in the afternoon he absented himself altogether from the meeting, and put
a wet bandage round his throat.   This threw the labor mainly
upon me, though our sterling friends, S. S. Foster and J. W.
Walker, made long and able speeches, which aided me considerably.   The enthusiasm was general and very great.   We
continued our meeting through the next day, with a large and
most intelligent audience, and made a powerful impression.
Douglass was much improved, and spoke with inimitable humor,
showing up the religion of the South in particular, and of the
country in general.   At the close, Dr. Richmond (one of our
most intelligent and active come-outers, last from the Liberty
party) offered a series of resolutions, strongly commendatory to
Douglass and myself, which were unanimously adopted by a
tremendous ' Ay!'—after which six cheers were given in the
heartiest manner.   Altogether, it was the most interesting meeting I have ever attended in this country.   . . ."

That week they attended commencement at the
famous anti-slavery college, Oberlin, where among the
graduates of this year they met Miss Lucy Stone.
Nearly three thousand people listened to their debate,
with President Mahan, who defended the Constitution of the United States as anti-slavery.   Then
came one immense meeting after another in various
places, including Salem, where "The rain poured
down in torrents, giving us all a pretty thorough baptism ; but the people would not disperse ; and we
looked the storm out of countenance and wound up
gloriously."   Their arrival in Cleveland had been
announced in one of the Liberty party organs, the
"Plain Dealer," by a paragraph headed, "The Menagerie Coming," and saying that "Garrison, Douglass, Foster, (and, we expect, Satan also), are to be

here on Saturday next, and open at 7 o'clock in the evening in their big tent, and continue their harangues over the Sabbath. This trio have made sale for a great many unmerchantable eggs in other places."

Their meetings on Sunday were so crowded that they had to go out from the church into the grove. Neither the big tent nor the eggs seem to have been on hand ; but on Monday Garrison was attacked by a fever, which kept him prostrate for five weeks ; while Douglass and Foster went on to a series of conventions which began at Buffalo, September 14, and closed with the month at Albany, after taking in Rochester and Syracuse.

The publication of the "North Star" was now announced, under circumstances which it is my duty to try to present in a different light from that thrown upon them in the really noble work above quoted. It must be remembered that Garrison had been consulted when the project was first entertained, and had spoken of it editorially in a way likely to hinder it from succeeding. I do not think that Douglass was under any obligation to consult him again, especially as this was not even suggested by the givers of the five hundred pounds. This money, as stated in an article published in London, July 24, and reprinted two months later by the "Liberator," was sent on the express understanding that Douglass might, if he had no immediate use for it, have it invested "under trustees of his own choosing," for his own permanent benefit and that of his children ; but that "If at any future time he should consider it advisable to establish a newspaper of his own, the capital so invested shall be available for that purpose." He was the

only man in America who had any right to decide
what should be done with this gift. Of course, he
was under great obligations for what Garrison had
done for him individually, as well as for his race.
But we must not forget that he had made some return
in the praises given to the " Liberator " and its editor
in a widely circulated book, and in speeches applauded
by great multitudes. Garrison would undoubtedly
have said, " If you owe anything to me, pay it to our
cause." That cause had no more faithful servant
than the man who risked his life at Pendleton and
Manayunk; who labored so diligently as repeatedly to
exhaust his mighty strength ; who spent year after
year, without complaint, in journeys which seldom
allowed him to be with his family ; who deliberately
exposed himself to be sent back into slavery, in its
most cruel form, rather than keep back facts which
might help on the work ; who had come back to
danger, ignominy, and privations in America, instead
of remaining abroad with his family in luxury,
safety, and honor ; and who now chose to put his
entire fortune into an enterprise of doubtful prospects,
but of possible benefit to his race, rather than lay it
aside for his permanent comfort and that of his
children. Douglass had now paid all his debts to
Garrison ; and there was a large balance due him on
the other side.

He still considered himself pledged to devote the
money to the purpose for which it was originally
subscribed, as soon as he could find a favorable
opening. He declined a place on the " Liberator,"
for this would not have been what was designed by
the donors. In August we find him almost decided

to become an associate editor of the "Ram's Horn,"
and write regularly for the "Standard," both which
journals were published in New York City. On
October 1, however, the "Liberator" announced
that he was about to publish a new paper at Cleveland,
called the "North Star." This notice was probably
given in consequence of a letter which he wrote after
September 12, the day when Garrison was taken sick.
At all events, Douglass had at that time been only
thirty-six hours in the city ; and his new scheme can
scarcely have been sufficiently matured to make it
necessary to say much about it. There would have
been very little to complain of, if Garrison had, as he
said, heard nothing about it before his illness ; but it
is altogether probable that the violence of the attack
caused him to forget what had been told him just
before his sickness by Douglass, according to a statement made by the latter that winter.

The reader is now requested to compare carefully
two letters. Rev. S. J. May wrote to Garrison, on
October 8, from Western New York, that

" Frederick Douglass was very much troubled that he did
not get any tidings from you when he reached Syracuse on the
24th of September. He left you reluctantly, yet thinking that
you would follow on in a day or two ; and as he did not get
any word from you at Waterloo, nor at Auburn, he was almost
sure he should meet you at my house. His countenance fell,
and his heart failed him, when he found me likewise in sad
suspense about you. Not until he arrived at West Winfield
did he get any relief, and then through the 'Liberator' of
the 23d."

This letter had, I fear, been read by Garrison, when

he wrote, twelve days later, from Cleveland, which
he had not quitted, to his wife thus :

" Is it not strange that Douglass has not written a single
line to me, or to any one in this place, inquiring after my health,
since he left me on a bed of illness ? It will also greatly
surprise our friends in Boston to hear that, in regard to his
project for establishing a paper here, to be called the ' North
Star ' . . . he never opened to me his lips on the subject, nor
asked my advice in any particular whatever ! Such conduct
grieves me to the heart. His conduct about the paper has
been impulsive, inconsiderate, and highly inconsistent with his
decision in Boston. What will his English friends say of such
a strange somerset ? I am sorry that friend Quincy did not
express himself more strongly against this project in the
' Liberator.' It is a delicate matter, I know, but it must be
met with firmness."

We must remember that Douglass had at first given
up his own wishes in deference to Garrison's advice,
and had spent months in deliberation before he
finally decided to use money which had been put
entirely at his own disposal, in the way originally
selected by the givers. Was this " impulsive " or
" inconsiderate ? " And what need was there for
" firmness," or for a single word against the publication from Mr. Quincy, who was temporarily editing
the " Liberator ? " The " North Star " was soon to
appear, and the only question was whether it should
be a success or a failure. Is it necessary to say which
result would have been for the good of the cause ?
Did Douglass deserve nothing but opposition in his
new career? A dozen friendly words might have
brought him a thousand subscribers. It is sad not
to find them in the early numbers of the " North

Star," nor in the long editorial which Garrison wrote, as he resumed his charge of the "Liberator," on January 7, 1848. A week later he reprinted, without comment, the statement of Mrs. Chapman that a subscription list for the " North Star " had been hung up in the Anti-Slavery Bazaar at Boston. She also expressed her hopes for the new editor thus :

" Let him be, as heretofore, proof against every form of temptation, and a long and glorious career, like that of Clarkson (whose past is already sealed) and Garrison (whom God preserve to a like late and faithful ending) lies before him. More fortunately circumstanced than Toussaint," . . . " may his success be made proportionate to his ability by his devotedness and perseverance to the end."

But it was not until January 28 that the " Liberator " acknowledged that

" The facility with which Mr. Douglass has adapted himself to his new and responsible position, is another proof of his genius, and worthy of especial praise. His editorial articles are exceedingly well written ; and the typographical, orthographical, and grammatical accuracy, with which the " North Star " is printed, surpasses that of any other paper ever published by a colored man."

He had already made up his mind that Western New York, where he had often spoken acceptably, would give him an even better field than Ohio ; and thus, as he says himself in "Life and Times" (p. 295), " From motives of peace, instead of issuing my paper in Boston, among New England friends, I went to Rochester, New York, among strangers." This last word is amply justified by Miss Holley's letter, which will be found in another chapter. The first number of the "North Star" appeared accordingly at Rochester, on December 3, 1847. Mr. Delany, who had edited the "Mystery," and who was not prevented by the complete blackness of his skin from afterwards becoming a major in our army, was associated with Douglass; and there were agents in Pennsylvania, Ohio, and Michigan, as well as in New England. The first article is an account of the convention of colored people which opened October 6, at Troy, where Douglass exhorted them to come out of the pro-slavery churches, and said, that "His right arm should wither before he would worship at their blood-stained altars." The next number, four weeks later, contains cordial notices from the Rochester dailies, the "New York Tribune," the "Standard," and the "Anti-Slavery Bugle," whose editor had warmly encouraged the plan of the new paper, and would have merged his own sheet in it if it had been published at Cleveland. The "Liberator" was still under the charge of Mr. Quincy, who had promptly acknowledged his friend's "eminent ability to man any breach that calls for a ready mind and a strong arm," and who now said that the "North Star's" "literary and mechanical execution would do honor to any paper, new or old, anti-slavery or pro-slavery, in the country." It was certainly a much more interesting paper, for general readers, than the "Liberator," whose subscribers must have been largely actuated by a sense of duty. There were not so many long contributions about visionary schemes; and there was a great abundance of selections from the brightest and ablest authors of the day, like Parker, Longfellow, Sumner, Douglas Jerrold, Dickens, Thackeray, Macaulay,

Howitt, Emerson, Lamartine, and Andersen. In fact, the main difficulty I found, in looking over the "North Star," was the constant temptation to linger over interesting extracts. To a poor family, who had little reading matter besides, its arrival must have been the great event of the week, especially as there were many valuable suggestions on practical points, while ample notice was taken of all important events, for instance the dethronement of Louis Philippe. Its chief editor had the advantage of a great gift, which he had already shown on the platform, and which is manifest on every page of his books, that of always knowing how to interest people. Even his boldest utterances were made attractive. Publishing this paper was, to quote his own words to me, " almost the wisest thing I ever did." He had to keep hard at work reading and thinking, collecting new matter and revising his old views. He was still a staunch disunionist ; and the Harrisburg riot had been praised by a Pennsylvania newspaper, which declared that " Douglass is a darkey and a tool for the enemies of our country." . . . " He lets no opportunity pass without giving our country a stab. It is unnecessary to say that he also stabs Democrats at every corner, and is armed to the shirt-collar with treason." He was now in the region where the Liberty party had its main strength ; and the necessity of meeting its arguments led him to test repeatedly the strength of his own position. He was as firm in it, however, in 1848, as ever before.

He had scarcely started the " North Star," when he made a long journey as a lecturer, speaking in January at the Bazaar in Boston, in April at various points in Ohio, and on May 9 at the annual meeting of the

A. A. S. S. in the Broadway Tabernacle, in New York City. Before copying the account of his speech, written down that day on the platform by Henry C. Wright, one of an audience of nearly three thousand, I must give a word or two of explanation. John P. Hale, who had but just before been nominated for the Presidency by the Liberty party, had lost his election as a member of the House of Representatives, because he opposed the annexation of Texas, but had recently been chosen Senator. Soon after he took his seat in Washington an attempt was made to rescue seventy-five slaves, among whom were three young girls of remarkable beauty. The vessel in which they fled was brought back; and popular indignation against the captain was expressed in a shameful riot. This disorder gave Hale a good opportunity for beginning an attack upon the whole system of slavery. His colleagues were too angry, however, to let him do more than begin; and his purpose was not understood by the Abolitionists. Such was the state of things when, according to Wright's letter,

"Frederick Douglass now takes the platform, and is welcomed with applause. The assembly is now fixed in its close attention, and Frederick is going on to show up the cowardly and sneaking conduct of John P. Hale, in bringing in a bill to protect property, and not daring to stand up and fearlessly advocate the right of slaves to run away, and the right and duty of Abolitionists to protect them. Frederick is describing 'Punch's' portraits of Brother Jonathan, with the devil hovering over him, eying with satisfaction passing events. The audience give him great applause. He is speaking to great effect, portraying the wrongs of the colored population of this nation. His eloquence sways the great assembly with him. He denounces the Northerners, who swear to support the

Constitution, as the real slave-holders of the country. It is good to listen to him. He shows up the Northern apologists of slavery as those whose smiles he does not want. He pledges himself to denounce those enemies of God and man, who swear to support the Constitution, as his enemies. Frederick has got the audience into a great state of glorification ; and he is now showing that there is no way to abolish slavery except by the dissolution of the Union. There, he is done ; and the meeting is breaking up. It has been a pleasant and profitable time."

Douglass now enlarged his aims so far as to include a new reform, even more unpopular than abolitionism. Women were then excluded, throughout the United States, not only from the suffrage, but from almost every lucrative or honorable employment, while their pay, in such occupations as were left open to them, was but scanty. They had scarcely any opportunity to get a thorough education, and their attempts at public speaking met with violent opposition, as we have seen to have been the case with Abby Kelley and Angelina Grimké. A married woman could own nothing, not even her daily earnings or her clothes ; and her husband or father might take away her children   Efforts had been made from time to time, by Frances Wright, the Grimké sisters, Ernestine L. Rose, and other women individually, to right these wrongs, but there was no concerted movement before 1848. Then a " Woman's Rights Convention " met, on July 19, at Seneca Falls, on a call sent out by Lucretia Mott, Elizabeth Cady Stanton, and two other ladies. A declaration of independence, closely copied from that adopted in 1776, was signed by a hundred men and women, and among the names is that of

Frederick Douglass.   He took part with Mrs. Stanton
in a proceeding which she described, on March 31,
1888, before the International Council of Women at
Washington, as follows :

"I wanted to demand the right of suffrage then and there,
because I saw that was the fundamental right out of which all
others would necessarily flow, so I drew up, myself, a very
short resolution, and my husband told me, 'Now, you make the
whole thing ridiculous.   So long as you advocate simply rights
of education, rights of property, rights of children, and all that
sort of thing, it is very well, but the idea of demanding the
right of suffrage!'   And Lucretia Mott said the same thing,
and all the convention ; those who were interested in it were
opposed to this resolution.   So I seemingly gave it up, but
when I got into the convention I determined to push forward
my resolution ; but, unfortunately, I had never said a word in
public, and how to put two sentences together I did not know.
So I surveyed the convention, and there I saw one man,
Frederick Douglass, and I knew that Frederick, from personal
experience, was just the man for the work ; so I read my resolution, and then I hurried to his side, and whispered into his
ear what I wanted said ; and he went along awhile very well,
but he didn't speak quite fast enough for me, nor say all I
wanted said ; and the first thing I knew I was on my feet
making a speech for that resolution, and Frederick Douglass
and I carried the whole convention, and the resolution was
passed unanimously."

Another of the speakers on this fortieth anniversary of the reform, said, in reply :

"There are few facts in my humble history to which I look
back with more satisfaction than to the fact, recorded in the
history of the Woman Suffrage Movement, that I was sufficiently
enlightened at that early day, and when only a few years from
slavery, to support your resolution for woman suffrage.   I have
done very little in this world in which to glory, except this one

act—and I certainly glory in that. When I ran away from slavery, it was for myself ; when I advocated emancipation, it was for my people ; but when I stood up for the rights of woman, self was out of the question, and I found a little nobility in the act."

Scarcely was the convention of 1848 finished, when he wrote an editorial, ending thus :

" Standing as we do upon the watch-tower of human freedom, we cannot be deterred from an expression of our approbation of any movement, however humble, to improve and elevate the character of any members of the human family. While it is impossible for us to go into this subject at length, and dispose of the various objections which are often urged against such a doctrine as that of female equality, we are free to say that in respect to political rights, we hold woman to be justly entitled to all we claim for man. We go further, and express our conviction that all political rights which it is expedient for man to exercise, it is equally so for woman. All that distinguishes man as an intelligent and accountable being, is equally true of woman ; and if that government only is just which governs by the free consent of the governed, there can be no reason in the world for denying to woman the exercise of the elective franchise, or a hand in making and administering the laws of the land. Our doctrine is that ' Right is of no sex.' We, therefore, bid the women engaged in this movement our humble God-speed."

The Seneca Falls convention had adjourned on July 20, to reassemble on August 2, in Rochester ; and there we find the editor of the " North Star " advocating " the emancipation of women from all the artificial disabilities imposed by false customs, creeds, and codes." We also read that " In answer to the many objections made by gentlemen present to granting to women the rights of suffrage, Frederick Douglass replied in a long, argumentative, and eloquent appeal for the complete equality of women in all the rights that belong to any human soul. He thought the true basis of rights was the capacity of individuals ; and as for himself, he should not dare claim a right that he would not concede to women." One active worker in the cause wrote soon after to another, " Can you tell me of any paper that advoc~ ~es our claims more warmly than the ' North Star ? ' " (" History of Woman Suffrage." Vol. i, pp. 67–91, 802–810.)

One week later he was present at a convention, with whose objects he had not full sympathy. Many of our best and ablest men had supposed that they could do better work against slavery by remaining Whigs or Democrats, than by becoming either Garrisonians or members of the Liberty party, which latter broke up in 1847 into two factions with different candidates for the Presidency. Thus, the antislavery champions were scattered about in five hostile camps. Four of these detachments united in 1848 to form the Free Soil party. Early in that year, Lewis Cass, who had declared himself opposed to that attempt to check the extension of slavery, known as the Wilmot Proviso, was nominated on a pro-slavery platform by the Democratic party, which had taken the lead in annexing Texas, as well as in making war on Mexico, and which was now determined to carry slavery into new territory. The anti-slavery Democrats of New York, nicknamed " Barnburners," on account of their desire to reform the civil service, were so badly treated in the nominating convention that they withdrew in disgust, and recommended for President Martin Van Buren, who had been elected

by the Democrats in 1836, had been re-nominated in
1840, but not elected, and would have been chosen as
the party candidate in 1844, if he had been sufficiently
in favor of annexation and war. Mean time, General
Taylor, a slave-holder who had never cast a vote or
held any civil office, and who had no scruples about
taking a nomination from anybody, was put up,
merely to catch votes, by the Whigs, who refused to
frame any platform, and voted down resolution after
resolution against the extension of slavery. Taylor's
position was described in the "Biglow Papers" as
"frontin' South by North," and his letters were
parodied thus :

> " Ez to my princerples, I glory
>   In hevin' nothin' o' the sort ;
>   I ain't a Wig ; I ain't a Tory ;
>   I'm jest a candidate in short.
>   Thet's fair an' square an' parpendicler ;
>   But if the public cares a fig
>   To hev me an'thin' in particler,
>   Wy, I'm a kind o' periwig."

Foremost among those members of the Whig convention, who had protested against the retirement of
the party into neutrality about all political questions,
was Henry Wilson ; and he now took the lead in a
movement for coöperating with the Barnburners in
forming a new party. A convention to meet for this
purpose, in Buffalo, early in August, was planned ;
and the suggestion was accepted by a mass-meeting
of citizens of Ohio of all parties opposed to the
extension of slavery, which met in Columbus at the
same time that Van Buren was nominated by the
Barnburners. The plan was also indorsed by a con-

vention of the Liberty party at Columbus, with Salmon P. Chase in the chair. A fourth convention, that same month, June, 1848, was held, in opposition to the extension of slavery, at Worcester, where speeches were made by Sumner, Giddings, and Charles Francis Adams, and delegates from each of the three parties were appointed for Buffalo. Daniel Webster was at first inclined to favor the movement ; and it had the steady support in New York of Bryant, Dix, and Tilden.

When the convention met at Buffalo, on August 9, Frederick Douglass was present as a spectator ; and the mention of his name was received with loud cheers ; but he declined the invitation to speak. He was still too much of a disunionist to join any party; and he was soon confirmed in this position by the platform as well as by the nomination for the Presidency. It was proposed to prohibit slavery in all free territory, to make no more compromises with its supporters, and to relieve the general government of all responsibility for its continuance ; but at the same time it was recognized as a State institution, which should not be interfered with by Congress ; and Van Buren had made so many concessions to the South, that it was a great mistake to prefer him to Hale at Buffalo. He received five times as many votes as the candidate of the Liberty party had done four years before ; and the agitation soon carried Chase, Seward, and Sumner into the Senate ; but the Garrisonians held, with the "North Star," " That the Free Soil movement ought not to be considered as the real anti-slavery movement of the country." It was looked upon more favorably than

the Liberty party had ever been ; but the feeling
about Van Buren among Abolitionists was what
Lowell expresses thus :

" I swan, I'm clean disgusted.
He ain't the man that I can say, is fittin' to be trusted;
He ain't half anti-slav'ry 'nough ; nor I ain't sure, as some be,
He'd go in fer abolishin' the Deestrict o' Columby.

    *   *   *   *   *   *   *

An' then, another thing, I guess, though mebby I am wrong,
This Buff'lo plaster ain't a goin' to dror almighty strong."

A resolution, indorsing the new party, was passed
in the colored people's convention, which met early
that September at Cleveland ; but the president, Mr.
Douglass, had his dissent recorded formally. He
succeeded in carrying an amendment, by which women
were made members ; and there was no opposition to
the address, drawn up by him, and saying, " We ask
that the doors of the school-house, the workshop, the
church, the college shall be thrown open as freely to
our children as to the children of other members of
the community." His speech presented what is still
an advanced idea of education, thus :

" Try to get your sons into mechanical trades. Press them
into the blacksmiths' shops, the machine shop, the joiner's
shop, the wheelwright's shop, the cooper's shop, and the
tailor's shop." . . . . " Every blow of the sledge hammer,
wielded by a sable arm, is a powerful blow in support of our
cause. Every colored mechanic is, by virtue of circumstance,
an elevator of his race. Every house built by black men is a
strong tower against the allied hosts of prejudice. It is
impossible for us to attach too much importance to this aspect
of the subject. Trades are important. Wherever a man may
be thrown by misfortune, if he has in his hands a useful trade,
he is useful to his fellow-man, and will be esteemed accord-

ingly.   And of all men in the world who need trades, we are the most needy."

While traveling, in consequence of this convention, on one of the steamers which ran between Cleveland and Buffalo, he gave a lecture at the invitation of some of the other passengers.   He closed by saying, that he should be happy to hear from any slave-holder in reply ; and he may possibly have mentioned that there was one already trying to apologize for his position in the "North Star."   One of the audience told him indignantly, that no white man would con-descend to argue with a nigger.   "My dear father was as white as you are," rejoined Douglass.   "If you cannot condescend to argue with my negro blood, please reply to the European blood."

On returning home, he found that the color-prejudice had shown itself in a peculiarly base and cruel form.   His family had followed him to Roch-ester ; and his daughter, Rosetta, then nine years old, had been accepted as a pupil in a private school, kept by a Christian lady and near his house, which was on high ground not far from Mount Hope cemetery. He was happy in the thought, that his child was having advantages which he had lost.   The little girl did not seem happy, however ; and he soon found that she was kept in a room by herself, a prisoner on account of her color, not permitted to see or hear any of the other pupils, but obliged to recite and take a recess by herself.   He complained to the teacher of this cruel fraud, but was told that it was necessary for the good of the school.   He in-sisted that the other girls should be asked, whether they had any objection to his daughter's company ;

and it was found that none of them had yet been
contaminated by the popular prejudice. The teacher
now declared that she could not let Rosa be with
them, unless all their parents were satisfied ; and
strong objection was made by one of the fathers,
whose house stood next to that of Douglass. After
this he had to have his children taught at home by a
governess from England. There was no other school
open to them, except a very poor one kept up for
colored people only at the other side of the city ; and
the boys were even younger than the girl. That
winter, however, he took the lead in an agitation
which did not cease until all children were permitted
to enter the Rochester schools without distinction of
color, a reform not yet accomplished at Washington.
He also opposed all restrictions at theaters, lecture-
rooms, and other public places ; and colored travelers
soon told him, that they felt the influence of his paper
within a radius of fifty miles.

On the Friday after the slave-holder without opinions was elected President, it was declared in the
" North Star " that " The cry of disunion shall be
more fearlessly proclaimed till slavery be abolished,
the Union dissolved, or the sun of this guilty nation
go down in blood." At the meeting of the A. A. S. S.
in New York city, an address was made on Wednesday evening, May 9, 1849, by Douglass, who
condemned the project of circulating tracts and the
Bible amongst the slaves. "Give them freedom
first," he said, "and then they will find the Bible for
themselves. The owners of slaves dread nothing
more than that any of their slaves should learn to
read. That instant he feels the fetters that bind

him." He then "went on to censure the religionists, who conferred honors on the spillers of blood ; for instance, on Zachary Taylor, who sent the hound on the track of the Indian."

The "North Star" had not met with so warm a welcome from the Garrisonians as from men who were trying, like Gerrit Smith, Horace Mann, Chase, Sumner, Seward, Giddings, and Palfrey, to turn the whole force of the Constitution against slavery. The necessity of defending his position against the arguments of his new friends forced Douglass to look beyond the narrow limits of Garrisonian orthodoxy. Even as early as February, 1849, he made an important concession to the Free Soilers. He said in his paper that " On a close examination of the Constitution I am satisfied that, if strictly construed, according to its reading, it is not a pro-slavery instrument." He still held, however, that " The original intent and meaning " . . . "makes it a pro-slavery instrument, such a one as I cannot bring myself to vote under or swear to support." Two days after the speech in New York City, just quoted, he held a public debate there with the editor of the " Northern Star and Colored Farmer," who, about this time, changed the name of his paper to avoid any confusion with its rival. Mr. Ward was a negro of the purest blood, and the force of his arguments is acknowledged by his mulatto antagonist to have been so great as ultimately to have made a permanent conquest. The conversion was far from sudden, however, and we find the little remnant of the Liberty party persuaded by Gerrit Smith, on July 3, 1849, to resolve unanimously "That the Phillipses, and Quinceys, and

Garrisons, and Douglasses, who " . . . "chime in
with the popular cry that the Constitution is pro-
slavery, do thereby, notwithstanding their anti-
slavery hearts, make themselves practically and
effectively pro-slavery."

The controversy which now took place between
the author of this resolution and Douglass must have
stimulated the growth of the seed sown by the
" Colored Farmer." The arguments brought forward
by the leader of the Liberty men had much to recommend them besides their intrinsic truth. He had
been eagerly observing the course of politics for
more than twenty years, and from an independent
standpoint. He had been working busily for the
slave ever since 1830, siding for a while with Garrison, but soon leaving him to organize that series of
appeals to the ballot-box, which at last was answered
by a final verdict against slavery. His vast wealth
was still freely given to the disunionists, as well as to
colonizationists and laborers in his own path. The
temperance, peace, and woman's rights movements
found him among their earliest and most zealous
advocates. His princely hospitality welcomed to his
board the illiterate negro missionary, the medium,
the Catholic priest, the fugitive slave, and the blind
beggar ; politicians of all parties, proselyters of all
sects, and agitators for every novelty. Again and
again he gave away farms so freely that he issued
deeds to three thousand colored people between 1845
and 1849, and then he began a fresh series of presents
of land to white men. Soon after we find him giving
twelve thousand dollars to set free a friend who had
been put in prison for aiding fugitives ; and he

subscribed ten thousand at one time for the deliverance of Kansas. The comparatively small assistance which he gave from time to time to the " North Star," would undoubtedly have been continued if it had never shifted its place ; and we know too much about its editor's independence of character to admit that he could ever have disguised his opinions in order to get aid from any quarter. He was too able a man to continue long a disunionist, after he had a chance to see both sides of the case ; but it is no discredit to him, if he was strongly influenced by the personal worth of a philanthropist without bitterness, whose burning zeal for religion and reform was never darkened by any ambition or intolerance.

The cost of publishing the " North Star " was about eighty dollars a week, and the number of subscribers was so small that, on May 5, 1848, a call for more money was issued in its columns. The editor had mortgaged his house, and was " heavily in debt," when his friend, Miss Julia Griffiths, afterward Mrs. Crofts, a lady of some literary ability and great energy, came over with her sister from England. On Thursday, May 24, 1849, these ladies were with Mr. Douglass, going down the Hudson from Albany to New York, on the steamer " Alida," when he ventured to go with them to the dinner-table. He was taken away by force and obliged to leave the cabin, but they followed at once, and went on to New York, hungry and indignant. Miss Julia's zeal and business ability soon caused the mortgage to be released, all the debts to be paid, and the circulation to rise, in a single year, from two thousand to four thousand copies. She remained for some years in Rochester, where she became an active officer of the Ladies' Anti-Slavery Society, and edited an annual called " Autographs for Freedom." It was, I presume, in her company, that Mr. Douglass, now sole editor, went in June to Niagara Falls, where he was treated like a prince on one side of the river, and like a Pariah on the other. The color-line seems to have been simply the boundary of the United States.

The influence of the Garrisonians was never large enough to be compared with that of the Southern disunionists, and these latter excited so much alarm in 1850 as to cause Congress to adopt a compromise which threatened to throw open the territories to slave-holders, and ensured the passage of a new law against fugitives, much worse than that which had sent Douglass abroad. Webster had spoken in behalf of these measures on March 7, and had won great applause at the North, especially from merchants who wished to please Southern customers, and manufacturers who hoped to gain Southern votes for a return to the high duties which had been given up in 1846. The leaders of both of the great parties were bidding against each other, at the expense of the slaves, for the support of the slave-holder. Thus the political and business influences were so strongly on the side of slavery as to give it almost complete control of both the press and the pulpit. One sign that public opinion condemned the Abolitionists was the license given to the rioters against them in New York City. Leading newspapers announced the annual meeting of the A. A. S. S. in language intended to collect a mob. On the first morning, that of May 7, but very few colored people were present, and they took care to keep near the doors. In one of the front seats on the platform, however, sat Frederick Douglass, " with brows knit, fiery eyes looking daggers, scorn upon his thick curled lips, and, lurking in his sable, woe-begone visage, the traces of malignity, disappointment, and despair." Thus speaks one of the pro-slavery papers, and another calls him " the master-genius of the crowd." Phillips and Lucretia Mott were also on the platform, and so was a gambler named Rynders, who had been the leader of the riot against Macready, a year before, in Astor Place, and who was afterward made marshal of the district by Buchanan. His band of rowdies was before him, waiting for a signal, which he gave in consequence of an attack on President Taylor by Garrison. The uproar was now furious, and the police were evidently under orders not to repress it. At last, Rynders was induced, by the promise that one of his supporters should be heard on the platform, to allow Garrison to conclude. Dr. Furness, whose recollections have been freely drawn upon by those who would describe the scene, was also permitted to speak ; and then came a fellow named Grant, who tried to prove that a negro is a kind of monkey. His own adherents soon got tired of hearing him, and then Douglass seized his opportunity. "Captain Rynders," said he, "Do you think that I am a monkey ? " " Oh no," replied Rynders, " you are half a white man." "Then I am half man and half monkey ? " " Yes." " And half brother to Captain Rynders ? "

The whole audience united in laughter and applause. Douglass now had the floor, and went on

to attack a critic of Garrisonianism, whom he knew
to be hated by the rioters before him, Horace
Greeley, who had recently said in his paper that the
blacks did nothing for themselves. "When I first
came North," said Mr. Douglass, "I went to the most
decided anti-slavery merchant in the North, and
sought employment on a ship he was building, and
he told me that if he were to give me work every
white operative would quit; and yet Mr. Greeley
finds fault with us that we do not help ourselves."
This criticism pleased Rynders, who bore that gentleman no good will; and he added a word to Douglass's
against Greeley. "I am happy," said Douglass, "to
have the assent of my half-brother here," pointing to
Rynders, and convulsing the audience with laughter.
After this, Rynders, finding how he was played with,
took care to hold his peace; but some one of Rynders'
company in the gallery undertook to interrupt the
speaker. "It's of no use," said Mr. Douglass; "I've
Captain Rynders here to back me. We were born
here," he went on to say. "We have made the
clothes you wear, and the sugar that you put into
your tea; and we mean to stay here and do all we can
for you." "Yes," cried a voice from the gallery,
"and you'll cut our throats!" "No," said the
speaker, "we'll only cut your hair." When the
laughter ceased, Mr. Douglass proceeded to say:
"We mean to stay here, and do all we can for every
one, be he a man or be he a monkey," accompanying
these last words with a wave of his hand toward
the quarter whence the interruption had come. He
concluded with saying that he saw his friend, Samuel
Ward, present, and would ask him to step forward.

All eyes were instantly turned to the back of the platform, or stage rather, so dramatic was the scene, and there, amidst the group, stood a large man, so black that, as Wendell Phillips said, when he shut his eyes you could not see him. " Had I observed him before, I should have wondered what brought him here, accounting him as fresh from Africa." He belonged to the political wing of the Abolition party (Gerrit Smith's), and had wandered into the meeting, never expecting to be called upon to speak. At the call of Frederick Douglass he came to the front, and as he approached, Rynders exclaimed, " Well, this is the original nigger ! " " I've heard of the magnanimity of Captain Rynders," said Ward ; " but the half has not been told me." And then he " went on with a noble voice, and his speech was such a strain of eloquence as I never heard excelled before or since."

" There are more than fifty people here," said he, " who may remember me as a little black boy running about the streets of New York. I have always been called nigger, and the only consolation that has been offered me for being called nigger, was that, when I die and go to heaven, I shall be white. If "—and here, with an earnestness of tone .and manner that thrilled us to the very marrow, he continued—" if I cannot go to heaven as black as God made me, let me go down to hell, and dwell with the devils forever ! " The effect was beyond description. " This gentleman," he said, " who denies our humanity, has examined us scientifically ; but I know something of anatomy. I have kept school, and I have had pupils, from the jet-black up to the soft dissolving views ; and I have seen white boys with retreating foreheads and projecting jaws, and, as Dickens says in 'Nicholas Nickleby' of Smike, 'you might knock here all day,' tapping his forehead, 'and find nobody at home.'" In this strain he went on ruling the large audience with Napoleonic power. Coal-black as he was, he was an emperor. When he ceased speaking the time had expired for which the Tabernacle was engaged, and we had to adjourn. "Never was there a grander triumph of intelligence of mind over brute force. Two colored men, whose claim to be considered human was denied, had, by mere force of intellect, overwhelmed their maligners with confusion."

The victory would have been complete if the politicians and merchants, whom Rynders served, had not ordered him to go back to the Tabernacle next day, and not let any one speak. Burleigh's voice was drowned that day by shouts of, "Oh, let Douglass shave that man, and make a wig for Garrison!" Even Phillips was silenced by cries of, "This is an imposition!" "A white-washed nigger instead of a black one!" "Put him out!" "Put the red-head down!" No hall or church in the city could be obtained for completing the business of the society, which had to elect its officers and pass its resolutions in a private parlor.

Such manifestations of sympathy with the South in the greatest city in the Union, encouraged Congress to pass the Fugitive Slave Bill, which provided that the trial should be summary, that no one arrested under it should be heard before a jury or allowed to testify in his own behalf, and that any attempt to prevent kidnapping might be punished by fines amounting to two thousand dollars, and also by six months in prison. More than forty colored people left Boston within three days after the signing of the bill, on September 18, 1850; while the pastor of the Colored Baptist Church in Rochester fled with every other member, except two, out of a hundred and fourteen, to Canada. The little girls in that city used to wonder every morning, whether they should see Mr. Douglass that day in the street, or hear that he had been carried off during the night. Many free negroes were enslaved; but he was able not only to protect himself but to save others. He was an active agent of the Underground Railroad; and a large room in his house was always ready for fugitives. Once he had eleven there together; and John Brown made them a speech. When any new arrival took place, the little Douglass boys would go to and fro collecting funds, to pay the fare on the steamer across Lake Ontario. Several instances of the way in which Douglass helped men who were in especial danger may be found in the " Life and Times ; " and there was also one case in which he took charge of a very small fugitive in petticoats, on the cars. He took a seat beside the child, saying very kindly, " Well, my little girl." The reply was in an indignant whisper, " I'm a boy."

The "swarthy Ajax," as he was now called, put forth all his powers of argument, repartee, ridicule, and denunciation against the supporters of the wicked law. Once, when he was speaking in Rochester, he called out, " Is there a single man here, who would sell his brother into bondage ? " " I would," said a fellow who stood in the rear. " Then turn your face to that wall," thundered the orator. He spoke with

Wendell Phillips, Theodore Parker, and Charles
Francis Adams, on October 14, before one of the
largest and noblest meetings ever held in Faneuil
Hall. He found time even then to appear with
Sojourner Truth before the Woman's Rights Conven-
tion, which was held in Worcester, October 23 and 24,
with the result of leading Mrs. Taylor, afterwards
Mrs. J. S. Mill, to write a powerful article in the
"Westminster Review." But at the close of the
month he was back in Boston, active in the defense of
William and Ellen Craft.

These two slaves had made their escape, eighteen
months before, when she traveled North as a white
gentleman in delicate health, and took her husband
as her servant. They were picked out for the first victims in Boston ; but they had too many friends there.
She was secreted at once ; and he was urged to fly ;
but he declared that he had run far enough already.
He even refused to be bought, and insisted that he
wanted to test the law. He is said to have been the
coolest man in Boston ; and it was all his friends
could do to persuade him to keep out of sight, and
carry several dirks and pistols. The slave-hunters
were themselves arrested, for calling him a thief, and
were followed about the streets by hooting crowds.
The Vigilance Committee met every night in a darkened room, and there it was finally agreed, in the
presence of Douglass, that a deputation should be
sent to warn the hunters to leave the town. The
name of Theodore Parker was proposed ; but Mr.
Slack said it would be better not to have any clergyman appointed. "And then," says Douglass, "I got a
peep into Parker's soul." He said, " This committee

can appoint me to no duty that I will not perform."
The passage quoted from his journal, in the memoir by
John Weiss, shows that he did the duty so faithfully
that the birds of prey fled from Boston the next afternoon.

On the very day when Parker spoke thus to the
other members of the Vigilance Committee, George
Thompson arrived in Boston from England. A
reception was given him in Faneuil Hall on November 15, but a party of pro-slavery men entered before
Garrison had half-finished his address of welcome,
and not another word of it reached the ears of the
audience. Phillips tried to get a hearing, but his
voice was drowned by continuous cheers for Daniel
Webster, a common way in those days of answering
anti-slavery speeches. Mr. Thompson himself was
greeted by all sorts of noises. Dogs were heard to
bark, cocks to crow, and ducks to quack. Yankee
Doodle was whistled furiously, and there were loud
questions about how many babies Queen Victoria
had, and how she was treating the Irish and the Hin-
doos. The member of Parliament soon left in disgust, and then Mrs. Abby Folsom was persuaded to
offer some inappropriate and inaudible remarks.
Theodore Parker came forward and stood for some
time, pointing to the portrait of Washington, while
no one could hear a word, except the loud cries that
he had better go and buy a bottle of Bogle's Hyper-
ion Fluid, a kind of hair-oil then in vogue. Neither
Parker Pillsbury nor Elizur Wright had any better
success, and Douglass stood for some time, pointing
his finger at the audience, with the utmost contempt,
amid a perfect storm of hisses, and shouts of " Hot

Corn," "Charcoal," etc. All sorts of things were thrown at him, and a man who stood near by was hit by one of the big copper cents, then current. Big and little fights were now going on all over the hall ; hats were smashed ; canes were being flourished briskly ; women fled with screams; and there were dances, accompanied by imitations of the Indian war-whoop. At last the biggest policeman in Boston stepped out upon the platform, and made a historic speech, the only one which had been heard from there since Garrison was first interrupted. " Gentle-men," said Captain Adams, " I am requested by the Marshal to inform you that this meeting is now adjourned."

There had been no change of feeling since the slave-hunters were driven away, but they and the dis-unionists were considered equally worthy of execra-tion by many a Bostonian. The North did not like to return fugitives, but it was much too anxious to keep at peace with the South ; and it was high time to speak as Frederick Douglass did at Rochester, on December 1, 1850, when he said :

" While this nation is guilty of the enslavement of three mil-lions of innocent men and women, it is as idle to think of hav-ing a sound and lasting peace, as it is to think there is no God to take cognizance of the affairs of men. There can be no peace to the wicked, while slavery continues in the land. It will be condemned ; and while it is condemned, there will be agitation. Nature must cease to be nature ; men must become monsters ; humanity must be transformed ; Christianity must be exterminated ; all ideas of justice and the laws of eternal goodness must be utterly blotted out from the human soul ; ere a system so foul and infernal can escape condemnation, or this guilty republic can have a sound, enduring peace."

CHAPTER VII.

WITH THE MEN WHO ABOLISHED SLAVERY.

> " Against his sovereign, Douglas ne'er
> Will level a rebellious spear."
> —" Lady of the Lake."

THE " North Star " fully justified its name by
enabling its editor to guide fugitives to freedom ;
and it also helped him to free himself from a
peculiarly Southern view of the United States Constitution, which deprived the Garrisonians of the
influence they deserved, and to rise to that higher view
which soon gained the supremacy at the North. Our
estimate, not only of his mental caliber, but of his
fidelity to his cause, will depend largely on our
opinion about this question ; and it must therefore be
examined thoroughly.

The Abolitionists were either disunionists, or else
Free Soilers and Liberty party men, according to
their view of the Constitution as pro-slavery or anti-
slavery. Douglass had been attacking it as pro-
slavery ever since his first speech in 1841 ; but on
May 7, 1851, when the A. A. S. S. was obliged to
meet in Syracuse, because no suitable place could be
found in New York City, a resolution was proposed,
indorsing the " Liberator " and other papers as anti-

190

slavery organs. Some one asked why the paper
edited by Frederick Douglass was not on the list.
Then he declared that he preferred to be left out, for
he had more sympathy with those Abolitionists who
were willing to vote, than with those who would not.
He had then been carrying on his paper for three
years and a half. How he thought at that time may
be imagined from what he said, a few years later,
in a lecture, entitled " The Anti-Slavery Movement,"
and published in Rochester, 1855. In speaking of
" the different anti-slavery sects," he says :

"I shall consider, first, the Garrisonian Anti-Slavery Society.
I call this the Garrisonian Society, because Mr. Garrison is,
confessedly, its leader. This Society is the oldest of modern
anti-slavery societies. It has, strictly speaking, two weekly
papers, or organs, employs five or six lecturers, and holds
numerous public meetings for the dissemination of its views.
Its peculiar and distinctive feature is its doctrine of ' No union
with slave-holders.' This doctrine has, of late, become its bond
of union, and the condition of good fellowship among its members. Of this Society I have to say, its logical result is but
negatively anti-slavery. Its doctrine of ' No union with slave-
holders,' carried out, dissolves the Union, and leaves the slaves
and their masters to fight their own battles, in their own way.
This I hold to be an abandonment of the great idea with which
that Society started. It started to free the slave. It ends by
leaving the slave to free himself. It started with the purpose
to imbue the heart of the nation with sentiments favorable to
the abolition of slavery, and ends by seeking to free the North
from all responsibility for slavery, other than if slavery were in
Great Britain, or under some other nationality. This, I say, is
the practical abandonment of the idea with which that Society
started. It has given up the faith that the slave can be freed
short of the overthrow of the Government; and then, as I
understand that Society, it leaves the slaves, as it must needs

leave them, just where it leaves the slaves of Cuba, or those of Brazil.   The nation, as such, is given up as beyond the power of salvation by the foolishness of preaching; and hence, the aim is now to save the North, so that the American Anti-Slavery Society, which was inaugurated to convert the nation, after ten years' struggle, parts with its faith, and aims now to save the North.   One of the most eloquent of that Society, and the man who is only second to Mr. Garrison himself, defines the Garrisonian doctrine thus: ' All the slave asks of us is to stand out of his way; withdraw our pledge to keep the peace on the plantation; withdraw our pledge to return him; withdraw that representation which the Constitution gives in proportion to the number of slaves; and without any agitation here, without any individual virtue, which the times have eaten out of us, God will vindicate the oppressed by the laws of justice which he has founded.   Trample under foot your own unjust pledges; break to pieces your compact with hell, by which you become the abettor of oppression.   Stand alone, and let no cement of the Union bind the slave, and he will right himself.'

" That is it. ' Stand alone.'   The slave is to ' right himself.' I dissent entirely from this reasoning.   It assumes to be true what is plainly absurd, and that is, that a population of slaves, without arms, without means of concert, and without leisure, is more than a match for double its number, educated, accustomed to rule, and in every respect prepared for warfare, offensive or defensive.   This Society, therefore, consents to leave the slave's freedom to a most uncertain and improbable, if not an impossible, contingency.   As a mere expression of abhorrence of slavery, the sentiment is a good one; but it expresses no intelligible principle of action, and throws no light on the pathway of duty.   Defined, as its authors define it, it leads to false doctrines and mischievous results.   It condemns Gerrit Smith for sitting in Congress, and our Saviour for eating with publicans and sinners.   Dr. Spring uttered a shocking sentiment when he said, if one prayer of his would emancipate the slaves, he would not offer that prayer.   No less shocking is the sentiment of the leader of the disunion forces, when he says, that if one vote of his would emancipate every slave in this country, he would not cast that vote. Here, on a bare theory, and for a theory which, if consistently adhered to, would drive a man out of the world—a theory which can never be made intelligible to common sense—the freedom of the whole slave population would be sacrificed.

"But again: 'No union with slave-holders.' I dislike the morality of this sentiment, in its application to the point at issue. For instance: A. unites with B. in stealing my property, and carrying it away to California, or to Australia; and, while there, Mr. A. becomes convinced that he did wrong in stealing my property, and says to Mr. B., 'No union with property-stealers,' and abandons him, leaving the property in his hands. Now, I put it to this audience, has Mr. A. in this transaction met with the requirements of stringent morality? He certainly has not. It is not only his duty to separate from the thief, but to restore the stolen property to its owner. And I hold that in the Union, this very thing of restoring to the slave his long-lost rights can better be accomplished than it can possibly be accomplished outside of the Union. This, then, is my answer to the motto, 'No Union with slave-holders.'

"But this is not the worst fault of this Society. Its chief energies are expended in confirming the opinion, that the United States Constitution is, and was, intended to be a slave-holding instrument—thus piling up, between the slave and his freedom, the huge work of the abolition of the Government, as an indispensable condition to emancipation. My point here is, first, the Constitution is, according to its reading, an anti-slavery document; and secondly, to dissolve the Union, as a means to abolish slavery, is about as wise as it would be to burn up this city, in order to get the thieves out of it. But again, we hear the motto, 'No union with slave-holders;' and I answer it, as that noble champion of liberty, N. P. Rogers, answered it with a more sensible motto, namely—'No union with slave-holding.' I would unite with anybody to do right, and with nobody to do wrong. And as the Union, under the Constitution, requires me to do nothing which is wrong, and gives me many facilities for doing good, I cannot go with the American Anti-Slavery Society in its doctrine of disunion."

A more complete statement of his position was made in 1860, when, in reply to the attack made upon his views by George Thompson, he delivered a speech, entitled "The Constitution of the United States : is it Pro-slavery or Anti-slavery ?" He meets the principal objections of the Garrisonians to the Constitution thus :

"It gives representatives to the South for three-fifths of its slaves; but what does that amount to ? It is a downright disability laid upon the slave-holding States, one which deprives those States of two-fifths of their natural basis of representation. Instead of encouraging slavery, the Constitution encourages freedom, by giving an increase of two-fifths of political power to free over slave States."

There is also a clause about importation of persons ; but

"It should be remembered that this very provision, if made to refer to the African slave-trade at all, makes the Constitution anti-slavery instead of pro-slavery; for it says to the slave States, the price you will have to pay for coming into the American Union is, that the slave-trade, which you could carry on indefinitely out of the Union, shall be put an end to in fifty years, if you come into the Union." . . . "It looked to the abolition of slavery rather than to its perpetuity."

There is also a clause about suppressing riots :

"I will be generous here, as well as elsewhere, and grant that it applies to slave-insurrections. Let us suppose that an anti-slavery man is President of the United States, (and the day that shall see this case is not distant) ; and this very power of suppressing slave-insurrection would put an end to slavery." . . . "If it should turn out that slavery is a source of insurrection, that there is no security from insurrections while slavery lasts, why the Constitution would be best obeyed by putting an end to slavery."

This prophecy was made on March 26, 1860, before Lincoln was even nominated. Of the so-called " Fugitive slave clause," it is correctly remarked that here, as in the other three cases, there is nothing in the Constitution to show that slaves were thought of. There was an attempt to make the words plainer ; but it failed. " The Convention would not consent to the idea, that property in man should be admitted into the Constitution." As the clause stands, it can refer only to apprentices and others who have bound themselves over to service ; the words " Person held to service or labor in one State, under the laws thereof," did not, in the opinion of Douglass, apply to the slave ; for " He is not described in it. He is a simple article of property."

It would, I suspect, have been better to say that, as the slave was here, and in the clauses about representation and importation, acknowledged to be a person, he was entitled to the full benefit of the Fifth Amendment, which declares that " No person shall " . . . " be deprived of life, liberty, or property, without due process of law." As soon as these words could be appealed to before unprejudiced judges, they would have amply protected fugitive slaves ; and their surrender, as well as every other attempt to assert a right of property in man, would have become illegal as soon as the Supreme Court should give due heed to a fact which was stated in the Senate by the author of the Fugitive Slave Bill in 1850 ; namely, that there was not " A single State in which the insti-

tution is established by positive law." What Douglass thought of the guarantees in the Constitution is
stated as follows in the speech of 1860, which, it must
be remembered, was directed against Thompson,
rather than Garrison :

"Its language is, ' We the people ; ' not we the white people,
not even we the citizens, not we the privileged class, not we
the high, not we the low, but we the people ; not we the horses,
sheep, and swine, and wheelbarrows, but we the people, we the
human inhabitants ; and, if negroes are people, they are
included in the benefits for which the Constitution of America
was ordained and established. But how dare any man who
pretends to be the friend to the negro thus gratuitously concede
away what the negro has a right to claim under the Constitution ? Why should such friends invent new arguments to
increase the hopelessness of his bondage ? This, I undertake
to say, as the conclusion of the whole matter, that the constitutionality of slavery can be made out only by disregarding the
plain and common-sense reading of the Constitution itself ; by
disregarding and casting away as worthless the most beneficent
rules of legal interpretation ; by ruling the negro outside of
these beneficent rules ; by claiming everything for slavery ; by
denying everything for freedom ; by assuming that the Constitution does not mean what it says, and that it says what it does
not mean ; by disregarding the written Constitution, and inter-
preting it in the light of a secret understanding. It is in this
mean, contemptible, and underhand method that the American
Constitution is pressed into the service of slavery. They go
everywhere else for proof that the Constitution is pro-slavery,
but to the Constitution itself. The Constitution declares that
no person shall be deprived of life, liberty, or property, without
due process of law ; it secures to every man the right of trial
by jury, the privilege of the writ of *habeas corpus*—that great
writ that put an end to slavery and slave-hunting in England ;
it secures to every State a republican form of government.
Any one of these provisions in the hands of Abolition States-

men, and backed up by a right moral sentiment, would put an
end to slavery in America."

He concludes with these arguments to prove that,

" The way to abolish slavery in America is to vote such men
into power, as will use their powers for the abolition of slavery.
. . . " My argument against the dissolution of the American
Union is this : It would place the slave system more exclusively under the control of the slave-holding States, and withdraw it from the power in the Northern States which is
opposed to slavery. Slavery is essentially barbarous in its
character. It, above all things else, dreads the presence of an
advanced civilization. It flourishes best where it meets no
reproving frowns, and hears no condemning voices. While in
the Union it will meet with both. Its hope of life in the last
resort is to get out of the Union. I am, therefore, for drawing
the bond of the Union more closely, and bringing the slave
States more completely under the power of the free States.
What they most dread, that I most desire. I have much
confidence in the instincts of the slave-holders. They see that
the Constitution will afford slavery no protection, when it shall
cease to be administered by slave-holders. They see, more-
over, that if there is once a will in the people of America to
abolish slavery, there is no word, no syllable in the Constitution
to forbid that result. They see that the Constitution has not
saved slavery in Rhode Island, in Connecticut, in New York, or
Pennsylvania ; that the free States have increased from one up
to eighteen in number, while the slave States have only added
three to their original number. There were twelve slave States
at the beginning of the Government: there are fifteen now.
There was one free State at the beginning of the Government:
there are eighteen now. The dissolution of the Union would
not give the North a single advantage over slavery, but would
take from it many. Within the Union we have a firm basis of
opposition to slavery. It is opposed to all the great objects of
the Constitution. The dissolution of the Union is not only an

unwise but a cowardly measure—fifteen millions running away from three hundred and fifty thousand slave-holders. Mr. Garrison and his friends tell us that while in the Union we are responsible for slavery. He and they sing out 'No union with slave-holders,' and refuse to vote. I admit our responsibility for slavery while in the Union; but I deny that going out of the Union would free us from that responsibility. There now clearly is no freedom from responsibility for slavery to any American citizen short of the abolition of slavery. The American people have gone quite too far in this slave-holding business now, to sum up their whole business with slavery by singing out the cant phrase, 'No union with slave-holders!' To desert the family-hearth may place the recreant husband out of the presence of his starving children, but this does not free him from responsibility. If a man were on board of a pirate ship, and, in company with others, had robbed and plundered, his whole duty would not be performed simply by taking the long-boat and singing out, 'No union with pirates.' His duty would be to restore the stolen property. The American people in the Northern States have helped to enslave the black people. Their duty will not have been done until they give them back their plundered rights. Reference was made at the City Hall to my having once held other opinions, and very different opinions to those I have now expressed. An old speech of mine, delivered fourteen years ago, was read to show, I know not what, that I am not infallible. If so, I have to say in defense that I never pretended to be. Although I cannot accuse myself of being remarkably unstable, I do not pretend that I have never altered my opinion both in respect to men and things. Indeed, I have been very much modified both in feeling and opinion within the last fourteen years. When I escaped from slavery, and was introduced to the Garrisonians, I adopted very many of their opinions, and defended them just as long as I deemed them true. I was young, had read but little, and naturally took some things on trust. Subsequent experience and reading have led me to examine for myself. This has brought me to other conclusions. When I was a child, I thought and spoke like a child.   But the question is not as to what were my opinions fourteen years ago, but what they are now.   If I am right now, it really does not matter what I was fourteen years ago.   My position now is one of reform, nct of revolution ; I would act for the abolition of slavery through the Government—not over its ruins.   If slave-holders have ruled the American Government for the last fifty years, let the anti-slavery men rule for the next fifty years.   If the South has made the Constitution bend to the purposes of slavery, let the North now make that instrument bend to the cause of freedom and justice.   If three hundred and fifty thousand slave-holders have, by devoting their energies to that single end, been able to make slavery the vital and animating spirit of the American Confederacy for the last seventy-two years, now let the freemen of the North, who have the power in their own hands, and who can make the American Government just what they think fit, resolve to blot out forever the foul and haggard crime, which is the blight and mildew, the curse and the disgrace of the whole United States."

Douglass said, in March, 1860, what was not admitted even then by the Garrisonians, although it had been urged repeatedly during the previous twenty years, first by the Liberty party men, then by the Free Soilers, and finally by the Republicans. The Constitution was no finality, but merely an instrument for enabling the majority to carry out its will with due respect for individual rights.   If the Constitution seemed pro-slavery, it was only because that was the opinion of the majority.   There never was any reason to doubt that, as soon as slavery should be condemned by the people, the Constitution would either be acknowledged to be anti-slavery or else would be made so.   The Abolitionists wou'd not have been prevented by it from adopting measur s which would ultimately have put an end to slavery. All they needed was a continual gain in strength ; and it was the probability that the Constitution would soon be interpreted in their favor, which caused the Southerners to acknowledge its anti-slavery tendencies by seceding.

The fact that secession led to emancipation is sometimes brought up as proof that the Garrisonians were right. But secession would not have destroyed slavery, if the seceders had not been slave-holders. If it had been the Abolitionists who seceded, it would have been their cause which was lost. What actually destroyed slavery was that feeling which Garrison and Phillips had done their best to root out, that love for the Union which insisted on preserving it at any cost, even that of resorting to emancipation as a war measure. Most of the men who fought to free the slave would have fought against any attempt to break up the Union for his benefit. Suppose New England had seceded because of the Fugitive Slave Bill. Attempts would certainly have been made to execute it, and would have been resisted sternly. The conflict would soon have become bloody, and there would have been an uprising of the people, like that in 1861. The only difference is that the Southern soldiers would have been supported by those of the Western and Middle States, as well as by the regular army ; the anti-slavery Confederacy would have fallen ; abolitionism would have been suppressed as treason ; and slavery would have gained a new lease of life. Or if we suppose simply that all the anti-slavery men had become non-voting disunionists, but had never been able to persuade a single State to secede, it is by no means improbable that there would be a slave-holder in the White House to-day. In order to do full justice to the men who kept abolition-ism sufficiently on constitutional ground to secure a final triumph, I must take the liberty of comparing those who would not even acknowledge them as fel-low-soldiers in the army of freedom, to the old man who is said to have been so much annoyed by the howling of a dog on his door-step, one winter's night, that he jumped out of bed and rushed into the snow. By and by his wife called out to know what he was doing. " Only trying to freeze this blamed dog to death."

The facts of history justified Douglass in saying what he did, in 1882, of the movement with which he refused to work in 1848 :

" Anti-slavery thus far had been only sheet lightning; the Buffalo convention sought to make it a thunderbolt." . . . . . . " This Buffalo convention of Free Soilers, however low was their standard, did lay the foundation of a grand superstructure. It was a powerful link in the chain of events by which the slave system has been abolished, the slave emancipated, and the country saved from dismemberment." (" Life and Times," pp. 314, 315.)

He says, in a letter not before printed :

" I was a non-voter in 1848, though deeply interested in the Free Soil movement, inaugurated in the Buffalo convention in that year. Before 1852 I became a sound convert to the doc-trine of the unconstitutionality of slavery and the duty of voting against slavery."

He adds that he gave " active support to all the candidates nominated thereafter, from Hale to. Lincoln."

The " North Star " changed its name at the time
that its editor changed his views.   He says that there
were " I know not how many other stars in the newspaper firmament," and in order to avoid confusion,
the name of " Frederick Douglass's Paper " was
adopted at the beginning of the fourth volume, in
December, 1850.   In 1852 it contained more news,
more poetry, more humor, more about politics, and
more about Woman's Rights and other new reforms
than had been found in the " North Star."   Mr. Ward
was prominent among the colored contributors, and
among the white ones were J. G. Birney and Gerrit
Smith.   The friend last named was president of the
New York State Anti-Slavery Society, which Douglass helped to revise and served as corresponding
secretary.   Its platform declares that slavery cannot
be made legal, and its first meeting was at Rochester,
on March 18, 1852, two days before the publication of
" Uncle Tom's Cabin."   That city was chosen as the
place for the subsequent meetings, which were not
numerous.

The Free Soilers gave a cordial welcome to their
new ally at the meeting of the Ohio Anti-Slavery
Society, on May 5, at Cincinnati, where he was made
vice-president ; and there Burleigh argued for disunion, while Julian defended the men who made him
one of their candidates in this year's campaign.   Our
Douglass devoted himself mainly to exposing the
short-comings of the Church, and his speech contained the following characteristic passage :

"In this connection I am always forcibly reminded of the
incomparable illustration of the principle of brotherly love in
the New Testament.   When the stranger fell among thieves,

and was left alone on the highways to perish, there came along
three persons, severally representing the classes in society.
First came the priest—evidently all priest and no humanity—
who passed by entirely ' on the other side,' and his successors
appear to have remained on the other side to this time.
[Laughter.]   Then came another, a deacon, probably; he
seemed half-man and half-priest, for he took a middle course,
and seemed wavering; but, unfortunately, the priest predom-
inated, and he followed ' in the footsteps of his illustrious predecessor' on the other side.   [Great laughter.]   But, my
friends, there next came that way a man, nothing but a man ;
yes, a regular human; [renewed laughter] and he went
straight up to the suffering stranger, bound up his wounds,
and attended to all his wants. [Laughter.] [The peculiar and
inimitable facial contortions setting off this narrative, can only
be imagined by those who have listened to Tom Corwin.]   I
can always distinguish the class of time-serving clergymen,
wherever I meet them, in the railroad car or steamboat—that
is, when they condescend to occupy the same car and cabin—
if they approach one of my color at all, the first question is—
not ' Do you love your neighbor, your brother man ? '   But,
' do you love God ? '   [Another unreportable expression of
countenance.]   But, my friends, let me be understood.   It is
the faithless and recreant priesthood I would hold up ; not
the true servants of an impartial God, who created us *all* in
his likeness.   I will never be driven off the platform of the
Christian religion in fighting slavery.   [Great applause.]   But
my heart goes out only to a practical religion.   I see in
this convention an exhibition of adherence to the vitality of
religion.   Christianity works thus, not alone with the rich and
strong, but it reaches its long, beneficent arm down to seize
and bear up the last link of humanity. [Applause.]   Such
Christianity is embodied in the great anti-slavery movement
of the nineteenth century—it is expressed in the resolution
before us.   I am heartily in favor of it."

It is sad to see that after this eulogy upon the Good

Samaritan, he failed to meet him at the convention of the A. A. S. S. one week later in Rochester. There he had to defend his change of views, and hear himself denounced as a deserter by Garrison, Phillips, Remond, Mrs. Abby Kelley Foster, and her husband, Stephen. Among other offenses were his advocating the Homestead Bill and his praising Kossuth. He was so provoked at Remond's thanking God for not being the son of a slave, that he made this allusion to the occupation of his critic's father, " I thank God that I am neither a barber nor the son of a barber." Another colored man compared him to a castaway, who had been picked up by the ship of which Garrison was captain, had tried in vain to get himself into command, and then had stolen a boat and fled. Garrison believed so firmly in disunionism, that it seemed to him impossible that any of his disciples had found a single error in the creed. He thought it his conscientious duty to bring a charge of mercenary motives against the friend, who had founded the " North Star " with money which he might honorably have invested for the benefit of his family; who sank in the enterprise, before 1856, at least twelve thousand dollars of his own earnings, according to the testimony of a competent and trustworthy writer, in the Introduction to " My Bondage and my Freedom ; " and who had made his house not only a refuge for fugitives, but a free boarding-house for poor colored boys who were invited there to learn the trade of printing. No wonder that an exile from Hungary said to one of my friends with uplifted hands, " If I attend any more of your anti-slavery meetings they will make me a pro-slavery man."

Douglass said some years later, in his reply to George Thompson :

" No personal assaults shall ever lead me to forget that some who in America have often made me the subject of personal abuse, are at the same time, in their own way, earnestly working for the abolition of slavery.   They are men who thoroughly understand the principle that he who is not for them is against them ; but unfortunately they do not seem to understand that he who is not against them is on their side."

He has since remarked, that " Mr. Garrison sent a great many people to perdition who obstinately refused to go."   Among them, by the way, were Longfellow, Sumner, and Channing.   The columns of " Frederick Douglass's Paper," for 1852 and 1853, are entirely free from any bitterness against his assailants ; and in the latter year he said, at the May meeting, held at New York by the Tappans and other non-Garrisonian Abolitionists :

" I honor and respect Lewis Tappan ; I love and honor William Lloyd Garrison ; and may God have mercy upon me when I refuse to strike a blow against slavery in connection with either gentleman.   I will work with either ; and if the one discards me because I work with the other, the responsibility is not mine."

The Garrisonians, however, continued to attack him so fiercely that there seemed likely, as the " Syracuse Journal " said, " To be a war between the white and black roses."   Mrs. Swisshelm, who was in hearty sympathy with the anti-slavery movement, as well as with that in behalf of her sex, says in her own paper, the " Saturday Visitor : " " We do believe that the ' Liberator,' ' Standard ' and ' Freeman ' might be better employed than in black-balling a black man."

She adds, in reference to a charge about neglecting
Mrs. Douglass, which drew out an indignant letter of
denial from the latter, and is fully refuted by one
quoted at the close of the next chapter : " In all our
experience of very bitter newspaper warfare, we never
saw the equal of this ; and for all we can see, the three
able papers that have united to crush Mr. Douglass,
have failed to bring a particle of proof that he is not
as good and true as he is eloquent and energetic."
He finally found it due to his family as well as to
himself, that he should reply once for all. Twelve
columns of his paper are occupied with an answer
which meets all the charges, and declares that this is
done " not to re-open, but if possible to close up our
account with these anti-slavery journals. For ourselves," he adds, " we have not now, as we had not
in the beginning, the slightest wish to be embroiled
in personal conflict with anti-slavery men of any sort.
There is better work for all of us to do than to keep
up a warfare against each other."

CHAPTER VIII.

"THE MAN WHO IS RIGHT IS A MAJORITY."

THE kidnapper's dogma, that the Constitution is pro-slavery, was carried out by both of the great parties, in June, 1852, to its logical results, namely, that hunting after fugitives ought to be kept up, and agitation against slavery ought to be put down. It was these collars, showing ownership by the South, that were clasped about the necks of both of the favorite runners in the race to the White House, Pierce and Scott. Scarcely had this been done, when Douglass said, at the celebration of the Declaration of Independence :

"Fellow-citizens, above your national, tumultuous joy, I hear the mournful wail of millions, whose chains, heavy and grievous yesterday, are to-day rendered more intolerable by the jubilant shouts that reach them. If I do forget, if I do not faithfully remember those bleeding children of sorrow this day, 'may my right hand forget her cunning, and may my tongue cleave to the roof of my mouth !' To forget them, to pass lightly over their wrongs, and to chime in with the popular theme, would be treason most scandalous and shocking, and would make me a reproach before God and the world. My subject, then, fellow-citizens, is 'American Slavery.' I shall see this day and its popular characteristics from the slave's point of view. Stand-

207

ing there, identified with the American bondman, making his wrongs mine, I do not hesitate to declare, with all my soul, that the character and conduct of this nation never looked blacker to me than on this Fourth of July. Whether we turn to the declarations of the past or to the professions of the present, the conduct of the nation seems equally hideous and revolting. America is false to the past, false to the present, and solemnly binds herself to be false to the future. Standing with God and the crushed and bleeding slave on this occasion, I will, in the name of humanity which is outraged, in the name of liberty which is fettered, in the name of the Constitution and the Bible which are disregarded and trampled upon, dare call in question and denounce with all the emphasis I can command, everything that serves to perpetuate slavery, the great sin and shame of America! ' I will not equivocate ; I will not excuse ; ' I will use the severest language I can command ; and yet not one word shall escape me that any man, whose judgment is not blinded by prejudice, or who is not at heart a slave-holder, shall not confess to be right and just.

" But I fancy I hear some one of my audience say, it is just in this circumstance that you and your brother Abolitionists fail to make a favorable impression on the public mind. Would you argue more and denounce less, would you persuade more and rebuke less, your cause would be much more likely to succeed. But, I submit, where all is plain, there is nothing to be argued. What point in the anti-slavery creed would you have me argue ? On what branch of the subject do the people of this country need light ? Must I undertake to prove that the slave is a man ? That point is conceded already. Nobody doubts it. The slave-holders themselves acknowledge it in the enactment of laws for their government. They acknowledge it, when they punish disobedience on the part of the slave. There are seventy-two crimes in the State of Virginia, which, if committed by a black man (no matter how ignorant he be), subject him to the punishment of death ; while only two of these same crimes will subject a white man to the like punishment. What is this but the acknowledgment that the slave is a moral, intellectual, and responsible being. The manhood of the slave is conceded. It is admitted in the fact that Southern statute books are covered with enactments, forbidding, under severe fines and penalties, the teaching of the slave to read or write. When you can point to any such laws in reference to the beasts of the field, then I may consent to argue the manhood of the slave. When the dogs in your streets, when the fowls in the air, when the cattle on your hills, when the fish of the sea, and the reptiles that crawl shall be unable to distinguish the slave from a brute, then will I argue with you that the slave is a man.

" For the present, it is enough to affirm the equal manhood of the negro race. Is it not astonishing that, while we are plowing, planting, and reaping, using all kinds of mechanical tools, erecting houses, constructing bridges, building ships, working in metals of brass, iron, copper, silver, and gold ; that, while we are reading, writing, and ciphering, acting as clerks, merchants, and secretaries, having among us lawyers, doctors, ministers, poets, authors, editors, orators, and teachers ; that, while we are engaged in all manner of enterprises common to other men—digging gold in California, capturing the whale in the Pacific, feeding sheep and cattle on the hill-side, living, moving, acting, thinking, planning, living in families as husbands, wives, and children, and, above all, confessing and worshiping the Christian's God, and looking hopefully for life and immortality beyond the grave—we are called upon to prove that we are men ?

" Would you have me argue that man is entitled to liberty ? That he is the rightful owner of his own body ? You have already declared it. Must I argue the wrongfulness of slavery ? Is that a question for republicans ? Is it to be settled by the rules of logic and argumentation, as a matter beset with great difficulty, involving a doubtful application of justice, hard to be understood ? How should I look to-day in the presence of Americans, dividing and subdividing a discourse to show that men have a natural right to freedom, speaking of it relatively and positively, negatively and affirmatively ? To do so would be to make myself ridiculous, and to offer an insult to your understanding. There is not a man beneath the canopy of heaven that does not know that slavery is wrong for *him*.

"What! am I to argue that it is wrong to make men brutes, to rob them of their liberty, to work them without wages, to keep them ignorant of their relations to their fellowmen, to beat them with sticks, to flay their flesh with the lash, to load their limbs with irons, to hunt them with dogs, to sell them at auction, to sunder their families, to knock out their teeth, to burn their flesh, to starve them into obedience and submission to their masters? Must I argue that a system, thus marked with blood and stained with pollution, is wrong? No; I will not. I have better employment for my time and strength than such arguments would imply.

What, then, remains to be argued? Is it that slavery is not divine; that God did not establish it; that our doctors of divinity are mistaken? There is blasphemy in the thought. That which is inhuman cannot be divine. Who can reason on such a proposition? They that can, may; I cannot. The time for such argument is past.

At a time like this, scorching irony, not convincing argument, is needed. Oh! had I the ability, and could I reach the nation's ear, I would to-day pour out a stream of biting ridicule, blasting reproach, withering sarcasm, and stern rebuke. For it is not light that is needed, but fire; it is not the gentle shower, but thunder. We need the storm, the whirlwind, and the earthquake!"

On August 11, 1852, the Free Soil convention met at Pittsburgh; and Rochester sent a colored delegate who was obliged, both in going and returning, to take a steamboat between Buffalo and Cleveland, and each time to pass the night on deck. On his way back he tried to get breakfast in the cabin; but his chair was pulled out from under him by the captain, who had already collected the full fare for berth and meal and would refund nothing. The train for

Pittsburgh stopped for dinner at a hotel where he was
not allowed to eat, on which many of the other delegates rose from the table and refused to return.   On
their way back not one of them entered the hall—
dinner had been prepared for three hundred guests,
but it was left on the landlord's hands.

One of the first steps taken in the convention was
to make Douglass a secretary by acclamation; and no
sooner did he enter the hall than he was invited to
speak by so many enthusiastic voices, that the white
man, who had the floor, was obliged to surrender it
at once to his dusky superior.   The latter was dressed
like Daniel Webster—in white trowsers and a blue
coat with brass buttons, "indicative," says an
unfriendly reporter, "of the bronze in his face."
There was a great deal more of iron in his blood than
in Webster's that summer.   There he stood, holding
in his hand a pamphlet, by Gerrit Smith, which he
was about to recommend to his audience, taken, as he
said, wholly by surprise, but bringing down the
house repeatedly, as he spoke thus :

"I am, of course, for circumscribing and damaging slavery
in every way.   But my motto is extermination." . . . "The
slave-holders not only forfeit their right to liberty, but to life
itself.   The earth is God's ; and it ought to be covered with
righteousness, not slavery."

Of the Fugitive Slave Bill he said, suiting the action
to the word :

"It is too bad to be repealed, a law fit only to be trampled
under foot.   The only way to make the Fugitive Slave Law a
dead letter is to make half a dozen or more dead kidnappers."
. . . "The man who takes the office of a bloodhound ought to
be treated as a bloodhound ; and I believe that the lines of

eternal justice are sometimes so obliterated that it is necessary to revive them by deepening their traces with the blood of a tyrant." . . . "This vile, infernal law does not interfere with singing of psalms, or anything of that kind, but with the weightier matters of the law, judgment, mercy, and faith." . . . "Had it been a law to strike at baptism, for instance, it would have been denounced from a thousand pulpits; and woe to the politician who did not come to the rescue." . . . "It has been said that this law is constitutional. If it were, it would be equally the legitimate sphere of government to repeal it. I am proud to be one of the disciples of Gerrit Smith, and this is his doctrine; and he only utters what all law writers have said, who have risen to any eminence. Human government is for the protection of rights, and not for the destruction of rights. Suppose you and I made a deed to give away two or three acres of blue sky, would the sky fall?" . . . "The binding quality of law is its reasonableness. I am safe, therefore, in saying that slavery cannot be legalized." . . . "You are about to have a party; but I hope not such a party as will gather up the votes here and there, in order to be swallowed up at a meal by the great parties." . . . "I want to be always independent, and not hurried to and fro into the ranks of Whigs and Democrats. It has been said that we ought to take the position of the greatest number of voters. That is wrong. It was said, in 1848, that Martin Van Buren would carry a strong vote in New York. He did, but he almost ruined us. He merely looked into the pig-pen to see how the animal grew, but the table was the final prospect he had in view. He regarded the colored population as fatlings to be devoured. Numbers should not be looked to so much as right. The man who is right is a majority. We, who have God and conscience on our side, have a majority against the universe."

It will be noticed that this speech contains an idea which was also put into the words, "One with God is a majority." In both forms it was, I think, original with Mr. Douglass.

He is said to have made "The one aggressive speech in the convention ;" but it is to be remembered that Gerrit Smith also advocated resisting the wicked law by force. The suggestion of this veteran of the war against slavery, in favor of declaring that political rights are "irrespective of sex or color," was not incorporated in the platform ; but the convention did agree that Christianity and humanity alike demanded the abolition of slavery. Of the Fugitive Slave Bill they spoke thus, We "demand its immediate and total repeal," and "We deny its binding force." The motto adopted for the campaign was, "Free Soil, Free Speech, Free Labor, Free Men." It was in full conformity with these principles that Hale was nominated for President, and Julian for Vice-President, without opposition ; and the men were worthy of the cause.

Such a nomination for President, and such a platform, were too good to be popular in 1852. Neither the Fugitive Slave Bill, nor "Uncle Tom's Cabin," could overcome the determination of the North to make every sacrifice then demanded for the preservation of the Union. The Democrats, who had bolted four years before, now went back so generally that New York gave Hale but little more than one-fifth as many votes as had been given to Van Buren. The Whigs stood firmer, but even in New England the Free Soil vote was less in 1852 than in 1848. The sum total of 290,000, obtained by Van Buren, shrank to 156,000, which was only about five per cent. of the whole number of votes. The little band of anti-slavery Congressmen did, however, receive some important accessions ; and among them was Gerrit

Smith, who owed his election very largely to the efforts of the Rochester editor. The latter's relations with Garrison were still friendly enough for them to appear together as speakers, at the meeting held at Syracuse, October 1, 1852, with Gerrit Smith in the chair, to commemorate the rescue, one year previous, of a fugitive slave named Jerry McHenry. Rev S. J. May has given, in his "Recollections of the Anti-Slavery Conflict," a vivid account of the exploit, in which he and Gerrit Smith took prominent parts. The celebration in 1852 was in the engine-house, just completed by the New York Central Railroad.

What Douglass said about Garrison among his opponents, on May 11, 1853, has been given in the last chapter ; and on that same day we find him once more on the platform of the A. A. S. S., in New York City. Henry Ward Beecher said there, that he had rather wait seventy-five years for slavery to be abolished by Christianity, than have emancipation decreed in only fifty years from mere motives of a selfish commercial interest. The next speaker was Douglass, and he began by saying that, " If the reverend gentleman had worked on plantations where I have been, he would have met with overseers who would have whipped him in five minutes out of all his willingness to wait for liberty." The boldness of this rebuke is all the more remarkable, because the man who gave it continued in these words :

" No colored man with any nervous sensibility can stand before an American audience, without an intense and painful sense of the disadvantages imposed by his color. He feels little borne up by the brotherly sympathy and generous enthusiasm which give wings to the eloquence and strength to the hearts of other men, who advocate other and more popular causes. The ground which a colored man occupies in this country is, every inch of it, sternly disputed. Sir, were I a white man speaking for the rights of white men, I would in this country have a smooth sea and a fair wind. It is perhaps creditable to the American people (and I am not the man to detract from their credit), that they listen eagerly to the report of wrongs endured by distant nations. The Hungarian, the Italian, the Irishman, the Jew and Gentile, all find in this goodly land a home; and when any of them or all of them desire to speak, they find willing ears, warm hearts. and open hands. For these people, the American people have principles of justice, maxims of mercy, sentiments of religion, and feelings of brotherhood in abundance. But for my poor people (alas, how poor), enslaved, scourged, blasted, overwhelmed, and ruined, it would appear that America had neither justice, mercy, nor religion. She has no scales in which to weigh our wrongs, and no standard by which to measure our rights. Just here lies the grand difficulty of the colored man's cause. It is found in the fact that we may not avail ourselves of the just force of admitted American principles. If I do not misinterpret the feelings and philosophy of my white fellow-countrymen generally, they wish us to understand distinctly and fully, that they have no other use for us whatever than to coin dollars out of our blood. Our position here is anomalous, unequal, and extraordinary. It is a position to which the most courageous of our race cannot look without deep concern. Sir, we are a hopeful people, and in this we are fortunate; but for this trait of our character we should have, long before this seemingly unpropitious hour, sunk down under a sense of utter despair. Look at it, sir, here upon the soil of our birth, in a country which has known us for two centuries, among people who did not wait for us to seek them, but who sought and found us, and brought us to their own chosen land, a people for whom we have performed the humblest services, and whose greatest comforts and luxuries have been won from the soil by our sable and sinewy arms. I say, sir, among such a people and with such obvious recommendations to favor, we are far less esteemed than the veriest stranger and sojourner. Aliens are we in our native land. The fundamental principles of the Republic, to which the humblest white man, whether born here or elsewhere, may appeal with confidence in the hope of awakening a favorable response, are held inapplicable to us. The glorious doctrines of your Revolutionary fathers, and the more glorious teachings of the Son of God are construed and applied against us. We are literally scourged beyond the beneficent range of both authorities—human and divine. We plead for our rights in the name of the immortal Declaration of Independence and of the written Constitution of government; and we are answered with imprecations and curses. In the sacred name of Jesus we beg for mercy; and the slave-whip, red with blood, cracks over us in mockery. We invoke the aid of the minister of Him who came 'to preach deliverance to the captive,' and to set at liberty them that are bound, and from the loftiest summits of this ministry comes the inhuman and blasphemous response, saying, if one prayer would move the Almighty arm in mercy to break our galling chains, that prayer would be withheld. We cry for help to humanity, a common humanity; and here, too, we are repulsed. American humanity hates us, scorns us, disowns and denies in a thousand ways our very personality. The outspread wing of American Christianity, apparently broad enough to give shelter to a perishing world, refuses to cover us. To us its bones are brass, and its feathers iron. In running thither for succor and shelter, we have only fled from the hungry bloodhound to the devouring wolf, from a corrupt and selfish world to a hollow and hypocritical church."

This passage was selected by the author as his contribution to "Autographs for Freedom," Volume ii., 1854. Miss Griffiths included in this year's collection a speech of Theodore Parker's, and also the poem on "Freedom," by Emerson. Each selection was accompanied by a fac-simile of the signature, and the book was handsomely bound and printed.

Among other portions of the address by Douglass, on May 11, 1853, are these :

"I have thus briefly given my view of one aspect of the present condition and future prospects of the colored people of the United States. And what I have said is far from encouraging to my afflicted people. I have seen the cloud gather upon the sable brows of some who hear me. I confess the case looks black enough. Sir, I am not a hopeful man. I think I am apt even to undercalculate the benefits of the future. Yet, sir, in this seemingly desperate case, I do not despair for my people. There is a bright side to almost every picture of this kind ; and ours is no exception to the general rule. If the influences against us are strong, those for us are also strong. But the inquiry, will our enemies prevail in the execution of their designs ? In my God and in my soul I believe they will not. Let us look at the first object sought for by the slavery party of the country, viz., the suppression of anti-slavery discussion. They desire to suppress discussion on this subject, with a view to the peace of the slave-holder and the security of slavery. Now, sir, neither the principal nor the subordinate objects here declared, can be at all gained by the slave-power, and for this reason : it involves the proposition to padlock the lips of the whites, in order to secure the fetters on the limbs of the blacks. The right of speech, precious and priceless, cannot, will not, be surrendered to slavery. Its suppression is asked for, as I have said, to give peace and security to slave-holders. Sir, that thing cannot be done. God has interposed an insuperable obstacle to any such result. ' There can be no peace,' saith my God, ' to the wicked.' Suppose it were possible to put down this discussion, what would it avail the guilty slave-holder, pillowed as he is upon the heaving bosoms of ruined souls ? He could not have a peaceful spirit. If every anti-slavery tongue in the nation were silent, every anti-slavery organization dissolved, every anti-slavery press demolished, every anti-slavery periodical, paper, book, pamphlet, or what not, were searched out, gathered together, deliberately burned to ashes, and their ashes given to the four winds of heaven, still, still the slave-holder could have ' no peace.' In every pulsation of his heart, in every throb of his life, in every glance of his eye, in the breeze that soothes, and in the thunder that startles, would be waked up an accuser, whose cause is, ' Thou art verily guilty concerning thy brother.' . . .

" Slavery has no means within itself of perpetuation or permanence. It is a huge lie. It is of the devil, and will go to its place. It is against nature, against progress, against improvement, and against the government of God. It cannot stand. It has an enemy in every bar of railroad iron, in every electric wire, in every improvement in navigation, in the growing intercourse of nations, in cheap postage, in the relaxation of tariffs, in common schools, in the progress of education, the spread of knowledge, in the steam engine, and in the World's Fair, now about to assemble in New York. and in everything that will be exhibited there.

" About making slavery respectable in the North, laws have been made to accomplish just that thing ; the law of 1850 and the law of 1793. And those laws, instead of getting respect for slavery, have begot distrust and abhorrence. Congress might pass fugitive slave laws every day in the year, for all time, if each one should be followed by such publications as ' Uncle Tom ' and the ' Key.' It is not in the power of human law to make men entirely forget that the slave is a man. The freeman of the North can never be brought to look with the same feeling upon a man escaping from his claimants as upon a horse running from his owner. The slave is a man, and no slave. Now, sir, I had more to say on the encouraging aspects of the times, but the time fails me, I will only say in conclusion, greater is He that is for us, than they that are against us ; and though labor and peril beset the anti-slavery movements, so sure as that a God of mercy and justice is enthroned above all created things, so sure will that cause gloriously triumph."

This meeting was as remarkable for tranquillity as

that in 1850 had been for disturbance. The anti-slavery cause was gaining in favor, though still under the ecclesiastical ban. Douglass set himself, in his paper, decidedly against giving any unnecessary excuse for such censures; but when he found himself branded as an infidel, which was the case down to the outbreak of the war, he said : " If the glory of American emancipation is to be given to infidels, it will be a killing sentence against the American Church." The best words I know of on this subject, however, were those which Lucy Stone, in her speech this very day, quoted from Sally Holley : "Let them call us infidels, if they please ; but, oh ! don't let them call themselves Christians."

The following description of the oratorical power of Douglass at this time was given by another colored man, Professor W. J. Wilson, in " Autographs for Freedom:"

" In his very look, his gesture, his whole manner, there is so much of genuine, earnest eloquence, that they leave no time for reflection. Now you are reminded of one rushing down some fearful steep, bidding you follow ; now of some delightful stream, still beckoning you onward. In either case, no matter what your prepossessions or oppositions, you, for the moment at least, forget the justness or unjustness of his cause, and obey the summons ; and loath, if at all, you return to your former post. Not always, however, is he successful in retaining you. Giddy as you may be with the descent you have made, delighted as you are with the pleasure afforded, with the Elysium to which he has wafted you, you return too often dissatisfied with his and your own impetuosity and want of firmness. You feel that you had only a dream, a pastime—not a reality. This great power of momentary captivation consists in his eloquence of manner, his just appreciation of words. In listening to him, your whole soul is fired, every nerve strung, every passion inflated, and every faculty you possess ready to perform at a moment's bidding. You stop not to ask why or wherefore. 'Tis a unison of mighty yet harmonious sounds that play upon your imagination; and you give yourself up for a time to their irresistible charm. At last, the cataract which roared around you is hushed, the tornado is passed, and you find yourself sitting upon a bank (at whose base roll but tranquil waters), quietly asking yourself, why, amid such a display of power, no greater effect had really been produced. After all, it must be admitted there is a power in Mr. Douglass rarely to be found in any other man."

Early in 1853 he published in his own paper a highly wrought story, which had already appeared in "Autographs for Freedom," entitled "The Heroic Slave." It is based on actual adventures of Madison Washington, who set himself free by his own courage some ten years before.

The colored national convention, which met that year in Rochester, on July 6, adopted an address, written by their champion, and containing this passage: "We are, and by right we ought to be American citizens. We claim this right; and we claim all the rights, privileges, and duties which properly attach to it." A resolution was also passed in favor of establishing an Industrial College, with an agricultural professor, and instructors "To superintend the practical application of natural philosophy to general smithing, turning, and cabinet making."

The author of this plan had written, four months before, a letter to Mrs. Stowe, which may be found in his "Life and Times" (pp. 323–327). He had been invited by her to a visit at her house, where he met a little girl who must, he thinks, have been the model for Eva in " Uncle Tom's Cabin ;" and during the interview he persuaded her to promise to use money, which she hoped to collect in Europe for the benefit of his race, in establishing what he calls, " A college where colored youth can be instructed to use their hands as well as their heads ; where they can be put in possession of the means of getting a living." One of his editorials, on March 18, was headed " Make your Sons Mechanics and Farmers, not Waiters, Porters, and Barbers." One passage, which may still be recommended to the attention of all men and women who send their children to our public schools, runs thus : " It is cruel, unnatural, brutal, and scandalous for parents to cast their offspring upon a selfish world without using every means in their power to give them useful trades." Our public schools are not yet fully up to the suggestions which he made nearly forty years ago, when he said in the number of his paper just referred to, " The education of the hands must precede that of the head."

It is also pleasant to find that he spoke strongly in favor of female compositors, in the Woman's Rights Convention, held in Rochester, November 30 and December 1, 1853, presided over by Rev. S. J. May, and attended by Rev. W. H. Channing, Rev. Antoinette L. Brown, Mrs. Stanton, Mrs. Bloomer, Mrs. Lucy N. Colman, and Miss Anthony. He also said, " Some one whispers in my ear, that as teachers, women get one-fourth the pay men do, while a girl's tuition is the same as a boy's."

Mrs. Colman, who did good work for abolitionism as well as for woman's rights, has kindly furnished

me with a letter of recollections, which has direct reference to this period :

"My intimate acquaintance with Frederick Douglass commenced in 1853; and, if we except the following year, 1854,
continued until the close of the war. Mr. Douglass was entirely
disfellowshiped by the Garrisonian party soon after his return
from England ; the establishing of a paper published and edited
by him, somehow, did not meet with Mr. Garrison's approval ;
and never did any party follow its leader more closely than the
Garrisonians followed him. Mr. Garrison did not allow a difference of opinion ; in his eyes such difference was not possible
in a true Abolitionist. The bitterness engendered by this
division had a marked effect upon Mr. Douglass's disposition ;
he is a man of very strong feeling ; and he had been petted and
almost owned by the prominent members of that class of Abolitionists. To find himself treated as though he had been false
to his race, because he had broken loose from leading strings,
and chose to work in his own way, was very hard ; but he was
equal to the situation, though his spirit was somewhat em-
bittered.

" There was in one of those years, when the Unitarian Society
in Rochester was without a settled pastor, an attempt to hold
a series of Sunday meetings by one of the agents of the Abolitionists. Mr. Douglass did not attend these Sunday meetings ;
and we all knew that his absence was a great loss, as his popularity was such, that his presence, if advertised, would always
insure a large audience ; but he had a personal grievance with
the getter-up of these meetings, and was in no mood to go. A
murder had been committed some little time previous ; and
the guilty man (not a man in age), was condemned to the
gallows. Some of us, wholly opposed to capital punishment,
concluded to call a public meeting, and try to act upon the
people by the presence of extenuating circumstances, which
were many, so as to get our petition, for a change to imprisonment for life, largely signed. I went to Mr. Douglass, and succeeded in getting his name to the call, and a promise that he

would attend. Our advertisement was followed by a call of the largest kind to the people to go and take the meeting from the callers, and prevent any presentation of sympathy with a murderer. We, the callers of the meeting, came together at the hour and succeeded in appointing the officers, making Mr. Douglass president, when the house filled with a mob of men so violent that it seemed as though there might be murder there. Frederick Douglass then and there showed himself a man of almost superhuman power. His loud but melodious voice rose above the wild howl of those enraged men, and quieted them for some few moments (they would hear no other one), though they frequently threw at him the most insulting epithets; but they had come to break up the meeting and they succeeded. The Mayor, instead of protecting the meeting, ordered the lights in the hall put out and the meeting proper to disperse. Thus was free speech protected in those pro-slavery days; but good came to Mr. Douglass through that disgraceful mob. His name (that had been ignored for some years) found its way into the 'Liberator' and 'Anti-Slavery Standard' in words that gave him true honor; and many old friends forgot their animosity and greeted him as of old.

" Mr. Douglass had a fund of humor that, whatever the emergency, he could call upon; and he had a kind of venom so cruel, that I would feel for my bitterest enemy that was being stung by it.

" He was once invited to speak in a village west of Rochester, the place a Baptist church. After he had ascended the pulpit, the deacon of the church went to him and told him ' There was an unpleasant rumor abroad in that region concerning him, that he ought to clear up.' Mr. Douglass asked to be informed what it was, and the deacon said ' It is that you have married a white wife!' So when Mr. Douglass rose, he repeated what the deacon had told him and proceeded to 'clear it up.' He said he had been invited to give an anti-slavery lecture there, and had come prepared to do so; and he could not see in what way the color of his wife affected the subject. If his wife had chosen to marry him, he being colored, it was her business. The audience at this point were very sure that they would hear the confession from his own lips, that his wife was white. They were all excitement. ' Now,' said Mr. Douglass, ' If my wife could see, she could not help knowing that I was not a white man ; and yet she married me. Pray tell me what has her color to do with a lecture against slavery ? ' So he tantalized his audience with the subject till they supposed his next utterance would be an announcement that his wife was white, and then he would return to the subject and argue it out again, showing that his color, or that of his wife, had nothing to do with the subject that he came to discuss. At length, after the large audience wearied of the delay, Mr. Douglass decided that the color of his wife was not the business of the meeting, and dropped it without telling them ; and so they supposed his wife was white. The truth was, she was black as night; but the audience forgot to be angry as they listened to his lecture, so thrilling, so grand that even our Wendell Phillips, silver-tongued and graceful beyond description, ' the World's Orator,' could not more than equal it.

" I have heard Mr. Douglass tell a story in which his color was no longer of any use. Said he, ' I used to find myself favored with a double seat in the cars, very convenient when one is traveling at night; but recently I had an all-night ride before me, and prepared my bag for a pillow, covered my head with my shawl, and was about falling to sleep ; when some one shook me, saying at the same time, " Move along and give me a seat." I roused myself, took my cap as well as my shawl from my head, so that my hair would be observable, thinking that would be sufficient to insure me my resting place ; but a more severe shaking came and a peremptory command to move and give up one seat. Then I said very meekly ' I am a nigger.' " Go to —— with your nigger, move along and give me a seat ! " ' So,' said he, ' My color is no longer of any use.' "

Another lady answered my questions thus :

" I wish I had more facts of Frederick Douglass's life than I have. I knew him when he had just escaped from slavery, in Syracuse, where he first attracted immensely as a speaker. He was full of wit, humor, and satire, somewhat bitter at times, of commanding presence, and a magnificent voice, unsurpassed as an orator, especially when a little bit angry. 'One with God is a majority,' was said by him after a taunt from an opponent on the weakness of numbers and power of the Abolitionists. You know he went to England, and was bought and presented to himself by the English people. He was converted from the Garrisonians to the political party of anti-slavery by Gerrit Smith, who was always a firm friend. His recent autobiography will give you all the information there is about his public career, written in excellent taste. The paper you speak of I tried to subscribe for, but, owing to bad arrangements in the office, did not succeed. In fact, he was not methodical, or very practical. Susan B. Anthony used to say, ' He had a great deal of uncommon sense, but his wife more than her share of common sense.' Nothing that he has ever done or said is more admirable than the respect he always showed her, and his undeviating exaction of the same from others. She was an excellent house-wife and manager. I have been to his house in Rochester, saw her and the children. They are more like their mother as I remember them. The daughter, Rose, married a fugitive slave. A younger daughter died broken hearted during the John Brown raid; her father being obliged to fly to Europe, you remember, and Brown himself, who had been at his house, and to whom the child had become much attached, being hung, and the illustrated papers being scattered about so excited the child, that she drooped and died ; and he had only the grave to look upon when he returned. Douglass is a man of great natural refinement, perhaps from his white father, perhaps from a freak of nature. I think very little of heredity myself. Certainly the best in society and in life was what he liked best, and was always seeking. I think many colored people did not feel fully assured of his friendship to them, which was a great mistake. The wholesome truths he uttered seemed harsh, but he was and is a true friend to his race."

A pathetic circumstance about his child's grave is mentioned by Miss Holley, in the valuable letter from which I make another extract. The lines, there quoted from Campbell, are given precisely as they were afterward written out by Mr. Douglass, who has improved them greatly.

" Years went by, and the next meeting I recall with this heroic 'fugitive slave, whose romantic fortunes are indeed a miracle, was in the city of Rochester. He had a respectable residence in spacious grounds in the country, near the beautiful Mount Hope. I called on Mr. D. and his family whenever I visited Mount Hope, and well remember the tidiness and taste of the little parlor, the quiet, handsome library, with its attractive books and pictures—his daughters, Rosa, an intelligent school-girl, and the gentle, darling, little Anna, with her winning, modest shyness, but happy to trust the friendly face of the lady who held her small, soft, velvety hand kindly, while talking with her father and mother. Perhaps these were rare occasions to the little girl, for we never met any white lady caller; and the social isolation of Mr. Douglass—man of genius as he was, of distinguished presence and gracious manners, fit to adorn any circle—must have been torture. He told us sadly once, ' I live the life of a hermit here in Rochester.' Illustrious strangers, like James Russell Lowell and Frederika Bremer, traveling through Rochester, always called on Douglass, but Rochester people didn't. He was fortunate in the comfort of his home, made so by the nice and able house-keeping of Mrs. Douglass, who kept an inviting table, and the wardrobe of her family neat and presentable. She was ever attentive to warding off attacks of colds and rheumatism with warm changes of cloth-ing for Mr. D., at home and on his travels. But the anti-slavery families of Rochester, who formed, in those days, a superior and attractive circle (that included the Rev. Wm. H. Channing, and the new university professors), held shy from incur-ring popular odium by asking a black man to their social ever. ·

ing parties. I remember when Hon. George Thompson, of England, was in Rochester, a round of evening parties was given in his honor. Mr. and Mrs. Wilder gave the most elegant one in their large, handsome house. Mr. Thompson was in brilliant mood, sang delightful songs, told merry anecdotes, and talked charmingly. Still, I thought the company incomplete without the presence of Frederick Douglass. I was ashamed of the stupid prejudice that excluded him. A lively young gentleman said to me, 'To have Douglass here this evening might strangle the young infant University to death.' And yet the time may come when Rochester will be only known as the place where Frederick Douglass once lived. This color exclusion was keenly felt by so sensitive a nature as F. D.'s, admirably suited to enjoy and reciprocate the genial flow and glow of cultured society, by his rare innate refinement and the glimpses his peculiar experience had gained from association with our true American noblesse, who had thrown all their advantages of birth, wealth, and social position into the scale of humanity against the prevalent spirit of caste and prejudice.

" Of these conspicuously was the 'noblest name in the Empire State,' Hon. Gerrit Smith—that peerless philanthropist, whose princely fortune was devoted, beyond precedent, to the service of humanity, as simple, transparent and unaffectedly devout a follower of the Christian precepts of human brotherhood as Count Tolstoi, from whose table and delightful drawing-room Frederick Douglass was never made to feel the ban of color. That charming Peterboro' mansion dispensed generous and unique hospitality—alike to the beauty and chivalry of the city and the State, and to the lowly fugitive slave and his advocates, who stood nowhere else on such footing as in that splendid domain, inherited from the partner of John Jacob Astor. Gerrit Smith ever welcomed Douglass 'as a brother beloved.'

" So in Boston did the highest and proudest in family distinction, Wendell Phillips, condescend to him of low estate. His invalid, but magnificent-hearted wife, a cousin of Copley, the painter, precluded domestic entertainment. But on every steamboat, in every omnibus, railroad car, where Douglass was tabood, solely because of color, there was Wendell Phillips ready to take his seat beside his 'despised and rejected' brother, vastly to the annoyance of conductors and agents, who couldn't help feeling the scandal and disgrace of the miserable colorphobia, so pointedly rebuked. To crown all the rest, once in an anti-slavery family—too poor to offer two beds to their guests of a night—Wendell Phillips so far forgot the hateful proscription as to share the bed of Frederick Douglass. Mr. P. may have had this in his mind when later, in his exquisite addresses, he used to tell the anecdote of Washington making the chilled and sleepy negro servant of Colonel Pickering, watching with him in the same tent, lie down beside him and sleep out the night under the same blanket.

"I once heard Douglass in a speech in Rochester, in a strain of subdued yet powerful eloquence, say : 'I sometimes forget the color of my skin, and remember that I am a man. I sometimes forget that I am hated of men, and remember I am loved of God. Has the white man religious aspirations ? So have I. Thoughts that wander through eternity, affections that climb up and twine around the Universal Father.'

"While the *élite* of Rochester shrank from the social equality, implied in an invitation to its table, there were households, like Miss Porter's, that keenly enjoyed a chance call, or interview, with one known then to be 'a lion ;' and its diverse members would quickly assemble in the parlor to bask in the inimitable play and sparkle of his wit and fancy, or to be thrilled by his indignant and caustic allusions to passing events at home and abroad, whenever it was noised through the house that Frederick Douglass was calling on his friends. Chief of all these triumphs over 'race, color and previous condition of servitude' was that in the superb Corinthian Hall, then the handsomest audience chamber in all that part of the State. Its brilliantly-lighted interior was an enchantment to everybody, with the delicate and dainty white lilies pouring out of their lovely chalices the blazing gas-jets, upon rich and poor, white and black, high and low, assembled to hear the unsurpassed eloquence of Frederick Douglass, on the crime and shame of our country, which permitted, sanctioned, and defended, with all its machinery of government and religion, the horrible merchandise in men, women and children—himself but lately redeemed from the clutches of the foul demon of slavery by the philanthropy of English friends, who admiringly placed his bust in white marble on its grand Merchant's Exchange in London. Where could Campbell's stinging satire sound so impressively as from those lips in Corinthian Hall in 1850?

> " ' United States, your banner wears
> Two emblems—one of fame;
> Alas! the other that it bears
> Reminds us of your shame.

> " ' The white man's liberty in types
> Is blazoned by your stars;
> But what's the meaning of your stripes?
> They mean your negro's scars.'

" One incident of that Rochester life is indelibly engraved on my mind. My dear friend, Maria Porter, took me with her to ever holy Mount Hope. Her valued sister Jane's was the new grave we were visiting. As we stood there by it, I saw a small, newly-made mound, and knowing of no child's death in their circle, I asked in surprise whose grave is that? ' Why that is little Anna Douglass's. Mr. Douglass had selected no lot— and poor, dear, little Anna grieved herself to death with fright and terror over her father's flight to England, to escape the fate of old John Brown.

CHAPTER IX.

" BEWARE OF A YANKEE WHEN HE IS FEEDING."

FORTUNATE is the biographer whose hero supplies such headings for chapters. No words could better indicate the quarter from which suddenly came rein-forcements that completely changed the position of the Abolitionists. Previous to 1854 they were like the rebel Jews who resisted Titus, shut up in their holy city, surrounded by an overwhelming army of the heathen, fighting fiercely against the besiegers and even more fiercely among themselves. The parallel would be a closer one, if Jerusalem had held out long enough to find a friendly emperor mount the throne. Hitherto we have looked only at the little anti-slavery bands and the great pro-slavery host. We have not yet had much occasion to notice the existence of the neutral North. The number of Northerners who were in favor of slavery was small compared to that of the men who regretted its existence, but saw no way of getting rid of it; who found little fault with the Garrisonian principle, but much with the method; who kept aloof from the Free Soil party, because they were afraid of throwing away their votes; and who tried to elect one pro-slavery candidate after another, partly because he seemed less pro-slavery than his opponent, and partly

because they liked subordinate features of the platform. This neutral position was the most advanced
one which had yet been taken, except by isolated individuals, in the Northwest ; and this was the attitude
of the vast majority of the clergy, even in New
England where most of the ministers really sympathized with the slave, but not so warmly as to overcome the combined influence of dislike at those innovations which were allied with Garrisonianism, of
indignation at the censures which the Church
received from Abolitionists, and of deference to the
conservatism, not only of wealthy laymen, but of
leading divines. It was not because the Southerners
had so much cordial support, but because they had
so little active opposition at the North, that they were
able to pass the Fugitive Slave Bill, to recover hundreds of bondmen under it, and to elect a President
who wished to have it " respected cheerfully," with a
vote so large as seemed to have swept not only the
hostile Free Soilers out of existence as a party, but
also the lukewarm Whigs.

This victory of 1852 emboldened the South to
insist that slavery should be carried beyond the
boundary to which it had been restricted by the
Missouri Compromise of 1820, and should take
possession of a new region ten times as large as
Massachusetts, with a much less severe climate, and
with a soil fertile beyond comparison. Before the
close of 1853 it was proposed in Congress that the
compromise should be set aside, that settlers should
be allowed to bring their slaves into the Territories,
about to be organized under the names of Kansas
and Nebraska, and that the final decision, whether

these should form free or slave States, should be left
to be settled by the inhabitants.   This last principle,
known as that of " Squatter Sovereignty," had Senator
Douglas for a prominent advocate.   Opposition was
promptly made, not only by Sumner, Gerrit Smith,
and other anti-slavery Congressmen, but also by
Edward Everett, who had hitherto been on the other
side.   He now gave a strong indication of what a
change was going on in New England, by presenting
a remonstrance signed by more than three thousand
of her clergymen.   How large a part of these
petitioners were now opposing the slave power for
the first time may be imagined from the fact that the
indignation meeting, which was held in Faneuil
Hall, on the afternoon of February 23, 1854, had a
member of Congress, who had voted for the Fugitive
Slave Bill, in the chair, and all the speakers, as well
as some of the vice-presidents, had earned a place on
the " Liberator's " blackest list.   Similar meetings
were held so freely all over the North, that Senator
Douglas declared, some years later, that he could have
traveled from Boston to Chicago by the light of his
own burning effigies.   One half of the Northern Democrats voted with all the Northern Whigs and the
Free Soilers against the Kansas and Nebraska Bill in
the House of Representatives ; but it became a law,
at the same time that Anthony Burns was sent back
to slavery from Boston, and carried through the
streets by soldiers and armed policemen in open day.
   All the appeals of Garrison, Phillips, Douglass,
Beecher, and Mrs. Stowe, in behalf of the negro, had
awakened but little interest compared with that
called out by the attempts of the South to prevent

Northern white men from settling Kansas, and to drive them out by inroads of border-ruffians from Missouri, backed by federal troops. Public sentiment sanctioned not only the supply of rifles to emigrants, who flocked in from Massachusetts, Ohio, and other Northern States, but the formation of guerrilla bands under John Brown and other captains. The Fugitive Slave Bill was decided to be unconstitutional in Wisconsin; and laws to hinder its execution were passed by Michigan, as well as by the New England States. The Whigs united with the Free Soilers, and the new party took the name Republican in July, 1854. The outrages upon Free State settlers in that year and the next caused the anti-slavery vote of New England to rise from 57,143, in 1852, to 184,850 in 1855, and 307,417 in 1856. The figures for New York are 25,359, 136,698, and 276,004. The change throughout the Union was from 156,149 votes in 1852 to 1,341,264 in 1856. Eleven States were then carried for Fremont, whereas not a single electoral vote had ever been cast for any of the Free Soil or Liberty party candidates. The neutral North became anti-slavery, because it was not allowed to feed peaceably in Kansas.

How earnestly, and at the same time how sensibly, Douglass took part in this great struggle, may be judged from the speech which he delivered before a great audience in Chicago, early in September, 1854. I have taken care to copy all the boldest portions ; and there is also a cordial eulogium on Senator Douglas, closing with the remark that no one would think any the less of that name if it should be placed by the nation upon the scroll of Presidents. He begins by claiming to be an American citizen, and declaring that :

" The Constitution knows no man by the color of his skin. The men who made it were too noble for any such limitation of humanity and human rights. The word 'white' is a modern term in the legislation of this country. It was never used in the better days of our Republic, but has sprung up within the period of our national degeneracy." . . . " I am here simply as an American citizen, having a stake in the weal or woe of the nation in common with other citizens. I am not even here as the agent of any sect or party. Parties are too politic and sects are too sectarian, to select one of my odious class, and of my radical opinions, at this important time and place to represent them. Nevertheless, I do not stand alone here. There are noble-minded men in Illinois who are neither ashamed of their cause nor their company. Some of them are here to-night, and I expect to meet with them in every part of the State where I may travel. But, I pray, hold no man or party responsible for my words, for I am no man's agent, and I am no party's agent." . . . " It is alleged that I am come to this State to insult Senator Douglas. Among gentlemen that is only an insult which is intended to be such, and I disavow all such intention. I am not even here with the desire to meet in public debate that gentleman. I am here precisely as I was in this State one year ago—with no other change in my relations to you, or to the great question of human freedom, than time and circumstances have brought about. I shall deal with the subject with the same spirit now as then, approving such men and such measures as look to the security of liberty in the land, and with my whole heart condemning all such men and measures, as serve to subvert or endanger it. If Hon. S. A. Douglas, your beloved and highly gifted Senator, has designedly, or through mistaken notions of public policy, ranged himself on the side of oppressors and the deadliest enemies of liberty, I know of no reason, either in this world or in any other world, which should prevent me, or prevent any one else, from thinking so, or from saying so.

"The people in whose cause I come here to-night are not among those whose right to regulate their own domestic concerns is so feelingly, and earnestly, and eloquently contended for in certain quarters. They have no Stephen Arnold Douglas—no General Cass, to contend at North Market Hall for their popular sovereignty. They have no national purse, no offices, no reputation, with which to corrupt Congress, or to tempt men, mighty in eloquence and influence, into their service. Oh, no! They have nothing to commend them but their unadorned humanity. They are human—that's all—only human. Nature owns them as human—God owns them as human; but men own them as property, and only as property. Every right of human nature, as such, is denied them; they are dumb in their chains. To utter one groan or scream for freedom in the presence of the Southern advocate of popular sovereignty, is to bring down the frightful lash upon their quivering flesh. I know this suffering people; I am acquainted with their sorrows; I am one with them in experience; I have felt the lash of the slave-driver, and stand up here with all the bitter recollection of its horrors vividly upon me.

"There are special reasons why I should speak, and speak freely. The right of speech is a very precious one. I understand that Mr. Douglas regards himself as the most abused man in the United States; and that the greatest outrage ever committed upon him was in the case in which your indignation raised your voices so high that his could not be heard. No personal violence, as I understand, was offered him. It seems to have been a trial of vocal powers between the individual and the multitude; and, as might have been expected, the voice of one man was not equal in volume to the voices of five thousand. I do not mention this circumstance to approve it; I do not approve it. I am for free speech, as well as for free men and free soil; but how ineffably insignificant is this wrong done in a single instance, compared to the stupendous iniquity perpetuated against more than three millions of the American people, who are struck dumb by the very men in whose cause Mr. Senator Douglas was here to plead! While I would not approve the silencing of Mr. Douglas, may we not hope that this slight abridgment of his rights may lead him to respect in some degree the rights of other men, as good in the eye of Heaven as himself?

"Let us now consider the great question of the age, the only great national question which seriously agitates the public mind at this hour. It is called the vexed question, and excites alarm in every quarter of the country. . . .

"The proposition to repeal the Missouri Compromise, was a stunning one. It fell upon the nation like a bolt from a cloudless sky. The thing was too startling for belief. You believed in the South; and you believed in the North; and you knew that the repeal of the Missouri Compromise was a breach of honor; and, therefore, you said that the thing could not be done. Besides, both parties had pledged themselves directly, positively, and solemnly against re-opening in Congress the agitation on the subject of slavery; and the President himself had declared his intention to maintain the national quiet. Upon these assurances you rested, and rested fatally. But you should have learned long ago that men do not 'gather grapes of thorns, or figs of thistles.' It is folly to put faith in men who have broken faith with God. When a man has brought himself to enslave a child of God, to put fetters on his brother, he has qualified himself to disregard the most sacred of compacts: beneath the sky there is nothing more sacred than man, and nothing can be properly respected when manhood is despised and trampled upon. . . .

"It is said that slavery is the creature of positive law, and that it can only exist where it is sustained by positive law—that neither in Kansas nor Nebraska is there any law establishing slavery and that, therefore, the moment a slave-holder carries his slave into those territories, he is free and restored to the rights of human nature. This is the ground taken by General Cass. He contended for it in the North Market Hall, with much eloquence and skill. I thought, while I was hearing him on this point, that slave-holders would not be likely to thank him for the argument. Theoretically the argument is good; practically the argument is bad. It is not true that slavery cannot exist without being established by positive law. The instance cannot be shown where a law was ever made establishing slavery, where the relation of master and slave did not previously exist. The law is always an after-coming consideration. Wicked men first overpower, and subdue their fellow-men to slavery, and then call in the law to sanction the deed. Even in the slave States of America, slavery has never been established by positive law. It was not established under the colonial charters of the original States, nor the constitutions of the States. It is now, and has always been, a system of lawless violence. On this proposition I hold myself ready and willing to meet any defender of the Nebraska Bill. I would not even hesitate to meet the author of that bill himself. . . .

"He says he wants no broad, black line across this Continent. Such a line is odious, and begets unkind feelings between the citizens of a common country. Now, fellow-citizens, why is the line of thirty-six degrees, thirty minutes, a broad black line? What is it that entitles it to be called a black line? It is the fashion to call whatever is odious in this country, black. You call the devil black, and he may be; but what is there in the line of thirty-six degrees, thirty minutes, which makes it blacker than the line which separates Illinois from Missouri, or Michigan from Indiana? I can see nothing in the line itself which should make it black or odious. It is a line, that's all. If it is black, black and odious, it must be so, not because it is a line, but because of the things it separates. If it keeps asunder what God has joined together—or separates what God intended should be fused, then it may be called an odious line, a black line; but if, on the other hand, it marks only a distinction natural and eternal, a distinction fixed in the nature of things by the eternal God, then I say, withered be the arm and blasted be the hand that would blot it out. . . .

"Nothing could be further from the truth, than to say that popular sovereignty is accorded to the people who may settle the territories of Kansas and Nebraska. The three great cardinal powers of government are the executive, legislative, and judicial. Are these powers secured to the people of Kansas and Nebraska? You know they are not. That bill places the people of that territory as completely under the powers of the federal government as Canada is under the British crown. By this Kansas-Nebraska Bill the federal government has the substance of all governing power, while the people have the shadow. The judicial power of the territories is not from the people of the territories, who are so bathed in the sunlight of popular sovereignty by stump eloquence, but from the federal government. The executive power of the territories derives its existence not from the overflowing fountain of popular sovereignty, but from the federal government. The secretaries of the territories are not appointed by the sovereign people of the territories, but are appointed independently of popular sovereignty.

" But is there nothing in this bill which justifies the supposition that it contains the principle of popular sovereignty? No, not one word. Even the territorial counsels, elected, not by the people who may settle in the territories, but by only certain descriptions of people, are subject to a double veto power, vested first in a governor, whom they did not elect, and second in the President of the United States. The only shadow of popular sovereignty is the power given to the people of the territories by this bill to have, hold, buy, and sell human beings. The sovereign right to make slaves of his fellow-men if they choose, is the only sovereignty that the bill secures. In all else, popular sovereignty means only what the boy meant, when he said he was going to live with his uncle Robert. He said he was going there, and that he meant while there to do just what he pleased, if his uncle Robert would let him. . . .

" But it may be said that Congress has the right to allow the people of the territories to hold slaves. The answer is, that Congress is made up of men, and possesses only the right of men; and unless it can be shown that some men have a right to hold their fellow-men as property, Congress has no such right. There is not a man within the sound of my voice, who has not as good a right to enslave a brother man, as Congress has. This will not be denied even by slave-holders. Then I put the question to you, each of you, all of you, have you any such right ? To admit such a right is to charge God with folly, to substitute anarchy for order, and to turn earth into a hell. And you know better. Now, friends and fellow-citizens, I am uttering no new sentiments at this point, and am making no new argument. In this respect there is nothing new under the sun.

"Error may be new, or it may be old, since it is founded in a misapprehension of what truth is. It has its beginnings ; and it has its endings. But not so with truth. Truth is eternal. Like the great God, from whose throne it emanates, it is from everlasting unto everlasting, and can never pass away. Such a truth is a man's right to freedom. He was born with it. It was his before he comprehended it. The title-deed to it is written by the Almighty on his heart ; and the record of it is in the bosom of the Eternal ; and never can Stephen A. Douglas efface it, unless he can tear from the great heart of God this truth ; and this mighty government of ours will never be at peace with God, unless it shall, practically and universally, embrace this great truth as the foundation of all its institutions, and the rule of its entire administration. Now, gentlemen—I have done. I have no fear for the ultimate triumph of free principles in this country. The signs of the times are propitious. Victories have been won by slavery ; but they have never been won against the onward march of anti-slavery principles. The progress of these principles has been constant, steady, strong, and certain. Every victory won by slavery has had the effect to fling our principles more widely and favorably among the people. The annexation of Texas—the Florida war—the war with Mexico—the compromise measures, and the repeal of the Missouri Compromise have all signally vindicated the wisdom of the great God, who has promised to over-rule the wickedness of men for his own glory—to confound the wisdom of the crafty, and bring to naught the counsels of the ungodly."

Mr. Douglass tells me that during the tour through

Illinois which began thus, his namesake, whom he calls " an undersized Daniel Webster," refused to speak at Rockford, because he did not wish to encounter that " negro impostor who had been called in to hunt him down." They did finally meet at Freeport, where the Senator was " very courteous both in public and in private."

Our orator had hitherto trusted entirely to his gift for extempore speech, and had become so famous for his power of thinking on his legs, that Wendell Phillips spoke of him to a friend of mine, as " possessed of more genius than any other man in the anti-slavery ranks." When he assumed the responsibilities of editing the " North Star," he gave up parodies, used mimicry more sparingly, and began to write out portions of his addresses. After one of these experiments, in Western New York, he went home to spend the night with a Quaker, named Pliny Sexton. Anxiety to find out how well he had succeeded made him keep silent, and wait for his host to say something. There was nothing more than a Quaker meeting, however, until they were about to bid each other " Good-night." Then Pliny, who, by the way, was a Garrisonian, said, " Frederick, the poorest part of thy lecture was the written part."

On July 12, 1854, he took part, for the first time in his life, in the exercises of a college commencement. An invitation to deliver an address had come from a literary society in the Western Reserve College, then at Hudson, Ohio, but now at Cleveland. The President and the rest of the Faculty were much distressed at the invitation, as he found out afterwards ; and he did right in taking for his subject, the Claims of the

Negro. Unfortunately, however, he treated of the question ethnologically, and tried to prove, not only that the negro sprang from the same original ancestry as other men, but that he had a peculiarly close relationship with the ancient Egyptians. Neither of these opinions is now held by Douglass; but he did not change his mind about the builders of the pyramids, until he had made a journey to Egypt in order to satisfy himself on this point. He also made the mistake of merely reading his address; and it had much less effect than his extempore remarks at the collation afterwards. There is at least one fine passage, which ought still to be kept fresh in our remembrance, where he says, in regard to the supposition that the colored people may ultimately die out from among us:

" The statistics of the country afford no encouragement for such a conjecture. The history of the negro race proves them to be wonderfully adapted to all countries, all climates, all conditions." . . . " The poor bondman lifts a smiling face above the surface of a sea of agonies, hoping on, hoping ever. His tawny brother, the Indian, dies under the flashing glance of the Anglo-Saxon. Not so the negro; civilization cannot kill him. He accepts it, becomes a part of it." . . . " All the facts in his history mark out for him a destiny united to America and Americans. Now, whether this population shall, by freedom, industry, virtue, and intelligence be made a blessing to the country and the world, or whether their multiplied wrongs shall kindle the vengeance of an offended God, will depend upon the conduct of no class of men so much as upon the scholars of the country."

His most important publication previous to 1882 was the enlarged edition of the "Narrative," which appeared in 1855, under the title " My Bondage and

My Freedom," with an Introduction by Dr. James M'Cune Smith. There is a portrait, taken from a daguerreotype, and showing much sterner features than those which usher in the volumes of 1845 and 1882. The signature below indicates that his hand-writing had become less delicate and feminine than it was ten years before, and had acquired its present manly vigor. The dedication is to Gerrit Smith. The preface by Garrison, which had appeared in 1845, is omitted, with the letter from Phillips and the appendix about religion. The publishers were Miller, Orton, and Mulligan, in New York and Auburn; the volume contains nearly five hundred pages, including the Introduction and appendix; and the latter gives extracts from seven speeches, and also a letter to Thomas Auld. The account in the "Narrative," of the author's life up to 1841, was re-written, with frequent additions of graphic details, so as to be enlarged to a size almost three times as great as before, and to occupy about fifty per cent. more space in this version of 1855 than in that of 1882, which did not, I think, gain by abridgment. The period from 1841 to 1855 is given at much greater length in the version of 1882, however, than any part of it had ever been before; and described on the whole with greater vigor, although many character-istic passages have been omitted. This much has been said about "My Bondage and My Freedom," because it seems to have become rather a rare book, and its disappearance would be a great loss.

The most curious thing about this book is an opinion which was passed upon it by Garrison, and which is here quoted as an act of justice to those

philanthropic people who differed from him. George
Thompson gave " My Bondage and My Freedom " a
friendly notice in his own organ, but this led Garrison to write him a letter, part of which soon found
its way into the " Liberator," for January 18, 1856.
It is a protest against this " panegyric upon Frederick
Douglass's new volume, ' My Bondage and My Freedom,' a volume remarkable, it is true, for its thrilling
sketches of a slave's life and experience, and for the
ability displayed in its pages, but which, in its second
portion, is reeking with the virus of personal malignity towards Wendell Phillips, myself, and the old
organizationists generally, and full of ingratitude and
baseness towards as true and disinterested friends as
any man ever yet had upon earth." The only pages
which could possibly be referred to, acknowledge
that he went to Rochester " from motives of peace,"
say nothing about Phillips, speak of Garrison as " the
known and distinguished advocate " of the non-voting
principle, mention that " To abstain from voting was
to refuse to exercise a legitimate and powerful means
for abolishing slavery," and say, finally, " To those
with whom I had been in agreement and sympathy,
I was now in opposition. What they held to be a
great and important truth, I now looked upon as a
dangerous error. A very painful, and yet a very
natural thing now happened. Those who could not
see any honest reasons for changing their views, as I
had done, could not easily see any such reasons for my
change ; and the common punishment of apostates
was mine. The opinions first entertained were
naturally derived, and honestly entertained ; and I
trust that my present opinions have the same title to

respect." If there is any "virus" in these words it is only such as has always been greatly needed for the inoculation of reformers.

I am not aware that Douglass ever spoke more severely of Garrison than in 1879, when he said this :

" Massachusetts is a great State ; she has done many great things ; she has given to our country many scholars and states-men, many poets and philosophers, many discoverers and inventors ; but no son of hers has won for her a more enduring honor, or for himself a more enduring fame, than William Lloyd Garrison. No one of her sons has stamped his convictions in lines so clear, deep, and ineffaceable into the very life and future of the Republic. Of no man is it more true than of him—that being dead he yet speaketh. The lessons he taught fifty years ago from his garret in Boston are only yet half learned by the nation. His work will not stop at his grave. Our general has fallen ; but his army will march on. His words of wisdom, justice, and truth will be echoed by the voices of the millions, till every jot and tittle of all his prophecies shall be fulfilled. Mr. President, this is not the time and place for a critical and accurate measurement of William Lloyd Garrison ; but when it comes, no friend of his has need to fear the application to him of the severest test of honest and truthful criticism. He never refused to see, nor allow his readers to see, in the ' Liberator,' the worst that was thought, felt, and said of him. A candid examination of his character and his work in the world may disclose some things we would have had otherwise. Speaking for myself, I must frankly say I have sometimes thought him uncharitable to those who differed from him. Honest himself, he could not always see how men could differ from him and still be honest. To say this of him is simply to say that he was human ; and it may be added that when he erred here, he erred in the interest of truth. He revolted at halfness, abhorred com-promise, and demanded that men should be either hot or cold. This great quality of the man, though sometimes in excess, is one explanation of his wonderful and successful leadership. What it cost him in breadth and numbers, it gained him in condensation and intensity. He held his little band well in hand all the time, and close to his person; no leader was ever more loved by the circle about him. Absolute in his faith, no sect could proselyte him; inflexible in his principles, no party could use him; content with the little circle about him, he did not mingle directly and largely with the great masses of men. By one simple principle he tried all men, all parties, and all sects. They that were not for him, were against him. What his name stood for in the beginning, it stands for now, and will so stand forever. It is said that the wicked shall not live out half their days. This is true in more senses than one; for 'The coward and the small in soul scarce do live.' Mr. Garrison lived out his whole existence. For to live is to battle; and he battled from first to last. Although he had reached a good old age, time had not dimmed his intellect, nor darkened his moral vision, nor quenched the ardor of his genius. His letter, published three weeks before his death, on the exodus from Mississippi and Louisiana, had in it all the energy and fire of his youth. Men of three score and ten are apt to live in the past. It was not so with Mr. Garrison. He was during his latest years fully abreast with his times. No event or circumstance bearing upon the cause of justice and humanity escaped his intelligent observation. His letter written a few months ago upon the Chinese question was a crowning utterance. It was in harmony with the guiding sentiment of his life, 'My country is the world; and all mankind are my countrymen.' With him it was not race or color, but humanity."

One result of the publication of "My Bondage and My Freedom," was that a bookseller in Mobile, who had been a slave-holder, bought not only a copy which had been ordered but two others to supply possible customers. A clergyman in the city heard of this, sent his son to buy the books, and stirred up such an excitement against the bookseller that he was glad to steal away in a little sail-boat.

While still busy with the composition of this work, its author was invited by the members of the Legislature to address them, in March, 1855, in the Assembly Chamber at Albany. There he denounced not only the Nebraska and Fugitive Slave Bills, but also the indifference of the North to his people's wrongs. An eye-witness describes the rapt attention of the crowded audience for two hours and a half as the grandest scene he ever saw in the capital; and the Lieutenant-Governor said he would give twenty thousand dollars to be able to speak as powerfully. The May meeting of the A. A. S. S. in New York gave the orator an opportunity to defend a proposition which he had already submitted to them in writing, namely that, "The Garrisonian views of disunion, if carried to a successful issue, would only place the people of the North in the same relation to American slavery which they now bear to the slavery of Cuba or Brazil." He defended this proposition on May 10, in reply to the assertion of another fugitive from slavery, that the Union was of no value to colored people. Then, according to the "New York Daily News," "A grand and terrific set-to came off between Abby Kelley Foster, Garrison, and Frederick Douglass, who defended the Union while claiming rights for his people. He was insulted, interrupted, and denounced by the Garrison Cabinet, but stood amid them and overtopped them like a giant among pigmies." One thing said against him was, that he had no more right to call himself anti-slavery, than a

moderate drinker has to try to pass himself off for a
friend of temperance.

Soon after this debate, he told the colored men,
with whom he was holding a council to prepare for a
national convention in October, that he knew that his
plan of an industrial college was opposed by some of
the Abolitionist organs :

" But if the colored people would ever arrive at a respectable
place in society, they must do their own thinking. The colored
people are now the ' sick man ' of America; those who pretend
to be their friends measure their places and pat them on the
back; but when they step beyond that narrow place, their
friends become villifiers and enemies."

On June 26, 27, 28, there was a convention in Syracuse of men who had agreed, a year or two before, to
call themselves Radical Political Abolitionists. The
editor of " My Bondage and My Freedom," Dr. Smith,
presided ; and among other speakers were Douglass,
Gerrit Smith, Lewis Tappan, and Rev. S. J. May. Ten
States were represented, besides New York and
Canada. It was unanimously resolved that the members should do what they could to prevent the return
of fugitives ; but there was some difference of
opinion in consequence of a proposal to raise money
to enable John Brown, who was going out that fall to
join his sons in Kansas, to take out a good supply of
weapons. Douglass, who had known him well for
eight years, spoke earnestly in his behalf ; Tappan
and others were unwilling to encourage violence ; but
as a letter recently received from Hayti says : " The
collection was taken up with much spirit, nevertheless ; for Captain Brown was present and spoke for

himself; and when he spoke, men believed in the man."

The national colored convention came off, as proposed, in Philadelphia, and on the first day, October 16, there was an evident repugnance to the admission of the only delegate from Canada, Miss Shadd. Her sex was so much against her that Remond thought it best to make a compromise, which would give her a seat as a corresponding member. Douglass insisted on having this vote reconsidered; and his speech caused her to be recognized, by a majority vote, as a member in full standing. The "New York Tribune" had endorsed his plan for an industrial college as "the greatest and most comprehensive for elevating the colored race in this country yet proposed." Some members of the convention saw little need of such an institution, at a time when more than thirty per cent. of those of their brethren in the North who were trained in trades and professions were prevented, as Douglass himself had been, by the color prejudice from carrying them on. It was also urged that a college in one place would do little good at a distance; and much was said in favor of a mechanical bureau, which should employ teachers of special trades wherever such instruction might be demanded. There was also quite a controversy as to whether slavery could be abolished constitutionally; but here Douglass triumphed, with the aid of his friend, Dr. Smith, and his paper was formally acknowledged to be "our organ."

A long quotation has already been made from his pamphlet on "the Anti-Slavery Movement;" it also contains an expression of dissatisfaction with the

newly organized Republican party, of which he
says :

"It aims to limit and denationalize slavery, and to relieve the
Federal Government from all responsibility for slavery. Its
motto is, 'Slavery, Local; Liberty, National.' The objection
to this movement is the same as that against the American
Anti-Slavery Society. It leaves the slave in his fetters, in the
undisturbed possession of his master, and does not grapple with
the question of emancipation in the States."

His own preference, in 1855, was for the Liberty
party, which was " pledged to continue the struggle
while a bondman in his chains remains to weep.
Upon its platform must the great battle of freedom
be fought out, if upon any short of the bloody field.
It must be under no partial cry of ' No union with
slave-holders,' nor selfish cry of 'No more slavery
extension,' but it must be, ' No slavery for man under
the whole heavens.' "

His opinion of the Republican party was fully
justified in 1856, when its convention, at Philadelphia,
adopted a platform which had nothing to say against
the Fugitive Slave Bill, or in favor of emancipation
in the States ; while its candidate, Fremont, was
selected with no more reference to his record as an
Abolitionist than to his experience as a statesman.
So far at least as the conventions of 1852 and 1856
could be compared, there was perfect truth in the
statement of our editor in 1860: " The national
conventions, held successively in Pittsburgh, Philadelphia, and Chicago, have formed a regular descent
from the better utterances of 1848 at Buffalo." No
colored man spoke at Philadelphia, and but little
was said by Abolitionists. The candidates of the

other parties, however, for President were Fillmore,
who had signed the Fugitive Slave Bill, and Buchanan,
who was pledged to sustain it as well as to hinder
Kansas from entering the Union as a Free State.
Garrison acknowledged that if he could vote for any
one, it would be for Fremont ; and Douglass did all
he could to elect him.

Among the pilgrims to Rochester, in 1856, was Miss
Ottilia Assing, who afterwards published a German
translation of " My Bondage and My Freedom."
She says in her preface, dated 1858, that twenty
thousand copies of the original had already been
sold ; and she also praises the author for " his brilliancy, cheerfulness, and refinement in conversation,"
as well as for " his success in calling out others and
elevating them to his own height." His oratory was
" remarkable for complete mastery of his subject,
keenness in argument, and perfect moderation amid
all his passion. Often he will rise to a tragic grandeur, and then he will illuminate his position, as with
soldiers' torches, by brilliant flashes of wit. He will
speak to the heart of his hearer, and then divert him
with gay humor. All is fresh, original, and attractive. All these advantages are increased by a perfect
command of English, and a voice as tender, pleasing,
and flexible as any I ever heard."

The poor success of his lecture on Ethnology had
stimulated him to make another trial of his strength,
and his second attempt was a complete success. The
lecture on " Self-Made Men," which he wrote in 1855,
was in great demand at Lyceums, especially in the
West ; and he thus found himself eminent in a lucrative and honorable profession. It has not yet been

published, and the manuscript has undergone various changes in successive years of use. Among the most interesting passages are these :

" On the first point, I may say, that by self-made men, I mean precisely what the phrase itself imparts to the popular mind. They are the men who, without the ordinary helps of favoring circumstances, have attained knowledge, usefulness, power, position, and fame in the world. They are the men who owe nothing to birth, relationship, friendly surroundings, wealth inherited, or to early and approved means of education ; who are what they are, without any of the conditions by which other men usually achieve the same results. In fact, they are the men who come up, not only without the voluntary assistance or friendly co-operation of society, but often in open and derisive defiance of all the efforts of society to repress, retard, and keep them down. In a world of schools, academies, and other institutions of learning, they manage in some way to get an education elsewhere, and in other conditions hew out a way for themselves and become the architects of their own fortunes. In a peculiar sense they are indebted to themselves for themselves. If they have traveled far, they have made the road on which they traveled. If they have ascended high, they have built their own ladder. It is hard to fathom the depths from which some of these men have come. From the heartless pavements of the large and crowded cities—barefooted, homeless, and friendless—they have come. From hunger, rags, and destitution—motherless and fatherless—they come. From prisons, slavery, and the depths of infamy—they come. Flung overboard in the midnight storm, on the broad and tempest-tossed ocean of life, without oars, ropes, or life-preservers, they are the men who have bravely buffeted the frowning billows with their own sinewy arms, and have risen in safety, where other men, well supplied with the best appliances of safety and success have fainted, despaired, and gone down. Such men as these, whether we find them in one position or another, whether in the college or the factory, whether professors or plowmen, whether of Anglo-Saxon or Anglo-African origin, are self-made men, and are entitled to a certain measure of respect for their success. Though a man of this class may not claim to be a hero, and to be worshiped as such, there is genuine heroism in his struggle, and something of sublimity and glory in his triumph. Every instance of this kind is an example and a help to the race. It assures us of the latent powers and resources of simple and unaided manhood. It robs labor of pain and depression, dispels gloom from the brow of destitution, and enables men to take hold of the roughest and flintiest hardships incident to the battle of life, with lighter hearts, higher hopes, and with larger courage. . . .

" When we find a man who has ascended high beyond ourselves, who has a broader range of vision than we, and a horizon with more stars in it than we have, we may know that he has worked harder, better, and more wisely than we have. He was awake while we slept, was busy while we were idle, and wisely improved his time while we wasted ours. There is nothing good, great, or desirable in this world which man can possess, that does not come by labor, either physical, or mental. A man may, at times, get something for nothing, but in his hands it will amount to nothing. What is true in the world of matter is equally true in the world of mind. There is no growth without exertion, no polish without friction, no knowledge without labor, no progress without motion, no victory without conflict. The man who lies down a fool at night, hoping that he will awake wise in the morning, will rise up in the morning as he laid down in the evening. Faith itself does not seem worth much, if anything, in the absence of work. The preacher who finds it easier to pray for knowledge than to tax his brain with study, will find his congregation growing beautifully less, and his flock looking elsewhere for the mental food. Our colored ministers are somewhat remarkable for the fervor with which they pray for knowledge; but, thus far, they are not remarkable for any wonderful success; in fact, they who pray loudest seem to get least. They are able to give us abundance of sound for destitution of sense.

In every view we catch of the perfection of the universe, whether we look to the stars in the peaceful blue dome above us, or to the long line where land and water maintain eternal conflict—the lesson is the same. It is labor, movement, earnest work. These beautifully rounded pebbles which you hold in your hand, and marvel at their exceeding smoothness, were chiselled into their varied and graceful forms by the ceaseless action of countless waves. Nature is herself a great worker, and tolerates no contradictions to her wise example without certain rebuke. She follows inaction by stagnation, stagnation is followed by pestilence, and pestilence by death. General Butler, busy with his broom, could sweep yellow-fever out of New Orleans; but this dread destroyer returned when Butler and his broom were withdrawn, and the people piously ascribed to Divinity, what was simply due to dirt. From these remarks it will be seen that, allowing only ordinary natural ability and opportunity, we explain success by one word, and that is 'Work.' . . . .

" America, not without reason, is said to be pre-eminently the home and patron of self-made men. All doors fly open to them. They may aspire to any position. Courts, Senates, Cabinets, spread their rich carpets for their feet, and they stand among our foremost men in every honorable service. Many causes have made it possible and easy for this class to rise and flourish here, and first among these is the general respectability of labor. Search where you will, there is no country on the globe where labor is more respected, and the laborer more honored, than in this country. The conditions in which American society originated, the free spirit that framed its independence and created its government, based upon the will of the people, exalted both labor and the laborer." . . . " The principle of measuring and valuing men, according to their respective merits, is better established and more generally enforced and observed here than in any other country. In Europe, a king can make a belted knight, a marquis, duke, and a' that; but here, wealth and greatness are forced by no such capricious and arbitrary power. Equality of rights brings equality of dignity. . . .

" By these remarks, however, no disparagement of institutions of learning is intended. With all my admiration for self-made men, I am far from considering them the best made men. Their symmetry is often marred by the effects of their extra exertion. The hot rays of the sun and the long and rugged road in which they were compelled to travel have left their marks sometimes quite visibly and unpleasantly upon them. While the world values skill and power, it values beauty and polish as well. It was not alone the hard good-sense and honest heart of Horace Greeley, the self-made man, that made the ' New York Tribune,' but likewise the brilliant and thoroughly educated men silently associated with him. There was never a self-educated man, however well educated, who, with the same exertion, would not have been better educated by the aid of schools. It must be admitted that self-made men are not generally over-modest or self-forgetful men. Perhaps the peculiar resistance they meet in asserting their pretentions, may account for the loudness of their self-assertion. The country knows the story of Andrew Johnson by heart, and from his own lips. The very energies employed, the obstacles overcome, the heights to which some men rise, and the broad contrasts which life forces upon them at every step tend to make them egotistical. A man indebted to himself for himself, may naturally think well of himself. But this thing may be far overdone. That a man has been able to make his own way in the world, is an humble fact as well as an honorable one. It is, however, possible to state a very humble fact in a very haughty manner, and self-made men are, as a class, much addicted to this vice. In this respect they make themselves much less agreeable to society than they might otherwise be. One other criticism is often very properly made upon these men. Never having enjoyed the benefits of schools, colleges, and other institutions of learning, they display a contempt for them which is quite ridiculous. A man may know much about educating himself, and little about the proper means of educating others. He may be remarkably large but somewhat awkward ; swift but ungraceful; a man of power but deficient in the polish and amiable proportions of the affluent and regularly educated man. Generally, I think, self-made men answer this description."

CHAPTER X.

MR. DOUGLASS, himself, suggested this title for the chapter about a time when such a question might have been asked by many an Abolitionist besides Sojourner Truth. She interrupted him with it, as he was dwelling upon the darkness of the hour ; and he replied : "No, God is not dead ; and therefore it is that slavery must end in blood !" The warmth with which the South sanctioned the outrages in Kansas, applauded the striking down of Sumner in the Senate, threatened to secede in case Fremont was elected, and demanded the re-opening of the slave-trade, showed plainly that war might soon break out ; and the failure of the Republicans to carry Pennsylvania, New Jersey, Illinois, Indiana, and California, even on these plain and urgent issues, made it seem not un-likely that the contest would be between a united South and a divided North. War must come ; but would it abolish or perpetuate slavery ? This ques-tion could not always be answered confidently ; and Douglass was once hard at work in his sanctum in Rochester, mailing copies of his paper, and thinking gloomily of the future, when Beecher came in and asked him, what he thought of the prospects of the cause. "All is lost," was the reply. "No," said the preacher, "God reigns ! Sit down beside me, and let

me talk to you." Talk he did for twenty minutes,
about what might yet be hoped from the divine justice ; and when he went away, he left his friend so
much encouraged as to be almost a new creature.

There was not a bit of cowardice in the spirit in
which the champion of his race took the heavy blow
dealt at it in the Dred Scott decision. In the speech
which was prepared for the meeting at New York, in
May, 1857, of those Abolitionists who held slavery unconstitutional, and was published that year in a
pamphlet, he says :

" I own myself not insensible to the many difficulties and discouragements that beset us on every hand. They fling their
broad and gloomy shadows across the pathway of every thoughtful colored man in this country. For one, I see them clearly
and feel them sadly. Standing, as it were, barefoot, and
treading upon the sharp and flinty rocks of the present, and
looking out upon the boundless sea of the future, I have sought
in my humble way to penetrate the intervening mists and clouds,
and perchance to descry in the dim and shadowy distance the
white flag of freedom, the precise speck of time at which the
cruel bondage of my people should end, and the long entombed
millions rise from the foul grave of slavery and death. But
of that time I can know nothing, and you can know nothing.
All is uncertain at that point." . . . " We are told, in tones
of lofty exultation, that the day is lost, all lost ; and that we
might as well give up the struggle. The highest authority has
spoken. The voice of the Supreme Court has gone out over
the troubled waves of the national conscience, saying, ' Peace,
be still !' This infamous decision of the slave-holding wing of
the Supreme Court maintains " . . . " that slaves are property
in the same sense that horses, sheep, and cattle are property;"
. . . "that the right of the slave-holder to his slave does not
depend upon the local law, but is secured wherever the Constitution of the United States extends ; that Congress has no power to

prohibit slavery anywhere; that slavery may go in safety anywhere under the star-spangled banner ; that colored persons of African descent have no rights that white men are bound to respect."

He might be asked how he is affected by "this judicial incarnation of wolfishness ; " and he would answer :

" My hopes were never brighter than now. I have no fear that the national conscience will be put to sleep by such an open, glaring, and scandalous tissue of lies as that is, and has been, over and over again, shown to be. The Supreme Court of the United States is not the only power in this world. It is very great ; but the Supreme Court of the Almighty is greater. Judge Taney may do many things, but he cannot perform impossibilities. He cannot bail out the ocean, annihilate this firm, old earth, or pluck the silvery star of liberty from our Northern sky. He may decide, and decide again; but he cannot reverse the decision of the Most High." . . . " Man's right to liberty is self-evident." . . . " To decide against this right in the person of Dred Scott " . . . " is to decide against God." . . . " It is an attempt to undo what God has done, to blot out the broad distinction instituted by the Allwise, between men and things, and to change the image and superscription of the ever living God into a speechless piece of merchandise." . . . " In one point of view, we, the Abolitionists and colored people, should meet this decision, uncalled for and monstrous as it seems, in a cheerful spirit. This very attempt to blot out forever the hope of an enslaved people may be one necessary link in the chain of events preparatory to the downfall and complete overthrow of the whole slave system. The whole history of the anti-slavery movement is studded with proof, that all measures, devised and executed with a view to allay and diminish the anti-slavery agitation, have only served to increase, embolden, and intensify that agitation." . . . " It was so with the Fugitive Slave Bill ; it was so with the Kansas-Nebraska Bill ; and it will be so with this last and most shock-

ing of all pro-slavery devices, this Taney decision." . . .
" Come what will, I hold it to be morally certain that, sooner or
later, by fair means, or foul means, in peace or in blood, in judgment or in mercy, slavery is doomed to cease out of this otherwise goodly land, and liberty is destined to become the settled
law of this Republic."

As a justification for this view he appeals to the
tendencies of the age, and the character of the American people, and also to the fact that colored people
were citizens of several of the States which formed
the Constitution, and were therefore entitled to the
protection which it confers. He insists on the anti-
slavery character of the Constitution, when rightly
interpreted, and challenges any one who differs from
him to say in what particular that instrument sanc-
tions oppression :

" Where will he find a guarantee for slavery ? Will he find
it in the declaration that no person shall be deprived of life,
liberty, or property, without due process of law ? Will he find
it in the declaration that the Constitution was established to
secure the blessings of liberty ? Will he find it in the right of
the people to be secure in their persons, and papers, and houses,
and effects ? Will he find it in the clause, prohibiting the enactment by any State of a bill of attainder ? These all strike at
the root of slavery, and any one of them, but faithfully carried
out, would put an end to slavery in every State in the American Union."

This speech also contains the only verses of his
which I have read ; but they are not so good as his
prose. There is power, though, in this line :

" The pathway of tyrants lies over volcanoes."

On August 4, he spoke at Canandaigua, as he had

done there ten years and three days before, at the celebration of Emancipation in the West Indies. This speech was published in the same pamphlet with that on the Dred Scott decision. He complains justly that the white people in the United States had never shown any general appreciation of the grandeur of this act, and did not even then appear to care anything for the improvement of the morality, intelligence, and happiness of the freedman. The only question asked, even at the North, was still, "Did it pay?" He left the task of answering that question to Dr. Garnett, who was on the platform, and himself took the opportunity to give his hearers some timely advice, as follows :

" I know, my friends, that in some quarters the efforts of colored people meet with very little encouragement. We may fight; but we must fight like the Sepoys of India, under the white officers. This class of Abolitionists don't like colored anti-slavery fairs for the support of colored newspapers. They don't like any demonstrations whatever in which colored men take a leading part. They talk of the proud Anglo-Saxon blood as flippantly as those who profess to believe in the natural inferiority of races. Your humble speaker has been branded as an ingrate, because he has ventured to stand up on his own right and to plead our common cause as a colored man, rather than as a Garrisonian. I hold it to be no part of gratitude to allow our white friends to do all the work, while we merely hold their coats. Opposition of the sort now referred to, is partisan opposition ; and we need not mind it. The white people at large will not be largely influenced by it. They will see and appreciate all honest efforts on our part to improve our condition as a people. Let me give you a word of the philosophy of reform. The whole history of the progress of human liberty shows that all concessions, yet made to her august claims, have been born of earnest struggle. The conflict has been exciting, agitating, all-absorbing, and for the time being putting all other tumults to silence. It must do this, or it does nothing. If there is no struggle, there is no progress. Those who profess to favor freedom, and yet deprecate agitation, are men who want crops without plowing up the ground. They want rain without thunder and lightning. They want the ocean without the awful roar of its many waters. This struggle may be a moral one ; or it may be a physical one ; or it may be both moral and physical ; but it must be a struggle. Power concedes nothing without a demand. It never did, and it never will. Find out just what people will submit to, and you have found out the exact amount of injustice and wrong which will be imposed upon them ; and these will continue till they are resisted with either words or blows, or with both. The limits of tyrants are prescribed by the endurance of those whom they oppress. In the light of these ideas, negroes will be hunted at the North, and held and flogged at the South, so long as they submit to those devilish outrages, and make no resistance, either moral or physical. Men may not get all they pay for in this world ; but they must certainly pay for all they get. If we ever get free from all the oppressions and wrongs heaped upon us, we must pay for their removal. We must do this by labor, by suffering, by sacrifice, and, if needs be, by our lives and the lives of others."

I cannot say precisely what he did in 1858 to justify Miss Assing's statement that he " has spoken for seventeen years, but never repeated himself, nor lost his hold upon his audience. In all the North there is no city or village where the announcement of his name will not fill every place in the hall." Neither the woman's cause nor the slave's found in him a lukewarm advocate, however ; and it was in this year that a little magazine, called " Douglass's Monthly," and designed especially for circulation in England, made its first appearance. The first number was that for June ; the price was five shillings a year ; and Miss Griffiths, then in England, where she was married to Dr. Crofts, was a valuable contributor. The weekly paper, it may here be added, was merged in the " Monthly " in August, 1860.

The most important events in the life of Douglass in 1858 were not publicly known before October, 1859. During the latter part of 1847 he had spent a night in Springfield, Massachusetts, as the guest of John Brown, of whom there is a graphic account in the " Life and Times," (pp. 309-311). The conversation which then took place is related thus in an unpublished lecture by Douglass :

" He touched my vanity at the outset, in this wise : ' I have,' he said, ' been looking over your people during the last twenty years, watching and waiting for heads to rise above the surface, to whom I could safely impart my views and plans. At times I have been most discouraged, but lately I have seen a good many heads popping up, and whenever I see them, I try to put myself in communication with them.' John Brown's plan, as it was then formed in his mind, was very simple, and had much to commend it. It did not, as some suppose, directly contemplate a general uprising among the slaves, and a general slaughter of the slave-masters, but it did contemplate the creation of an armed force, which should constantly act against slavery in the heart of the South. He called my attention to a large map upon the wall, and pointed out to me the far-reaching Alleghanies, stretching away from New York into the Southern States. ' These mountains,' he said, ' are the basis of my plan. God has given the strength of these hills to freedom. They were placed here by the Almighty for the emancipation of your race. They are full of natural forts, where one man for defense will be equal to a hundred for attack. They are full of good hiding places, where a large number of brave men could be concealed and for a long time baffle and elude pursuit. I know these mountains well, and could take a body of men into them, and keep them there, despite all the efforts Virginia could make to dislodge and drive me out of them. My plan, then, is this: to take about twenty-five brave men into those mountains, and begin my work on a small scale, supply them with arms and provisions, and post them in companies of fives on a line of twenty-five miles. These shall for a time busy themselves in gathering recruits from the neighboring farms, seeking and selecting the most daring and restless spirits first.' In this part of the work, he said, the utmost care was to be taken to avoid treachery and discovery. Only the most conscientious and skillful of his men were to be detailed for this perilous duty. With care and enterprise, he thought, he could soon gather a force of one hundred hardy men, who would be content to lead the free and adventurous life to which he proposed to train them. When once properly drilled, and each man had found the place for which he was best suited, they would begin the work in earnest. They would run off the slaves in large numbers. They would retain the strong and brave, and send the weak ones to the North by the underground railroad. His operations would be enlarged with the increasing number of his men, and they would not be confined to one locality. He would approach the slave-holders in some cases at midnight, and tell them they must give up their slaves, and also let them have their best horses upon which to ride away. Slavery, he said, was a state of war, in which the slaves were unwilling parties, and that they, therefore, had a right to anything necessary to their peace and freedom. He would shed no blood, and would avoid a fight, except when he could not escape from it and was compelled to do it in self-defense. He would then, of course, do his best. This movement, he said, would weaken slavery in two ways. First, by making slave property insecure, it would make such property undesirable. Secondly, it would keep the anti-slavery agitation alive, and public attention fixed upon the subject, and thus finally lead to the adoption of measures for

abolishing the slave system altogether. He held that the anti-
slavery agitation was in danger of dying out, and that it needed
some such startling measures, as he proposed, to keep it alive
and effective. Slavery, he said, had nearly been abolished in
Virginia by the Nat. Turner insurrection; and he thought his
plan of operation would speedily abolish it in both Maryland
and Virginia. He said his trouble was to get the right kind of
men with which to begin the work, and the means necessary
to equip them. And here he explained the reason for his simple mode of living, his plain dress, his leather stock. He had
adopted this economy in order to save money with which to
arm and equip men to carry out his plan of liberation. This
was said by him in no boastful terms. On the contrary, he said
he had already delayed his work too long, and that he had no
room to boast either his zeal or his self-denial. From eight
o'clock in the evening till three o'clock in the morning, Captain
John Brown and I sat face to face, he arguing in favor of his
plan, and I finding all the objections I could against it. Now
mark! This conversation took place fully twelve years before
the blow was struck at Harper's Ferry, and his plan was even
then more than twenty years old. He had, therefore, been
watching and waiting all these years for suitable heads to rise
up, or ' pop up,' to use his expression, among the sable millions,
to whom he could safely confide his plan, and thus nearly forty
years had passed between this man's thoughts and his act."

One of the objections then made by Douglass
seems very shrewd, namely, that it would be difficult
for the band to find provisions. A somewhat similar
attempt, made in the Alps by Dolcino, during the
Middle Ages, failed from just this cause. The fanatics cut all who first met them to pieces; but they
could not collect food enough to save themselves
from being ultimately so reduced by starvation, as to
fall an easy prey. This would, I fear, have been the
fate of John Brown, if he had not been crushed by

superior numbers at once, as actually took place.
The plan which he finally adopted was far worse than
the original one ; but I do not think that he would,
under any circumstances, have been able to gather
recruits among the slaves fast enough to prevent being captured by the masters ; and if he had succeeded
in making his mountain-camp strong enough to resist
all other enemies, he would certainly have been conquered by famine. It is by no means strange that
Brown and other Northerners, who judged of the
slaves mainly from fugitives like Douglass and
Craft, imagined they would be more willing to rise in
revolt than proved to be the case, either at Harper's
Ferry or during the war ; but Douglass himself must
have understood the temper of the men among whom
he had been brought up. I suspect that in his relations
with Brown, as well as those previously with O'Connell, and afterwards with Butler, he allowed his sympathy with a benefactor of his race to carry him
beyond what would have been approved by his own
impartial judgment.

One of Brown's objects, it should be remembered,
was to increase the agitation about slavery ; and this
was much more desirable in 1847 than in 1859.
Almost anything would have been allowable to
arouse the North, while it remained in apathy ; but the
aggressions of the South had, before 1859, stirred up
so much opposition as to make nothing more necessary than that the Republican President should be
elected by an overwhelming majority, and that any
attempt at secession should be put down by a united
North. That no such attempt as was first planned,
or ultimately made, by John Brown could then have

promoted the attainment of these objects will, I hope, be plain enough as we go on.   Let me only add that I go thus fully into the matter, because it is due to Mr. Douglass that he should be freed from blame which has been cast upon him, for not going to Harper's Ferry.

He did assent to the original plan, proposed by a man, "whose mission seemed to him the only apology for his existence," and whose conviction was that "He had no better use for his life."   "I have talked with many men upon the subject of slavery," says our lecturer, "but I remember no one who seemed so deeply excited upon that subject as Captain John Brown.   He would walk the room with agitation at the mention of slavery.   He saw the evil through no mist, haze, or clouds, but in a broad light of infinite brightness, which left no line of its ten thousand horrors out of sight." . . .   "His zeal in the cause of freedom was infinitely superior to mine.   Mine was as the taper light : his was as the burning sun.   Mine was bounded by time : his stretched away to the silent shores of eternity.   I could speak for the slave : John Brown could fight for the slave.   I could live for the slave : John Brown could die for the slave."

"I not only did not aspire to the crown of martyrdom ; but I never prompted such aspirations on his part," adds Mr. Douglass.   He was much more fully in sympathy with the struggle in Kansas, and often got up public meetings which sent out money to help Captain Brown fight against border-ruffians.   Their defeat made it possible for the hero to get the men and money he needed for Virginia ; and in January, 1858, he came to his friend in Rochester, and told him that he wanted to spend several weeks with him, but would not stop unless he could be allowed to pay board. Douglass was glad to have him there, but had to take him on his own terms. There he stayed until late in February, employing part of his time in making out a constitution for the mountain-camp, and part in writing letters to Gerrit Smith, Mr. George L. Stearns, of Boston, and other friendly Abolitionists. His men were already drilling in Iowa; but he was in urgent need of money. He spoke now and then of the government arsenal at Harper's Ferry as a place where he could get weapons; but he seemed much more intent on plans for fortifications in the Alleghanies. He had so much to say about his plans, that they soon ceased to interest any one in the house, except the children, one of whom now says : " The sun seemed to rise and set to me in John Brown."

From Rochester he went to Peterboro, where he met Gerrit Smith, Mr. Sanborn, and Mr. Morton, on February 22. His friends tried to shake his purpose, but found him bent upon it, and finally concluded that, as the attempt would probably be made at all events, they had better have it a success. Stearns, Parker, Dr. Howe, and Higginson were of the same opinion in Boston; but Brown could get nothing more than a positive refusal out of Phillips and Garrison ; and these latter seem to me to have taken the wisest and kindest course. From Boston the Captain went on to Philadelphia, where, on March 10, he met several leaders of the colored people, including Douglass, who had, I presume, made an engagement to lecture as a pretext for the journey. That winter,

Brown led the most successful of his many expedi-
tions, that which set free eleven slaves in Missouri
and carried them to Canada.   On July 4, 1859, he was
at Harper's Ferry, where he hired the farm to which
his men and weapons were soon brought.

Douglass, meantime, had been hard at work as
editor and lecturer.   That spring he spoke in about
twenty cities in Michigan, Illinois, and Wisconsin.
A reception was given him, on February 1, in
Chicago, where he told about " Self-made Men ; " and
his whole trip was a pleasant one, except at Janesville.   There he and the two colored men who accompanied him were put at a table by themselves, in full
view of all the rowdies in the bar-room.   Douglass
soon said, loud enough to be heard by all the crowd,
that he had made a great discovery in the stable.
" I saw black and white horses eating there in peace,
out of the same trough ; and I infer that the horses
in Janesville are more civilized than the people."
The by-standers laughed good-naturedly ; and there
was no color-line across that dining-room afterwards.

May 12, 1859, we find him delivering a eulogy on
Judge William Jay, an early advocate of immediate
emancipation in the District of Columbia.   This address, which was prepared by the invitation of the
colored citizens of New York City, was printed that
year in pamphlet form, and seems to me his most
scholarly production.   The amount of information is
ample and the arrangement judicious, while the elevation of the author's views at this time appears in
the following passage :

" The subject of slavery is an exciting one.   Oppression is
apt even to make a wise man mad.   The bare relation of

master and slave, unaccompanied by its grosser manifestations of ignorance, depravity, cruelty, and blood, shocks and stuns the mind by its deformity. O'Connell used to say, that when he first heard the idea of property in man, it sounded to him as if some one was stamping upon the grave of his mother. The very thought chills the blood in the veins of the strong man, and stirs a fever in the blood of the age. The heart becomes sick and the spirit frantic with horror over its brutal atrocities and crimes. In writing upon a system of such boundless and startling enormity, where the wildest fancy is overmatched by the terrible reality, it is not easy to steer clear of exaggeration in individual cases. Some extravagance may, indeed be looked for and excused in treating of such a subject ; but such extravagance will be looked for in vain in the writings of Judge Jay on slavery. As a writer that can be said of him, which can be said of but few reformatory writers in any age : he not only relied implicitly upon and believed in the simple, undistorted truth, as the safest and best means of accomplishing his benevolent purposes, but was never, to the knowledge of any, tempted or driven by eager anxiety for immediate results into distortion or exaggeration. He had an earnest heart. It was always alive with the fires of justice and liberty ; but with all, he possessed that accurate and well-balanced judgment which controlled and directed wisely and discreetly all his writings on the subject of slavery. No fact, no statement of Judge Jay, how fiercely soever his opinions may have been combated, has ever been called in question." . . .

Douglass spoke this year on the anniversary of emancipation in the West Indies, at Geneva, New York, in company with Dr. Cheever, whose attempt to start a movement within the Church against slavery, was cordially praised in "Douglass's Monthly." A few days later came a summons which brought Douglass to his last meeting with John Brown, on Saturday, August 20. It was, as the lecturer says :

"In an old stone quarry on the Conecochege, near the town of Chambersburg, Pennsylvania. His arms and ammunition were stored in that town, and were to be moved on the night of our meeting to Harper's Ferry. In company with Shields Green, I obeyed the summons. Prompt to the hour we met the old Captain at the appointed time and place. He was accompanied by Mr. Kagai, his secretary. Our meeting was, in some sense, a council of war. Until that night I did not know that Captain Brown meant to depart from his old plan, already explained. We spent that night and the succeeding Sunday in conference on the question, whether the meditated blow at Harper's Ferry should be struck, or whether the old plan before described should be the one pursued. Captain Brown was for boldly striking Harper's Ferry at once, and running the risk of getting into the mountains afterward. Shields Green, who had come down with me, and Mr. Kagai remained silent and continued listeners to the discussion throughout, never venturing a word. It is needless to repeat here what was said—after what has happened. Suffice it to say that, notwithstanding all I could urge, my old friend Brown had resolved upon his course ; and it was idle to parley longer. I told him at last, that he was going into a steel trap, and that it was impossible for me to join him. He regretted my decision ; and we parted, he going to Harper's Ferry, and I going to Rochester. Thus far I have spoken exclusively of Captain Brown. Let me say a word now of his brave and devoted followers. Time fails me to do more than this. And first, a word of Shields Green, the young man who accompanied me to meet John Brown in the old stone quarry at Chambersburg. This man was, at that time, only a year from slavery in South Carolina. His love of liberty and hatred of slavery were attested by his escape from Charleston, and finding his way through innumerable dangers, to Rochester, where he lived in my family, and where he met the man with whom he bravely went to the scaffold. I said to him, when about to leave Captain Brown, ' Now, Shields, you have heard our discussion. If, in view of it, you do not wish to go to Harper's Ferry, you have but to say so, and you may go back with me to Rochester.' He answered; 'I believe I will go with the old man;' and go with the old man he did, and bore himself as bravely and grandly as any of the number. He went with him into the fight, and to the gallows, without a murmur. When Captain Brown was surrounded and at the mercy of the enemy, and all chances of escape were cut off, this man, Green, was already free and abroad in the mountains, with Osborn Anderson, and could, like Anderson, have made his escape. When asked to do so, however, he said, 'No! I will go down to the old man.' When in prison in Charleston, he could not see his old friend, but to those who spoke to him of the trouble brought upon him, he repeatedly said, 'I have no complaint to make against the old man.' If a monument is erected to John Brown, and one ought to be, the name and figure of Shields Green should have a conspicuous place upon that monument, for he was true to the 'old man,' when his cause was most desperate, and in the face of a death upon the gallows."

We also read that, at parting, John Brown " put his arms around me, in a manner more than friendly, and said : ' Come with me, Douglass, I will defend you with my life. I want you for a special purpose. When I strike, the bees will begin to swarm ; and I shall want you to help me hive them.' " He had already insisted that " The capture of Harper's Ferry would serve as notice to the slaves, that their friends had come, and as a trumpet to rally them to his standard." One of the prisoners, confined by him in the armory, Captain Dangerfield, says he was sure that " by twelve o'clock he would have fifteen hundred men with him, ready armed." He stated himself during the examination by Governor Wise, the day after his capture, that, " He confidently expected large reinforcements." Writers have wondered why he stayed at Harper's Ferry for twelve hours after taking the town, with his forces badly scattered, and without making any preparations for a retreat. It has also been asked, why he was there at all, especially as the mountains in the neighborhood are not particularly fit for guerrilla warfare. The best explanation, I think, is that he thought this stroke would set the bees swarming; and he was waiting to hive them. Alas, few bees would quit the old hive; and when great swarms did darken the sky, they were furious wasps and deadly hornets.

His heroism in the fight and the prison, at the trial and on the scaffold, are beyond all praise. No man ever died more nobly. But morality is no respecter of persons. Her authority ought not to be thrust aside in order to set up heroes for worship. Just before the anarchists were hung at Chicago, I was urged to defend their conduct, and told that they were no worse than John Brown, and every one approved of what he did. Let us see what was thought of it at the time. Mrs. Child wrote to Governor Wise, that no one in her "large circle of abolition acquaintances" expected the attack on Harper's Ferry; "nor do I know of a single person who would have approved of it." Garrison pronounced it "well intended, but sadly misguided." Whittier spoke, after the execution, of the "guilty means" and "the folly which seeks through evil, good." The "Independent" called John Brown "a lawless brigand." The "New York Tribune's" opinion about him and his companions was that: "They dared and died for what they felt to be the right, though in a manner that seems to us fatally wrong." This was said at the first; and an editorial after the execution runs thus: " Of course, we regard Brown's raid as utterly mistaken, and in its direct consequences pernicious," " a wrong way to rid his country of the curse," etc. Henry Wilson wrote at this time to the " Liberator," from Natick, in reply to Henry G. Wright, that:

> " Pending the recent election in New York, I addressed thousands of people in Brooklyn, Syracuse, Rome, Watertown, Auburn, Geneva, and other places, and during the canvass of two weeks everywhere expressed my ' regret and condemnation ' of his armed invasion of Virginia; and, during that time, I conversed with no one who did not regret and deplore it. And in this State, and in this town, where you declare the people approve of Brown's lawless act, I have met few, very few indeed, who approve that act. My conviction is that, while the people of Massachusetts are nearly unanimous in their sympathy for the fate of Brown, and in their admiration of his personal heroism, they are quite unanimous in their regret and condemnation of his lawless raid at Harper's Ferry."

Wilson stated afterward, in his " History of the Rise and Fall of the Slave Power " (Vol. ii, p. 587), that " Anti-slavery men generally regretted and condemned the invasion." The Republican platform of 1860 declares that, " We denounce the lawless invasion by armed force of the soil of any State or Territory, no matter under what pretext, as among the gravest of crimes;" and the candidate, Abraham Lincoln, said, in his famous Cooper Institute speech, that the Harper's Ferry affair " corresponds with the many attempts related in history at the assassination of kings and emperors. An enthusiast broods over the oppression of a people, till he fancies himself commissioned by Heaven to liberate them. He ventures the attempt, which ends in little else than his own execution. Orsini's attempt on Louis Napoleon and John Brown's attempt at Harper's Ferry were, in their philosophy, precisely the same." John Brown gave up his life gladly in hope of freeing the oppressed; so did the men who slew the Czar, Alexander II. He thought he was doing God service; and Paul thought the same while he was persecuting Christianity. Persecutors have usually fancied themselves in the right, but they have always been in the wrong; the motives of the revolutionist are nobler than those of the persecutor, but no individual motives have as high authority as the eternal and universal principles of morality. It is by the standard of these principles that we must judge whether it was right or wrong to set peaceable citizens of our country in deadly conflict among themselves and finally against our government's soldiers, to slay an unarmed colored man for trying to give the alarm, and to sacrifice twenty-five other victims. Who can tell how many happy homes would have been made desolate, if John Brown could have had any part of the success he expected? His attempt is all the less excusable, because it was made at a time when the interest of the anti-slavery cause demanded that nothing should be done to repel the crowds of new recruits, who had hitherto been neutral or hostile, and that no occasion should be given for pretending that Abolitionism was dangerous to the country's permanent peace and welfare. Nothing could have better suited the purpose, either of the Northerners who were hoping to defeat the anti-slavery candidates, or of the Southerners who were plotting secession. The John Brown pike was never flourished so vigorously as by Democratic stump-speakers. Meeting after meeting of the Abolitionists was broken up by such mobs as had not been met there since 1850. Emerson was silenced in Boston for opinions which had already caused the withdrawal of an invitation to lecture in Philadelphia. How Douglass and Sanborn suffered will have to be told more at length. Among other results of the Harper's Ferry tragedy were the expulsion of Northern business men by the dozen from Southern cities, and the withdrawal of Southern students by the hundred from Northern schools and colleges. What sympathy was expressed for John Brown served to bring undeserved blame upon the champions against slavery, and to exasperate their enemies. The elections in the fall of 1859, and the spring of 1860, showed a serious check in the growth of the party by which slavery was to be abolished.

One of John Brown's many mistakes was his leaving for capture by the Virginians, at the farm-house where he had been living, a carpet-bag containing letters implicating his Northern friends, and among them was Douglass, who says that, "When that bag was opened, there we were all sprawling." He had gone to Philadelphia to lecture ; and he hurried by night to Hoboken, where Miss Assing telegraphed to his son to secure his papers. It was not safe for him to take a train in New York City, but he was driven over to Patterson, a station on the Erie Railroad ; and thus he was able to return to Rochester in disguise. Scarcely had he entered his house, when his friends urged him to go to Canada, lest there should be a bloody conflict in his defense against the officers of the law. Buchanan's marshals are said to have been in Rochester within six hours after he left ; and Governor Wise made requisition on the executive, not only of New York but also of Michigan, where he hoped to be able to find his prey, and make the capture by means of agents who professed to be traveling in the interest of the Post-office Department. How thoroughly in earnest he was, may be judged from a speech which he made in Richmond, on December 21, at a reception given to two hundred medical students, who had just left the school at Philadelphia. The applause was tremendous as he said :

"Oh if I had had one good, long, low, black, rakish, well-armed steamer in Hampton Roads, I would have placed her on the Newfoundland Banks, with orders, if she found a British packet with that negro on board, to take him. And by the eternal gods he should have been taken—taken with very particular instructions not to hang him before I had the privilege of seeing him well hung."

Such was the danger which Douglass escaped by going to England. He took the steamer at Quebec, on November 12 ; and the place which he was to have occupied as a lecturer in the Parker Fraternity Course in Boston, had to be filled by Thoreau. who spoke enthusiastically of John Brown.

The passage across the ocean occupied fourteen stormy days ; and the fugitive feared that he was going into life-long exile. John Brown's attack on the slave-power showed that it held full possession of the national government, as it seemed likely to do for years to come. Public opinion was so much against the Abolitionists, that scarcely any one could see how brief would be the time, before they would have full justice. England was much more eager than America to hear about Harper's Ferry; and our lecturer found himself in great demand. On giving an account of the affair at Newcastle, on February 23, 1860, he declared that "Slavery might be put down by honestly carrying out the provisions of the Constitution." This great charter was then assailed as pro-slavery by George Thompson, in Glasgow, where Douglass replied on March 26, with arguments already quoted. He desired at this time to visit France; but the American minister, Dallas, who had been Vice-President, refused his application for a passport, and told him that he was not a citizen of the United States. The French minister at London granted a permit at once. Before the visit could be made news came of the death, on March 13, "of my beloved daughter, Annie, the light and life of my house."

The bereaved father returned at once, and found that he was in no particular danger at the North, where there had been a great change in public opinion about Harper's Ferry. The John Brown song was now sung in all the free States; and anti-slavery men were busy organizing the campaign in which they were to elect their President. The South hated the Abolitionists as bitterly as ever, and there was an armed riot at Knoxville, Tennessee, against a colored man, who was supposed to be Frederick Douglass. No notice of his return was taken, however, either by Wise or Buchanan. On August 1, 1860, he spoke at Geneva, New York, as he had done the year before. The Republicans had already adopted a platform which was sufficiently outspoken about the refusal to

admit Kansas, the slave-trade, the Dred Scott decision,
and the other attempts to carry slavery into the territories. John Brown was censured, as we have seen ;
and nothing was said about the Fugitive Slave Bill,
or the abolition of slavery, not even in the District of
Columbia. Lincoln owed his nomination largely
to not having gone so far in opposition to slavery as
Seward ; and the spirit of the convention was so cautious as to cause Giddings to retire in disgust.
Douglass pronounced this convention even more un-
satisfactory than that of 1856, and joined with others
of the Radical Political Abolitionists in nominating
Gerrit Smith, for President. The little band soon
received an important ally. Stephen S. Foster had
been for more than twenty years denouncing all
churches and parties with a vigor which had made
him suffer more persecutions than any other of the
Abolitionists. His influence among the Garrisonians
had been nearly equal to that of the leader whose
name they bore. The old Berserker now made his
first appearance as a politician, and, I think, his last
one. He actually started a movement which held a
convention at Worcester, on September 19 and 20, in
order " to organize a political party upon an anti-
slavery interpretation of the Constitution, with the
avowed purpose of abolishing slavery in the States as
well as the territories." Garrison called the whole
business " a farce," and Phillips " a nuisance." Lucy
Stone and Higginson spoke at Worcester, but in
opposition to Foster ; and his only supporter of much
importance was Douglass, who succeeded in carrying
a resolution endorsing the nomination of Gerrit
Smith. His language about the Garrisonians seems

to have been misunderstood ; and he gave an account
of his speech as follows, in the "Liberator," for October 26 :

" My objection to the American Anti-Slavery Society respected
its plan, not its life. So far from working for the annihilation
of that Society, I never failed, even in the worst times of my
controversy with it, to recognize that organization as the most
efficient generator of anti-slavery sentiment in the country."
. . . What had I said ? Why ; in substance this : That
the plan of operation adopted by the American Anti-Slavery
Society did not embrace the abolition of slavery by means of
the government, and that the Radical Abolition party was the
only organization which proposed such abolition. This is what
I said, and meant to say."

At the very time he wrote this letter, he received
one containing a proposition which I copy literally :

" I have been informed that you had an onely daughter, and
that you desire her to marry a whight man ; whereupon you
giv $15,000 or $20,000 dollars to any respectabl whight man
that would marry her and cherish her through life. If there is
any truth in this report, P. S. let me know and I will marry
your daughter on these conditions, and will endeavor to make
myself agreeable."

Douglass, in reply, remarks, that a man who was a
total stranger, ought to have given at least one reference, and then says :

" You date from Auburn, and tell me to direct to Auburn,
but do not name the street. Pardon me for regarding this as
a suspicious circumstance. You may be an inmate of the State
Prison, or on your way there, a fact which, you see, would interfere with the fulfillment of your part of the proposed bargain,
even if I could fulfill the part you assign to me. You want
$15,000 or $20,000. This is a common want ; and you are not

to blame for using all honorable means to obtain it. But candor requires me to state, that if you were in every respect a suitable person to be bought for the purpose you name, I have not the money to buy you. I have no objection to your complexion; but there are certain little faults of grammar and spelling as well as other little points in your letter, which compel me to regard you as a person, by education, manners, and morals, wholly unfit to associate with my daughter in any capacity whatever. You evidently think your white skin of great value. I don't dispute it : it is probably the best thing about you. Yet not even that valuable quality can commend you sufficiently to induce even so black a negro as myself to accept you as his son-in-law."

I presume it was about this time that Mrs. Douglass had occasion to engage a servant, and said to her : " I hope you have no prejudices about color. I have none myself."

Even friendship for Gerrit Smith did not prevent Douglass from finally deciding to do what he could, in his " Monthly " and on the platform, to elect Lincoln ; and he then threw himself into the contest "with firmer faith and more ardent hope than ever before."

The triumph of the Republicans provoked a movement toward secession ; and conservative people in the North were hoping to avert ·the danger by new compromises, when an Abolitionist meeting " to mark the anniversary of the Martyrdom of John Brown," was summoned to meet on December 3, in Tremont Temple, Boston. F. B. Sanborn was about to take the chair, when some well-dressed men, who wished to break up the meeting, insisted on having their own leader, a Mr. Fay, made president. This man proceeded to read resolutions denouncing John Brown, but had some trouble, either with his voice or his conscience, whereupon a glass of water was handed him by Douglass, who said, "If thine enemy thirst, give him drink." He was to have been the orator of the day, and he insisted on his right to the floor. At length he got a chance to say, amid constant inter-ruption :

"This is one of the most impudent, barefaced outrages on free speech I ever witnessed in Boston or elsewhere. I can make myself heard. I know your masters. I have served the same master that you are serving. You are in the service of the slave-holders. The freedom of all mankind was written upon the heart by the finger of God. It is said that the best way to abolish slavery is to obey the law. Shall we obey the blood-hounds of the law, who do the dirty work of the slave-catchers? If so then you are fit for your work. Mr. Norris, of New Hampshire asked Wade, of Ohio, in the Senate of the United States, if he would render his personal assistance to the execution of the Fugitive Slave Bill ; and that noble-hearted man and Christian gentleman replied ' I will see you d———d first.' Sir, there is a law which we are bound to obey, and the Abolitionists are most prompt to obey it. It is that law written in the Constitution of the United States, which includes all colors."

Here there was a long disturbance, ending with a cry of "Go on, nigger!" "If I were a slave-driver," said Douglass, "and had hold of that man for five minutes, I would let more daylight through his skin than ever got there before." "He has said the truth," interposed Fay; "for a negro slave-driver is the most cruel in the world." "Yes," said Douglass, "just as a northern dough-face is more contemptible than a southern slave-holder." Here the meeting was thoroughly broken up, but it was finally reorganized with another friend of the South, named Howe, in the chair. Douglass tried repeatedly to speak, but was interrupted by cheer after cheer, sometimes for the Union, sometimes for himself, and sometimes for South Carolina. He called himself for three cheers for liberty; and they were given unanimously; but three more followed for Governor Wise, who had threatened to hang him, as he did John Brown. At last his attempt to prevent his chair from being taken away for Mr. Howe brought about so much confusion that the hall was cleared by the police.

The next Sunday he gave his lecture on "Self-Made Men" before Theodore Parker's Society in the Music Hall, and before he closed, he said:

" The mortifying and disgraceful fact stares us in the face, that though Faneuil Hall and Bunker Hill Monument stand, freedom of speech is struck down." . . . " Even here in Boston, and among the friends of freedom, we hear two voices, one denouncing the mob that broke up our meeting on Monday as a base and cowardly outrage, and another deprecating and regretting the holding of such a meeting by such men at such a time. We are told that the meeting was ill-timed, and the parties to it unwise. Why, what is the matter with us? Are we going to palliate and excuse a palpable and flagrant outrage on the right of speech, by implying that only a particular description of person should exercise that right? Are we at such a time, when a great principle has been struck down, to quench the moral indignation which the deed excites by casting reflections upon those on whose persons the outrage has been committed? After all the arguments for liberty to which Boston has listened for more than a quarter of a century, has she yet to learn that the time to assert a right is when that right is called in question, and that the men of all others to assert it are the men to whom the right has been denied? "

Similar outrages took place soon after at the Janu-

ary meeting of the M. A. S. S., and at other anti-slavery conventions, for instance at Syracuse, and at
Albany, where Douglass was in serious danger,
and the Mayor had to call out the militia. John
Brown had given the North two songs, one saying
that his soul was marching on, and another, which I
heard sung in Boston by rioters, who would not let
Emerson speak, and which spoke thus of the anti-
slavery governor of Massachusetts:

"Tell John A. Andrew, John Brown 's dead!"

CHAPTER XI.

STATE after State was now seceding, to the open delight, not only of Phillips and Garrison but of Beecher and James Freeman Clark. Here, as well as in canonizing John Brown, the Abolitionists naturally made themselves obnoxious to the great majority of Northerners, who were determined that the Union should be preserved and the laws enforced. The loyalty, which hissed at disunionism in the North, soon found itself much better employed in shooting at it in the South. The capture of Fort Sumter brought about a great popular uprising, in which all differences between Republican and Democrat, Unionist and Abolitionist disappeared. The North was united at last against the slave-holders; and the end of slavery was near.

Douglass had tried, in the April number of his " Monthly," to convince other Abolitionists, that dissolution of the Union would not help their cause. He was preparing to sail on the 25th of that month to Hayti, in whose condition he has always taken great interest. But when the great news came, he gave up the trip. His May number came out with the figures of the American eagle and the star-spangled banner, placed at the head of the first column, and accompanied by the motto, " Freedom for all, or Chains for

284

all." Even then he told the colored men to form
militia companies at once, and make ready to obey
the summons to enlist. He spoke in favor of the war
on April 27, in Rochester, and often afterward in various parts of the North. He warned his hearers from
the first, that the contest would be long and bloody.
In his "Monthly" for October he says : "Our first
business is to save our Government from destruction."
He felt satisfied from first to last, that the mission of
the war was not only the salvation of the Union, but the
liberation of the slave ; though he "trusted less to
the virtue of the North than to the villany of the
South."

He was not repelled either by the outrages upon
fugitives to Union camps, or by occasional insults to
himself. When he was announced to lecture in Syracuse on Thursday, November 14, on "The Rebellion,
its Cause and its Remedy," placards were posted up,
headed, "Nigger Fred Coming," and evidently meant
to stir up a mob against "This reviler of the Constitution," "Traitor to his country," and "Arch-fugitive
to Europe." The Mayor called out not only the
entire police force, but also seventy special officers
and forty-five cadets with bayonets. There was no
disturbance either that night or the next, when Douglass delivered a lecture which was repeated that winter in Boston, in the Parker Fraternity Course, and
entitled "Life Pictures."

Early in the year 1862 he gave a lecture in the
Music Hall, Boston, in a course arranged by the
Emancipation League, recently formed to agitate for
abolition as a military necessity. Among the other
speakers were Conway, Greeley, Boutwell, and Phillips.

Douglass was also employed for some weeks by the League as a lecturer in varions parts of New England. The tenor of his remarks is shown in an address, which was given on January 14, in Philadelphia, and began thus : " He is the best friend of his country, who at this tremendous crisis dares to tell his country-men the truth, however disagreeable that truth may be." He then spoke of the duty of the North to arm its strong, black hand, as well as its soft, white one, against the rebels. He added : "I believed ten years ago, that liberty was safer in the Union than out of the Union ; but my Garrisonian friends could not see it, and in consequence dealt me some heavy blows. My crime was in being ten years in advance of them." He ended by saying : " I am for the war, for the Union, in any and every event."

On February 12, he made this protest in the Cooper Institute, against the talk about sending his people back to Africa :

" For a nation to drive away its laboring population is to commit political suicide." . . . " It is affirmed that the negro, if emancipated, could not take care of himself. My answer to this is, let him have a fair chance to try it. For two hundred years he has taken care of himself and his master into the bargain."

" Douglass's Monthly " was now published mainly for American readers, at the price of $1 a year, but still had agents in Great Britain. The reading matter was almost entirely about the war ; but the last of the sixteen pages was regularly occupied with circulars designed to encourage emigration to Hayti. In the number for May, 1862, however, the editor spoke with regret of a petition of colored people in Washington for aid to form colonies in Central America, and declared that "The estimate which shall be formed of the negro, and the place which he shall hold in the world's esteem, is to be decided here." . . . "The colored race never can be respected anywhere, till they are respected in America." "The true policy of the colored American is to make himself, in every way open to him, an American citizen, bearing with proscription and insult till these things disappear." The leading topic in the "Monthly" this summer was the duty of allowing the negro to fight in his own cause ; much is said about what had been done by colored soldiers under Jackson and Washington ; and the progress of the first experiment in South Carolina is recounted with eager interest.

The expectation that the Union would be restored by a single battle was wofully disappointed ; our progress during the first year was slight ; the repulse of our best army before Richmond, in June, 1862, showed the Confederacy to be still formidable ; and the North was so unwilling to free the slaves, as to give rise to fears that peace might yet be made at their expense. Such was the state of things when Douglass gave a Fourth of July oration at Himrod's Corners, a village in Western New York, which then consisted, he says, of "two taverns, one church, six neat, little cottages, one store, a huge pile of sawed wood for railroad purposes, and a celebration." An audience of two thousand people was soon collected in a pine grove, where he told them that all talk about the war's having any other cause than slavery was like "the Irishman's gun, aimed at nothing and hitting it every time." He then complained that the

Administration was fighting the rebels with the olive branch, instead of the sword, and that McClellan, who had wasted six precious months needlessly, and then allowed himself to be defeated by inferior forces, must be either a traitor or a military impostor. Lincoln he blamed for not adopting a decidedly anti-slavery policy; and his language was so severe as to call out a protest from one of his hearers. The audience was with the orator, however; and he had the pleasure of finding it wholly due to his own request, that the critic was patiently heard, and not handled roughly. Among the concluding passages of his oration are these:

" The only choice left to this nation is abolition or destruction. You must abolish slavery, or abandon the Union. It is plain that there can never be any Union between the North and the South, while the South values slavery more than nationality. A union of interest is essential to a union of ideas; and without this union of ideas the outer form of the Union will be but as a rope of sand." . . . "There is plausibility in the argument that we cannot reach slavery until we have suppressed the rebellion. Yet it is far more true to say that we cannot reach the rebellion, until we have suppressed slavery. For slavery is the life of the rebellion. Let the loyal army but inscribe upon its banner, Emancipation and protection to all who will rally under it; and no power could prevent a stampede from slavery, such as the world has not witnessed since the Hebrews crossed the Red Sea. I am convinced that this rebellion and slavery are twin monsters; that they must fall or flourish together, and that all attempts at upholding one, while putting down the other, will be followed by continued trains of darkening calamities, such as make this anniversary of our national independence a day of mourning instead of a day of transcendent joy and gladness." . . . "I have told you of great national opportunities in the past, a greater than any in the past is the opportunity of the present. If now we omit the duty it imposes, steel our hearts against its teachings, or shrink in cowardice from the work of to-day, your fathers will have fought and bled in vain to establish free institutions, and American republicanism will become a hissing and a by-word to a mocking earth."

On the following Monday he took part in a celebration, held by colored people, at Ithaca, in memory of the recent abolition of slavery in the District of Columbia. The day selected, July 8, 1862, was that on which New York decreed emancipation, sixty-three years before. The whole surrounding country, within a radius of a hundred miles, was nobly represented ; the procession, with bands of both colors, won the admiration of all beholders ; and the orator of the day was delighted with the change " since our first anti-slavery meeting there twenty years ago, when violence met us at every turn."

The preliminary declarations of the Administration, that the war was not against slavery, had been too literally taken in Great Britain ; her Abolitionists now out-garrisoned Garrison, and still thought our Union and slavery so closely incorporated, that they must survive or perish, be restored or abolished, together ; and her manufacturers could ill afford to be without American cotton. Her government had been too friendly to the rebels, especially in letting loose the Alabama ; and their recent victories made their recognition seem near at hand. To avert it, Beecher crossed the ocean in 1863. Douglass sent his protest in 1862. Immediately after Lincoln's first proclamation of emancipation on September 22, ap-

peared " The Slave's Appeal to Great Britain, by Frederick Douglass." The most important paragraphs
of the little pamphlet are as follows :

" Hear, I beseech you, my humble appeal, and grant this,
my earnest request. I know your power, I know your justice,
and, better still, I know your mercy; and with the more confidence I, in my imperfect speech, venture to appeal to you.
Your benevolent sons and daughters, at great sacrifice of time,
labor, and treasure, more than a quarter of a century ago,
under the inspiration of an enlightened Christianity, removed
the yoke of cruel bondage from the long bowed-down necks of
eight-hundred thousand of my race in your West India Islands ;
and later a few of them, in their generosity, unasked, with
silver and gold ransomed me from him who claimed me as his
slave in the United States, and bade me speak in the cause of
the dumb millions of my countrymen still in slavery. I am now
fulfilling my appointed mission by making, on the slave's behalf,
this appeal to you. I am grateful for your benevolence, zealous
for your honor, but chiefly now I am concerned lest, in the
present tremendous crisis of American affairs, you should be
led to adopt a policy which would defeat the now proposed
emancipation of my people, and forge new fetters of slavery
for unborn generations of their posterity.

" You are now more than ever urged, both from within and
from without your borders, to recognize the independence of
the so-called Confederate States of America. I beseech and
implore you, resist this urgency. You have nobly resisted it
thus long. You can, and I ardently hope you will, resist it
still longer. The proclamation of emancipation by President
Lincoln will become operative on the first of January, 1863.
The hopes of millions, long meted out and trodden down,
now rise with every advancing hour. Oh! I pray you, by all
your highest and holiest memories, blast not the budding hopes
of these millions by lending your countenance and extending
your honored and potent hand to the blood-stained fingers of
the impious slave-holding Confederate States of America. . . .

" I have no hesitation in saying that if you, Great Britain, had, at the outset of this terrible war, sternly frowned upon the conspirators, and given your earnest and unanimous sympathy and moral support to the loyal cause, to-day might have seen America enjoying security and peace, and you would not have been the sufferer that, in all your commercial and manufacturing interests, you now are. . . .

" Wanting a slave-holding constitution, the Southern States have undertaken to make one, and establish it upon the ruins of the one under which slavery can be discouraged, crippled, and abolished. The war, therefore, for maintaining the old against the new constitution, even though no proclamation of emancipation had been issued by the loyal government, under the old constitution, is essentially an anti-slavery war, and should command the ardent support of good men in all countries. What though our timid administration at Washington, shrinking from the logical result of their own natural position, did, at the first, refuse to recognize the real character of the war, and vainly attempted to conciliate, by walking backward to cast a mantle over the revolting origin of the rebellion ? What though they instructed their foreign agent to conceal the moral deformity of the rebels ? You could not fail to know that the primal causes of this war rested in slavery and a determination on the part of the rebels to make that stupendous crime and curse all controlling and perpetual in America. But I will not weary you with argument. The case is plain. The North is fighting on the side of liberty and civilization, and the South for slavery and barbarism. . . .

" No excuses, however plausible ; no distances of time, however remote ; no line of conduct, however excellent, will erase the deep stain upon your honor and truth, if, at this hour of dreadful trial, you interpose in a manner to defeat the emancipation of the American slaves. If at any time you could have intervened honorably in American affairs, it was when the Federal government was vainly endeavoring to put down the rebellion without hurting slavery. That gloomy period ended on the 22d of September, 1862. From that day our war has been invested with a sanctity which will smite as with death even the mailed hand of Britain, if outstretched to arrest it. Let this conflict go on ; there is no doubt of the final result ; and though it is a dreadful scourge, it will make justice, humanity, and liberty permanently possible in this country."

To his own fellow-citizens he wrote, about this time, as follows :

" What shall be done with the four million slaves, if they are emancipated ?   This question has been answered, and can be answered in many ways.   Primarily, it is a question less for man than for God,—less for human intellect than for the laws of nature to solve.   It assumes that nature has erred ; that the law of liberty is a mistake ; that freedom, though a natural want of the human soul, can only be enjoyed at the expense of human welfare, and that men are better off in slavery than they would be in freedom ; that slavery is the natural order of human relations, and that liberty is an experiment.—What shall be done with them ?

" Our answer is, Do nothing with them ; mind your business and let them mind theirs.   Your doing with them is the greatest misfortune.   They have been undone by your doings ; and all they now ask, and really have need of at your hands, is just to let them alone.   They suffer by every interference, and succeed best by being let alone.   The negroes should have been let alone in Africa, let alone when the pirates and robbers offered them for sale in our Christian slave-markets, (more cruel and inhuman than the Mohammedan slave-markets,) let alone by courts, judges, politicians, legislators, and slave-drivers, let alone altogether, and assured that they were thus to be let alone forever, and that they must now make their own way in the world, just the same as any and every other variety of the human family.   As colored men we only ask to be allowed to do with ourselves, subject only to the same great laws for the welfare of human society which apply to other men, Jews, gentiles, barbarian, Scythian.   Let us stand upon our own legs, work with our own hands, and eat bread in the sweat of our own brows. When you, our white countrymen, have attempted to do anything for us, it has generally been to deprive us of some right, power, or privilege, which you yourselves would die before you would submit to have taken from you. When the planters of the West Indies used to attempt to puzzle the pure-minded Wilberforce with the question, ' How shall we get rid of slavery ? ' his simple answer was, ' Quit stealing.' In like manner we answer those who are perpetually puzzling their brains with questions as to what shall be done with the negro, ' Let him alone, and mind your own business.' If you see him ploughing in the open field, leveling the forest, at work with ' a spade, a rake, a hoe, a pickaxe, or a bill,' let him alone : he has a right to work. If you see him on his way to school, with spelling-book, geography, and arithmetic in his hands, let him alone. Don't shut the door in his face, or bolt your gates against him ; he has a right to learn ; let him alone. Don't pass laws to degrade him. If he has a ballot in his hand, and is on his way to the ballot-box to deposit his vote for the man who, he thinks, will most justly and wisely administer the govern-ment which has the power of life and death over him, as well as others, let him alone ; his right of choice deserves as much respect and protection as your own. If you see him on his way to church, exercising religious liberty in accordance with this or that religious persuasion, let him alone. Don't meddle with him, nor trouble yourselves with any questions as to what shall be done with him.

" What shall be done with the negro, if emancipated ? Deal justly with him. He is a human being capable of judging be-tween good and evil, right and wrong, liberty and slavery, and is as much a subject of law as any other man ; therefore deal justly with him. He is, like other men, sensible of the motives of reward and punishment. Give him wages for his work, and let hunger pinch him if he don't work. He knows the differ-ence between fullness and famine, plenty and scarcity. ' But will he work ? ' Why should he not ? He is used to it, and is not afraid of it. His hands are already hardened by toil ; and he has no dreams of ever getting a living by any other means than by hard work. 'But would you turn them all loose?' Certainly. We are no better than our Creator. He has turned them loose, and why should not we? 'But would you let them all stay here?' Why not? What better is *here* than *there*? Will they occupy more room as freeman than as slaves? Is the presence of a black freeman less agreeable than that of a black slave? Is the object of your injustice and cruelty a more ungrateful sight than one of your justice and benevolence? You have borne the one more than two hundred years. Can't you bear the other long enough to try the experiment?" ("The Black Man, His Antecedents, His Genius, and His Achievements, by William Wells Brown, 1863," pp. 184-7.)

When the first of January dawned, it seemed still doubtful whether emancipation would really be proclaimed, as promised. The Tremont Temple, in Boston, was occupied all day by Abolitionists, who waited, hour after hour, hoping that the news would come. Among the speakers in the afternoon was Frederick Douglass, who declared that if free discussion of slavery had been allowed thirty years before, it would long ago have been abolished as peaceably as in the West Indies. He thanked God that he had lived to see the beginning of the end of the abomination. Emancipation might not seem a success at first; but he was sure it would be so in the end. Laughter and applause accompanied his declarations of the capacity of his race. When the people met again in the evening, they were very anxious; for nothing had been heard of the proclamation. Would it come? Why was it delayed? He did his best to cheer the audience; and so did Miss Anna E. Dickinson, then at the beginning of her great career. There was only one voice that any one really wished to hear; and that was silent. Hour after hour came and went ; and the shadows grew deeper and deeper around every heart. At last, a man hurried in, his face glorious with triumph, shouting : " It is coming ! It is on the wires ! "

All the audience were shouting or weeping for joy. Soon the proclamation was read aloud from the platform ; and then Douglass led in singing a hymn with the chorus, " This is the year of jubilee ! " The people were unwilling to leave the hall at midnight, when it was to be vacated according to agreement ; so they adjourned to the church belonging to the colored Baptists. There they stayed, and he among them, until day broke. Their day of independence had dawned at last.

His position, during the past ten years, that slavery was not to be abolished by denouncing but by enforcing the Constitution, was fully justified by the wording of both proclamations. The September one declared that the war had been and would be " prosecuted for the object of practically restoring " the Union ; and in January, emancipation was announced " as a fit and necessary war measure for suppressing said rebellion," and as " an act of justice, warranted by the Constitution upon military necessity." Lincoln's paramount object was still " to save the Union, and not either to save or destroy slavery ;" but in order to keep the Union alive he had to strike slavery dead. Mr. Douglass has recently been told " that he was wrong and Mr. Garrison right ; that the dissolution of the Union was the only way to free his race." His answer is : " Had the Union been dissolved, the colored people of the South would now be in the hateful chains of slavery. No, no, it was not the destruction

but the salvation of the Union that saved the slave."
It was that very determination to keep up the Union,
whatever else might go down, which Garrison and
Phillips had for so many years been trying to get out
of their way. The stone which they rejected became
the head of the corner. Whosoever fell upon it was
broken ; and it ground slavery to powder.

McClellan's disasters were largely due to his refusing to shelter fugitive slaves, or even to pay proper
attention to their reports. Similar unwillingness to
take any steps toward emancipation, made the North
long delay to follow the example promptly set by the
South in enlisting colored soldiers. Nothing shows
more clearly the unreasonableness of the color-prejudice than its standing in the way of calling upon
the free negroes in loyal States to help crush the rebellion. No one who knew anything about the Revolutionary War, or that of 1812, to say nothing of the Ma-
roons in Jamaica, could deny the ability of negroes to
fight ; they were much better fitted to withstand the
Southern climate, than any other men who could be enlisted ; and the need of more troops soon became so
urgent that those Northerners who were not Abolitionists might reasonably have been expected to say, as
" Punch " thinks they did: " It's better using niggers
up than citizens like us."

Conscription of whites had actually been resorted
to by Ohio, and was about to be imposed upon all
delinquent States by Congress, when, in January, 1863,
a permission to raise colored regiments was given to
Massachusetts, which had offered them in vain five
months before. Too many fugitives had been returned
by our army to make their brethren eager to enlist.

Only a hundred recruits were obtained during the first six weeks; and Governor Andrew said to Mr. Stearns, " I am afraid we shall have to give up our colored regiments." " I will raise one for you," was the reply, " if you will authorize it." " And when will you set about it ? " " To-morrow morning ! " It was ten degrees below zero, when Mr. Stearns started before day-break, and went straight to Rochester. The first man whom he enlisted was Charles Douglass, and the latter's father promptly published in his " Monthly " an address, which is dated March 2, and runs thus :

"*Men of Color to Arms*." . . . " Action ! Action ! not criticism, is the plain duty of this hour. Words are now useful, only as they stimulate to blows." . . . " There is no time to delay. The tide is at its flood that leads on to fortune. From East to West, from North to South, the sky is written all over, ' Now or Never.' Liberty won by white men would lose half its lustre. ' Who would be free, themselves must strike the blow.' ' Better even die free than live slaves.' This is the sentiment of every brave colored man amongst us." . . . " I have not thought lightly of the words I am now addressing you. The counsel I give comes of close observation of the great struggle now in progress, and of the deep conviction that this is your hour and mine. In good earnest then, and after the best deliberation, I now, for the first time during this war, feel at liberty to call and counsel you to arms. By every consideration which binds you to your enslaved fellow-countrymen,". . . " by every aspiration which you cherish for the freedom and equality of yourselves and your children, by all the ties of blood and identity which make us one with the brave black men now fighting our battles in Louisiana and South Carolina, I urge you to fly to arms, and smite with death the power which would bury the government and your liberty in the same hopeless grave." . . . " We can get at the throat of treason and slavery through the State of Massachusetts. She was first in the War of Independence," . . . "first to make the black man equal before the law, first to admit colored children to her common schools; and she was first to answer with her blood the alarm-cry of the nation, when its capital was menaced by rebels. You know her patriotic Governor; and you know Charles Sumner. I need not add more.

" Massachusetts now welcomes you to arms as soldiers. She has but a small colored population from which to recruit." . . . " Go quickly, and help fill up the first colored regiment from the North.". . . " I will not argue. To do so implies hesitation and doubt ; and you do not hesitate : you do not doubt. The day dawns : the morning-star is bright upon the horizon. The iron gate of our prison stands half open, one gallant rush from the North will fling it wide open, while four millions of our brothers and sisters shall march out into liberty. The chance is now given you to end in a day the bondage of centuries, and to rise in one bound from social degradation to the plain of common equality with all other varieties of men. Remember Denmark Vesey, of Charleston : remember Nathaniel Turner, of Southampton : remember Shields Green and Copeland, who followed noble John Brown and fell as martyrs for the cause of the slave. Remember that in a contest with oppression, the Almighty has no attribute which can take sides with oppressors. The case is before you. This is our golden opportunity. Let us accept it, and forever wipe out the dark reproaches unsparingly hurled against us by our enemies. Let us win for ourselves the gratitude of our country, and the best blessing of our posterity through all time."

It was largely due to this appeal, and those made by its author to individuals, that Massachusetts was able to send out the regiment which Colonel Shaw led to plant our flag upon Fort Wagner, first in the attack. Among the foremost who mounted upon the rampart was Sergeant-Major Lewis H. Douglass,

shouting, "Come on boys, and fight for God and
Governor Andrew!" His sword was shot from his
side; but both he and his brother Charles have sur-
vived the contest.

Their father was on the wharf when they left Boston;
and he did his best to help them and their comrades
depart in a spirit worthy of the cause. As he spoke
in public, a day or two before, he actually chuckled
with delight at the thought that men of his color,
and even of his own blood, were at last going to
stand equal with the whites on the field of honor. It
was anniversary week; and he had been regularly
invited in company with Senator Wilson, to address
the Emancipation League at a meeting where he was
chief speaker. On the evening after the regiment
had departed, Thursday, May 28, he came without
special invitation to the annual convention of the
Garrisonians, where he was recognized by the audience, who called him out. He said he felt inexpres-
sible pleasure in taking his place once more on the
freest platform in the world, and added :

"Emancipation is coming; and another question appears.
What shall be done with the slaves? Where shall we, the
colored people, stand? Shall we be wholly free, and equal at
the ballot-box, at the jury-box, and at the cartridge-box? The
negro may at first be better able to do justice to himself under
white officers; but there are men in the Fifty-fourth capable of
command; and promotion should be opened to them."

Some of the other members of the convention
thought he ought to have insisted on having colored
officers from the start. His own view was the wiser
one, as may be seen from a more deliberate statement.

On June 17, 1863, the citizens of Philadelphia obtained leave to raise colored regiments under the supervision of Major Stearns ; and a mass meeting was held in that city on July 6, when urgent calls for volunteers were made by Judge Kelley and Miss Anna E. Dickinson. Then Douglass came forward to meet the objection made by his people, that t'.ey ought first to be put on terms of equality with the whites, as regarded pay, bounty, rations, and right to choose officers out of the ranks.

" There is " [said he,] " something deep down in the soul of every man present, which assents to the justice of the claim thus made, and honors the manhood and self-respect which insists upon it. I say at once, in peace and in war, I am content with nothing for the black man short of equal and exact justice. The only question I have, and the point on which I differ from those who refuse to enlist, is whether the colored man is more likely to obtain justice and equality, while refusing to assist in putting down this tremendous rebellion, than he would be if he should promptly, generously, and earnestly give his hand and heart to the salvation of the country in this its day of calamity and peril. Nothing can be more plain, nothing more certain, than that the speediest and best possible way open to us to manhood, is that we enter this service. For my own part, I hold that if the Government of the United States offered nothing more as an inducement to colored men to enlist than bare subsistence and arms, considering the moral effects of compliance upon ourselves, it would be the wisest and best thing for us to enlist."

He then compared the attitude of the Jefferson Davis administration toward the negro with that then taken by the Government with which his hearers were " called upon to co-operate in burying rebellion and slavery in a common ground."

" Never since the world began was there a better chance offered to a long enslaved and oppressed people. The opportunity is given us to be men. With one courageous resolution, we may blot out the handwriting of ages against us. Once let the black man get upon his person the brass letters U. S., let him get an eagle on his button, and a musket on his shoulder, and bullets in his pocket ; and there is no power on the earth, or under the earth, which can deny that he has earned the right of citizenship in the United States." . . . " Do not flatter yourselves, my friends, that you are more important to the Government than the Government is to you. You stand but as the plank to the ship. This rebellion can be put down without your help. Slavery can be abolished by white men ; but liberty so won for the black man, while it may leave him an object of pity, can never make him an object of respect. Depend upon it, this is no time for hesitation. Do you say you want the same pay that white men get ? I believe that the justice and magnanimity of your country will speedily grant it. But will you be over-nice about this matter ? Do you get as good wages now as white men get, by staying out of the service ? Don't you work for less every day than white men get ? You know you do. But I hear you say you want black officers ? Very well ; and I have not the slightest doubt, that in the progress of this war we shall see black officers, black colonels, and generals even. But is it not ridiculous of us, in all at once refusing to be commanded by white men in time of war, when we are everywhere commanded by white men in time of peace ? "

Within a week after speaking thus, he was obliged, on his return home, to pass through the city of New York, while a mob of rioters against the conscription were murdering little children because they belonged to his race. On the first of August he wrote and published a letter to Major Stearns, which may be found in the " Life and Times " (pp. 382-4). Here he states that he had been obliged to decline an invita-

tion to speak at a meeting for promoting enlistments
at Pittsburgh :

"I must for the present leave to others the work of persuading colored men to join the Union army. I owe it to my long-
abused people, and especially to those already in the army, to
expose their wrongs and plead their cause. I cannot do that
in connection with recruiting. When I plead for recruits, I
want to do it with all my heart, without qualification. I cannot
do that now."

The original plan of using colored troops to garrison forts in unhealthy places, had not been followed.
They had been exposed in the open field to capture
by enemies, who had thus been enabled to carry out
the threat that negro prisoners should be sold into
slavery, if not slaughtered in cold blood. No attempt
at retaliation had been made by our Government;
and it looked as if, "The confiding colored soldiers
had been betrayed into bloody hands." He was soon
able to make this complaint at the White House,
where he also remonstrated against the delay in
rewarding colored soldiers with commissions, as well
as in making their pay equal to that of the whites.
In this last respect, justice was not done to the negro
even by a Republican Congress, until the Fort Wagner heroes had been more than a year under arms.
Douglass was so far satisfied with the goodness of
Lincoln's intentions, that he once more made up his
mind to get every black man he could into the army ;
and he accepted the offer of Secretary Stanton to
make him assistant to General Lorenzo Thomas, who
was recruiting troops on the lower Mississippi. A
commission as adjutant was promised, but it was
waited for in vain. Major Stearns went from his

work in Massachusetts and Pennsylvania to raise ten
regiments in Tennesee; but he resigned his commission, because, as he stated in March, 1864, "The Government has not kept its faith with the colored man
anywhere." Early that year, Douglass wrote him a
letter in which he speaks thus of his not having
joined General Thomas, the preceding fall : "I consider myself trifled with and deceived. How basely
have the black troops of Massachusetts been treated
by the General Government. The dead heroes at Fort
Wagner brought in debt for the shoes in which they
fought and fell!"

A full account of his interview with Lincoln is given
in his "Life and Times" (pp. 384–7): but it is interesting also to read what he said about it a few months
afterward. On Friday, December 4, 1863, he was
present at the Thirtieth Anniversary of the A. A.
S. S., which was held in Philadelphia, in a hall ornamented with the American flag and the motto, "Union
and Liberty." Many familiar speakers were heard
from the platform, and several comparatively new
ones. Among the latter was Senator Wilson, whose
speech was so well suited to the times that a demand
for three cheers was made by a colored man who had
sat hitherto silent on the platform. He was now recognized ; and as soon as the Senator had finished,
there were cries from different parts of the hall of
"Douglass! Douglass!" Then he spoke on the right
of the Southern negro to the ballot. During his
speech he referred to the time when he felt, on reaching Philadelphia, that he was rubbing against the wall
of his prison and could go no farther. Now he was
able to go back to Maryland, and even to Washington.

"I have been down there to see the President; and as you were not there, perhaps you may like to know how the President of the United States received a black man at the White House. I will tell you how he received me—just as you have seen one gentleman receive another" (great applause); "with a hand and a voice well-balanced between a kind cordiality and a respectful reserve. I tell you I felt big there." (Laughter.) "Let me tell you how I got to him; because everybody can't get to him. He has to be a little guarded in admitting spectators. The manner of getting to him gave me an idea that the cause was rolling on. The stair-way was crowded with applicants. Some of them looked eager; and I have no doubt some of them had a purpose in being there, and wanted to see the President for the good of the country. They were white; and as I was the only dark spot among them, I expected to have to wait at least half a day; I had heard of men waiting a week; but in two minutes after I sent in my card, the messenger came out, and respectfully invited 'Mr. Douglass' in. I could hear, in the eager multitude outside as they saw me pressing and elbowing my way through, the remark, 'Yes, d——n it, I knew they would let the nigger through,' in a kind of despairing voice—a Peace Democrat, I suppose." (Laughter.) "When I went in, the President was sitting in his usual position, I was told, with his feet in different parts of the room, taking it easy." (Laughter.) "Don't put this down, Mr. Reporter, I pray you; for I am going down there again to-morrow." (Laughter.) "As I came in and approached him, the President began to rise" (laughter), "and he continued rising, until he stood over me" (laughter); "and reaching out his hand, he said, 'Mr. Douglass, I know you; I have read about you, and Mr. Seward has told me about you;' putting me quite at ease at once.

"Now, you will want to know how I was impressed by him. I will tell you that, too. He impressed me as being just what every one of you have been in the habit of calling him—an honest man." (Applause.) "I have never met with a man who, on the first blush, impressed me more entirely with his sincerity, with his devotion to his country, and with his determin-

ation to save it at all hazards." (Applause.) "He told me,
(I think he did me more honor than I deserve,) that I had made
a little speech somewhere in New York and it had got into
the papers, and among the things I had said was this: that
if I were called upon to state what I regarded as the most sad
and most disheartening feature in our present political and military situation, it would not be the various disasters experienced
by our armies and our navies, on flood and field, but it would
be the tardy, hesitating, vacillating policy of the President
of the United States. And the President said to me, 'Mr.
Douglass, I have been charged with being tardy, and the like;'
and he went on, and partly admitted that he might seem slow;
but he said: 'I am charged with vacillating; but, Mr. Douglass, I do not think that charge can be sustained; I think it
cannot be shown that when I have once taken a position I
have ever retreated from it.'" (Applause.) "That I regarded as the most significant point in what he said during
our interview. I told him that he had been somewhat slow
in proclaiming equal protection to our colored soldiers and prisoners; and he said that the country needed talking up to that
point. He hesitated in regard to it, when he felt that the
country was not ready for it. He knew that the colored
man throughout this country was a despised man, a hated
man, and that if he at first came out with such a proclamation, all the hatred which is poured on the head of the negro
race would be visited on his administration. He said that
there was preparatory work needed, and that that preparatory
work had now been done. And he said, 'Remember this, Mr.
Douglass; remember that Milliken's Bend, Port Hudson, and
Fort Wagner are recent events; and that these were necessary
to prepare the way for this very proclamation of mine.' I
thought it was reasonable, but came to the conclusion that
while Abraham Lincoln will not go down to posterity as Abraham the Great, or as Abraham the Wise, or as Abraham the
Eloquent, although he is all three—wise, great, and eloquent, he
will go down to posterity if the country is saved, as Honest
Abraham" (Applause); "and going down thus, his name may

be written anywhere in this wide world of ours, side by side with that of Washington, without disparaging the latter." (Renewed Applause.)

In speaking of this interview, at the Abolitionist Reunion, in 1890, Douglass said that Lincoln was plainly aching to get hold of slavery, and that after asking, " Who is this Phillips who has been pitching into me ?" he added, " Well, tell him to go on. Let him make the people willing to go in for emancipation ; and I'll go with them."

About this time he delivered, in the hall where the anniversary was celebrated, a lecture which was repeated in Boston, on February 10, 1864, and elsewhere during the winter. His subject was, " The Mission of the War ;" and among the opening sentences are these :

" I look for no miracle to abolish slavery. The war looms before me simply as a grand national opportunity, which may be improved to national salvation or neglected to national destruction." . . . " Our destiny is not taken out of our own hands ; and it will not do to shuffle off our responsibilities upon the shoulders of Providence." . . . " We seem to have been especially chosen to strike this last blow to relieve the world of slavery. We stand in our lot to-day and wage war, not merely for ourselves but for the whole world, for unborn generations and for all time."

His hearers ought to make up their minds that this " shall be, and of right ought to be an abolition war ;" that there shall be no talk of any but " an abolition peace;" that all the slaves, even in loyal States, " shall be at once declared unconditionally and forever free;" that they " shall enjoy the most perfect civil and political equality, including the right of voting and

being voted for ; that this Government shall oppose
all schemes for colonizing colored Americans;" that
the people ought to pay them equal wages and give
them "an equal chance to rise;" and "that the freedom and elevation of white men are neither subserved
nor purchased by the degradation of black men, but
the contrary." . . . "I warn the Union party now,
as at the beginning of the war, that if they win they
are to do so with the aid of their black cards."

Two colored men who had been free before the
war, in New Orleans, and had rendered much aid to
the Union cause, were sent as delegates in behalf of
their race to Washington, and were invited to a dinner at the Parker House, in Boston, on April 12.
About eighty leading merchants and lawyers met
them there ; Governor Andrew was in the chair ; the
John Brown song was sung; and Garrison spoke of
the nearness of the time when the equality of blacks
and whites would be fully recognized. Then the
chairman said, "There is one man here who recognized that equality for himself more than twenty-five
years ago. And now here sits 'the Douglass in his
hall.'" Three cheers were then given for Douglass ;
and he made a speech in which he used the words,
"We Anglo-Saxons," and added :

"I see there is some smiling at my placing myself so conspicuously among the Anglo-Saxon race ; but I do it on the
best Copper-head authority. I was down in Maine not long
ago, and made a speech there, which some of the Republican
papers thought very good to prove that the negro had some
ideas as well as other men ; whereupon the Copper-head journal came out—'Douglass ? Why that proves nothing for the
negro race ; his speech proves nothing ; Douglass is a white
man.' Since then I have sat on the other side of the house."

He took no part in the attempt, made soon after, to set up Fremont as the anti-slavery candidate, but did his utmost to secure the re-election of Lincoln. The latter sent for him that summer to help organize a plan, somewhat like that first proposed by John Brown, for persuading the slaves to come more rapidly into the Union lines ; but such schemes were soon rendered unnecessary by the progress of the war

On the evening of the day, when he voted for Lincoln and Johnson, he was passing through the streets of Rochester, when he met four half-drunken rowdies who knew him, and shouted, " Here he is, the d——n nigger." One of them caught hold of him ; but the Douglass flung him off, and then said, with uplifted arm, " Come on. I am ready to settle this thing with you, now and here." They slunk away ; and he went on to hear the news about the election. He was asked for a speech ; and he made merely this reference to what had just taken place : " The returns indicate that Lincoln is elected, and I am sure he is ; for I judge by the behavior of some men, on the other side, who met me a few minutes ago."

He had already declared that he " had rather be the most whip-scarred slave in all the South, than the haughtiest master," and in the lecture which he delivered that winter on " William the Silent," he said:

" The Red Sea ever lies between the pilgrim and the promised land. War, war, grim, stern, and terrible, seems to be the inexorable condition exacted for every considerable addition to the liberties of mankind. The world moves, but only by fighting every inch of its disputed way. Right and wrong seem equally endowed with fighting qualities ; and if one does not prevail, the other will." . . . "The line over which oppression may not go must be marked with blood, first or last, to be respected."

He went on to Washington to see the inauguration in 1865, and was sitting in the Senate Gallery near the close of the session, when a white man came in behind him, put his hand on his shoulder, and said roughly, "What is your name?" His first impulse was to reply sternly; but after a glance at the questioner, he said, "as gently as any sucking dove," "Fred Douglass, Sir." "What! the original Fred Douglass?" "The original Fred Douglass, Sir." "Oh," faltered the would be negro-driver, and sneaked out, amid a general titter.

As he said in his speech about Lincoln, in 1888 :

"I felt at that time, there was the spirit of murder here in the District of Columbia" . . . "I kept close to the carriage nearly up to the hub in mud, for I was afraid, every step we took, that something would happen to that good and glorious man. Well, when we got to the east portico of the Capitol, there I saw Mr. Lincoln in his true light."

It is to his confession, that it would have been just and righteous for God to permit the war " to continue till all the wealth piled up by two hundred years of bondage shall have been wasted, and each drop of blood drawn by the lash shall have been paid for by one drawn by the sword," that our orator refers, as he goes on to say: "Those words rang out over that throng; and they went over the country as never words went before; and they silenced all murmurs. They came down on the land like the summer's thunder-shower on the parched ground; and a new life began."

Just before the ceremony, he was pointed out by
Lincoln to Andrew Johnson, who gave him a look
which was plainly, as he said on the spot, not that of
a friend of the colored race. No one of that race had
ever ventured to attend a reception at the White
House, and no one would accompany him there the
evening after the inauguration. He made up his
mind to see that the rights of his race were recognized, and took his place in the long column which
entered the White House. At the door were two
policemen who seized him rudely by the arm, and
told him to stand aside, for their orders were to let
no one of his color in. It seemed to be only the
White House still. He assured them that he was
personally known to the President; and then they
offered to lead him in; but he was led into a passage by which visitors were moving out. As soon as
he saw the trick, he halted, and declared that he
should not leave until he saw the President. He was
soon able to send in word, and was admitted. Long
before he reached Lincoln, the latter, recognizing him,
said, in a loud voice, " Here comes my friend Douglass," and asked his opinion of the inaugural address,
which Douglass pronounced "a sacred effort." It
turned out that no such orders had been given : the
officers were merely following the old usage. " I
have found in my experience," says our author in
relating this incident, " that the way to break down
an unreasonable custom, is to contradict it in practice." (" Life and Times," pp. 405–7.)

Richmond was soon taken ; and there was a jubilee
meeting in Faneuil Hall, on Tuesday afternoon, April
4. Among the speakers were Robert C. Winthrop and

also the colored man, who twenty-five years before, while waiting behind his chair in New Bedford, had been so entranced by his brilliant conversation as almost to forget his duties. Now he had his full share of the applause as he said :

" I tell you the negro is coming up. He is rising, rising. Why, only a little while ago, we were the Lazarus of the South; the Dives of the South was the slave-holder. But now a change has taken place. That rich man is lifting up his eyes in torments down there, and seeing Lazarus in Abraham's bosom; and he is all the time calling on Father Abraham to send Lazarus back. But Father Abraham says, ' If they hear not Grant and Sherman, neither will they be persuaded, though I send Lazarus unto them; ' I say, we are 'way up yonder now, no mistake."

Eleven days later, he spoke at another meeting of a very different character, under circumstances which a friend who was present relates thus :

" Rochester Court-house never held a larger crowd than was gathered to mourn over the martyred Lincoln. The meeting was opened by the most eloquent men in the bar and the pulpit with carefully prepared and earnestly uttered addresses. All the time the people were not aroused. Douglass, who told me he should not speak because he was not invited, sat crowded in the rear. At last the feeling could be restrained no more; and his name burst upon the air from every side, and filled the house. The dignified gentlemen who directed had to surren- der. Then came the finest appeal in behalf of the father of his people, who had died for them especially, and would be mourned by them as long as one remained in America who had been a slave. I have heard Webster and Clay in their best moments, Channing and Beecher in their hightest inspirations; I never heard truer eloquence ! I never saw profounder impres- sion. When he finished, the meeting was done."

CHAPTER XII.

MUCH as the colored man was talked about by
members of all parties, he was not allowed to say much
for himself until after the war. Then the negro vote
became vitally important, not only for restoring the
South to the Union, but for maintaining the supremacy
of the Republicans. They have had no more loyal
adherents than the followers of Douglass. Hitherto
he had been nothing more than a corporal in a forlorn hope ; but now he was the general in command
of a great army of voters. He was right in saying
that Andrew Johnson was not the Moses of the
colored people, as he called himself, but only a would-
be Pharaoh. Their real Moses had carried them safe
through the Red Sea, and is still leading them to and
fro in the wilderness.

His possession of this foremost place is largely due,
of course, to his oratory, in regard to which Colonel
T. W. Higginson, who owes to him, in great measure, his defeat as candidate for a seat in the present
Congress, writes me thus : " I have hardly heard his
equal, in grasp upon an audience, in dramatic presentation, in striking at the pith of an ethical question, and in single illustrations and images, as ' For
the negro the Republican party is the deck ; all else

312

is the sea.'" He had shown himself a statesman
also, by choosing the very path which finally led to
emancipation. His firmness in this course, in spite of
the opposition of those who had been his best friends,
displayed such an independence of character as made
it impossible for him to be contented with merely following any one. His advice on practical matters has
been sound ; his treatment of difficult questions has
been so thorough, that a legal friend thinks he would,
with special training, have made an excellent judge ;
and he has never let any thought of personal risk or
loss come between him and his people's cause.

He proved himself fully aware of what that cause
really demanded, when he took part with Phillips,
Foster, Anna E. Dickinson, and Remond, in defeating,
by a vote of more than two to one, the attempt made
by Garrison, in New York, on May 9 and 10, 1865, to
dissolve the American Anti-Slavery Society. Its
object could not be said to have been attained, even
in the narrowest sense, until the adoption of the
Thirteenth Amendment seven months later ; and
nothing would have been better for the colored
people than to have had their champions keep up an
organization without political bias or party limits.

Three months later he wrote a letter, published in
the "Liberator" for September 29, and giving his
reasons for declining to act as an officer of the
"Educational Monument Association." This was a
plan for collecting money from white people, as well
as colored, to build a college exclusively for colored
people as a Lincoln memorial. He is decidedly in
favor of having his people show their gratitude to
Lincoln by erecting a monument with their own

money ; but this scheme looks to him " like an attempt to wash the black man's face in the nation's tears." . . . " I am for washing the black man's face, that is educating his mind," he says, but not for " sending around the hat to a mourning public." And then, again, " I am not for building up perma- nent separate institutions for colored people of any kind," but "am opposed to doing anything looking to the perpetuity of prejudice." . . . " When I go for anything, I like to go strong ; and when I cannot go thus, I had better not go at all."

The willingness of the whites to allow the colored people to continue in a degraded condition soon became so apparent, as to make him withdraw his opposition to associated efforts by his people under temporary emergencies. This change of view is expressly stated in his address on October 1, at the dedication of the Douglass Institute, in Baltimore. He could not but be grateful for having his own name given to a hall opened at the cost of $16,000, in the city where he had been a slave, by an association of colored men for the intellectual culture of their race and his. Such institutions were peculiarly needed ; because :

" It is the misfortune of our class, that it fails to derive due advantage from the achievements of its individual members." . . . " Wealth, learning, and ability made an Irishman an Eng- lishman. The same metamorphosing power converts a negro into a white man in this country. When prejudice cannot deny the black man's ability, it denies his race and claims him as a white man." . . . " The public has sternly denied the represen- tative character of our distinguished men. This makes it nec- essary for the credit of the colored people that they should keep up institutions, like this one, where they may feel themselves limited by 'no caste, or sect, or color,' where their souls may be thrilled with heavenly music and lifted to the skies on the wings of poetry and song. Here we can assemble and have our minds enlightened upon the whole circle of social, moral, political, and educational duties.". . . "Here may come all who have a new and unpopular truth to unfold and enforce" . . . " Here, from this broad hall, shall go forth an influence which shall at last change the current of public contempt."

This wicked feeling was encountered in the White House, on February 7, 1866, when a committee, appointed by a colored convention of delegates from twenty States, attempted to persuade Johnson to withdraw his opposition against granting the suffrage to freedmen, or even giving persons of every race and color full protection from the laws, especially in the form of power to enforce contracts, to inherit property, and to testify in court. Frederick Douglass, who appeared that day in company with his son, Lewis, reminded Johnson that he had power to bless or blast a whole race, and said : "Your noble and humane predecessor placed in our hands the sword to assist in saving the nation ; and we do hope that you, his able successor, will favorably regard the placing in our hands the ballot with which to save ourselves." The ex-slave-holder replied by comparing himself to Moses, and complaining of so great a hostility between the poor whites and the negroes as to make it impossible to let " both be thrown together at the ballot-box." . . . " The query comes right there, whether we don't commence a war of races." He also recommended the colored people to leave the country. His unwillingness to let any one talk but

himself, was so great as to oblige the delegation to
make their reply in print. They ask him : " How
can you, in view of your professed desire to promote
the welfare of the black man, deprive him of all
means of defense ? " . . . " Can it be that you recommend a policy which would arm the strong and cast
down the defenseless ?   Experience proves that those
are most abused who can be abused with the greatest
impunity.   Men are whipped oftenest who are
whipped easiest.   Peace between races is not to be
secured by giving power to one race and withholding
it from another, but by maintaining a state of equal
justice."   It is also shown that the blacks can never
" be removed from this country without a terrible
shock to its prosperity and peace," and that it would
be a national infamy for them to be " driven into exile,
for no other cause than having been freed from their
chains."   (" Life and Times," pp. 426-8.)

The House of Representatives had already proposed an Amendment to the Constitution, providing
that if any State should refuse to grant the ballot to
colored citizens, its number of Congressmen should
be reduced proportionately.   Douglass and the other
delegates published a formal protest against the
language, as implying the right of a State to disfranchise on account of color ; and they labored individually to impress this view upon the Senators.
Sumner and others declared that the Amendment did
not go far enough ; while all the Democrats thought
it went too far.   As first drafted, it was voted down
in the Senate, but was subsequently revived with an
introductory section which guaranteed full protection
to all persons, and forbade that the privileges of

citizens of the United States should be abridged by any State. This was all the people were then willing to grant ; and it was not until after violent opposition in New Jersey and Ohio, as well as in the White House, that the Fourteenth Amendment became part of the Constitution. The guarantee of the suffrage had to be left for the Fifteenth, which was adopted in 1870 ; but care was taken from the first, that no State which had seceded should be allowed to resume its functions until it had effaced the color-line from its constitution.

The final adoption of the suffrage amendment was largely due to the action of the National Loyalist's Convention, which met in Philadelphia in September, 1866. Douglass was appointed as a delegate by his fellow-citizens of Rochester, almost all of whom were white. They had previously offered to nominate him for Congress ; and Theodore D. Weld had come to the city to urge him to accept the honor ; but he had refused, on the ground that he should probably be defeated and his failure would injure the cause. He did, however, set out for Philadelphia ; but other delegates on the same train sent a committee to represent to him that his recognition, as a member, would fatally injure the Republican party at the elections for Congress that fall, and the good of his people's cause required him to give up going. He replied that they might as well ask him to blow out his own brains. The only result of his staying away, to the party, would be its condemnation for hypocrisy and cowardice. " But ignoring the question of policy entirely, and looking at it as one of right and wrong, I am bound to go into that convention ; not to do so would contradict the principle and practice of my life."

When he met with the other members at Independence Hall, where they were to organize for marching two by two through Philadelphia, he was very coldly received by most of the delegates ; but General Butler and a few others were cordial. He had been told the night before that he would not be allowed in the procession, lest it should be mobbed ; he was the only colored member, and it seemed likely that he must walk alone if he went at all. Theodore Tilton, then an influential editor, volunteered to take his arm ; and his presence in the procession called out nothing but applause. During the march he received a cordial greeting from the daughter of his former mistress, Mrs. Lucretia Auld. The convention was soon found to be fatally divided on the suffrage question, and the president finally declared it adjourned. It was at once re-organized, however, and earnest speeches in favor of enfranchisement were made by Miss Dickinson as well as by Douglass.

What the latter thought about the questions of the hour, may be judged from the following account by Miss Holley, of his speech the next summer :

"The first day of August, 1867, I joined a party of ladies and gentlemen to hear Frederick Douglass speak at Watkins, N. Y. It was an open air meeting, with an audience of two thousand people. When Douglass was demanding for the negro equality before the law, that government should know no distinction of color, no white, no black man, a man in the audience cried out, ' That's a damnable sentiment.' To which Douglass replied, ' Take care ; lest it damn you !' The negro had been thought ' a natural born Christian.' " " ' If you smite him on one cheek, he will turn the other also ; ' but the war had shown he would fight. He was philosopher enough not to fight when he had no reasonable prospect of whipping anybody. Douglass liked people who would fight—didn't admire sheep-like natures. Fighting was the most respectable thing in the country. The man who could fight the best was most likely to be President.

" The Copper-heads were saying all over the country that he was no negro. ' Then,' said he, ' as a white man I have no objection to negro equality before the law.' He did not believe it would lessen his chances for the Presidency! The negro would not refuse him his vote on account of his complexion. The negro race were in this country, and here they would remain ; it was inevitable. They would not wear out ; they would not die out ; and, now slavery is abolished, they would not fade out. The question was, should they remain as a blessing or a curse ? Those Democrats in the Constitutional Convention at Albany, laboring to keep equal rights from the negro by urging a separate vote on the suffrage amendment, were trying to preserve the accursed system of slavery. He spoke of white-coated Greeley and the noble character of Gerrit Smith being thrust between miserable Jeff. Davis and the honest, hot indignation of the North. Douglass did not like it ; did not think we ought to forget what Jeff. Davis had done ; his release was an outrage. Douglass believed the Almightly gave us memory for a purpose—to remember just such things. Even Christianity did not ask us to forgive without repentance. Douglass didn't wish to forget Andersonville, Belle Isle, Libby Prison. All over the country, on the cars and in steamboats, in city streets, in private homes, he met wounded and crippled soldiers, maimed and marred, armless, legless men, marks of Jeff. Davis's crime and malignant character. A government that don't hate traitors, can't love loyal men. This Government does not know how to punish traitors. A man who loves liberty strongest and best is the one who hates and detests slavery and treason the worst. The negro owes nothing to the Republican party, nothing to the popular religion of this country. Douglass thought this Government had as much reason to be grateful to the negro, as the negro had to be grateful to this Government. Abraham Lincoln did not let the oppressed go free until the safety of this Government demanded it. Like Pharaoh of old, it was the awful suffering that came upon him. Emancipation was owing to the irresistible logic of events. The negro owed gratitude and thanks to Almighty God.

"Douglass then introduced his newly arrived, dear brother, Perry, from whom he had been separated forty years. He had often tried to find him; had sent agents down South again and again, but never could get any trace of him. Slavery hid him away forty years—whelmed him in its loathsome, bitter flood. He spoke of his unspeakable joy in his being restored to him again. The sight of those two long-parted brothers standing side by side—one with his culture and courage, the other in his truth and affection—moved the audience to tears. It seemed a picture for an artist. It was the first time Perry ever heard Frederick make a public speech; it was a great event to him. Perry said he was in Texas when emancipation was proclaimed, and overheard his master say he had run his property into Texas and then he could run it into Cuba. Then Perry said he knew something was wrong about master, and he made up his 'mind never to go on the water.' Perry was older than Frederick, and smaller and darker. He went to reside in Rochester near his brother. His honest face won interest and confidence at first sight, which his good-sense and religious trust confirmed."

Earnestly as the Douglass threw himself into the battle for the ballot, he was not indifferent to the sight of injustice anywhere. The outrages upon the Chinese made him accept them as sufferers from the same prejudices as his own people; and he undertook to defend both races by the same noble arguments. The lecture which he delivered in 1867 before the Parker Fraternity, in Boston, is entitled "The Composite Nation;" and he maintains that our ca-

pacity to become "the most perfect national illustration of the unity and dignity of the human family," is
largely due to our being "the most conspicuous
example of composite nationality in the world." In
Wales and the Highlands of Scotland, the people
boast that they are of pure blood and were never
conquered ; "but no man can contemplate them
without wishing that they had been conquered."
Only one-fifth of the population of the globe are
white, and are they to turn out the other four-fifths
everywhere ? " I know of no rights of race superior
to the rights of humanity." The Chinese are likely
to be even more difficult to deal with than the negro.
The latter "took his pay in religion and the lash. The
Chinaman is a different article, and will want the
cash." He "has notions of justice that are not to be
confused or bewildered by any of our 'Cursed be
Canaan' religion."

" Chattel-slavery, kingcraft, priestcraft, pious frauds, intolerance, persecution, suicide, assassination, repudiation, and a
thousand other errors and crimes have all had their defenses
and apologies. Prejudice of race and color has been equally
fortunate. The two best arguments in its defense are, first, the
worthlessness of the classes against which it is directed, and,
second, that the feeling itself is entirely natural. The way for
any people to overcome the first argument is, to begin to work
for the elevation of those they have deemed worthless, and thus
make them worthy of regard ; and they will soon become
worthy and not worthless. As to the natural argument it may
be said that nature has many sides. Many things are, in a
certain sense, natural, which are neither wise nor best. It is
natural to walk ; but should men, therefore, refuse to ride ? It
is natural to ride on horseback ; shall men, therefore, refuse
steam and rail ? Civilization is itself a constant war upon

some forces in nature ; shall we, therefore, abandon civilization and go back to savage life ? Nature has two voices : the one is high, the other low ; one is in sweet accord with reason and justice, the other is apparently at war with both. The more men really know of the essential nature of things, and of the true relation of mankind, the freer they are from prejudices of every kind. The child is afraid of the giant form of his own shadow ; it is natural ; but he will part with his fears when he is older and wiser. So ignorance is full of prejudice, but it will disappear with enlightenment. But I pass on. I have said that the Chinese will come, and have given some reasons why we may expect them in very large numbers in no very distant future. Do you ask if I would favor such immigration ? I answer, I would. Would you admit them as witnesses in our courts of law ? I would. Would you have them naturalized, and have them invested with all the rights of American citizenship ? I would. Would you allow them to vote ? I would. Would you allow them to hold office ? I would. . . .

" Our Republic is itself a strong argument in favor of cosmopolite nationality. It is no disparagement to Americans of English descent, to affirm that much of the wealth, leisure, culture, refinement, and civilization of the country are due to the arm of the negro and the muscle of the Irishman. Without these races, and the wealth created by their sturdy toil, English civilization had still lingered this side of the Alleghanies, and the wolf would still be howling on their summits. To no class of our population are we more indebted for valuable qualities of head, heart, and hand than to the Germans. Say what we will of their lager, their smoke, and their metaphysics, they have brought to us a fresh, vigorous, and child-like nature, a boundless faculty in the acquisition of knowledge, a subtle and far-reaching intellect, and a fearless love of truth. Though remarkable for patient and laborious thought, the true German is a joyous child of freedom, fond of manly sports, a lover of music, and a happy man generally. Though he never forgets that he is a German, he never fails to remember that he is an American. . . .

"But it is said that the Chinaman is a heathen, and that he will introduce his heathen rights and superstitions here. This is the last objection which should come from those who profess the all conquering power of Christian religion. If that religion cannot stand contact with the Chinese religion, or no religion, so much the worse for those who have adopted it. It is the Chinaman, not the Christian, who should be alarmed for his faith. He exposes that faith to great dangers by exposing it to the freer air of America. But shall we send missionaries to the heathen, and yet deny the heathen the right to come to us? I think that a few honest believers in the teachings of Confucius would be well employed in expounding his doctrines amongst us. . . .

"Let the Chinaman come; he will help to augment the national wealth. He will help to develop our boundless resources; he will help to pay off our national debt. He will help to lighten the burden of our national taxation. He will give us the benefit of his skill as a manufacturer and as a tiller of the soil, in which he is unsurpassed. Even the matter of religious liberty, which has cost the world more tears, more blood, and more agony than any other interest, will be helped by his presence. I know of no church, however tolerant, of no priesthood, however enlightened, which could be safely trusted with the tremendous power which universal conformity would confer. We should welcome all men of every shade of religious opinion, as among the best means of checking the arrogance and intolerance which are the almost inevitable concomitants of general conformity. Liberty always flourishes best amid the clash and competition of rival religious creeds."

support of Grant in 1868 election

Active support was given in 1868 by Douglass and other colored men to General Grant, not merely because he had been a firm friend to their race, but because his opponent had failed to put down the draft-riot, in which their orphan asylum was burned. A friend of mine was sitting in a parlor-car when the

porter came by, offering to embellish the boots of the
passengers with either a Grant polish or a Seymour
shine, whichever they might prefer.   " No," said she,
" when the colored orphan asylum was burned in
New York, that was a Seymour shine ! "

How fully Douglass shared this view may be judged
from the speech he made the year previous at Watkins, as well as from that which was delivered at
Arlington on Decoration Day, 1871, and which is
printed in his " Life and Times " (pp. 461-3).   It was
then that he said, " We are here to applaud
manly courage, save as it has been displayed in a
noble cause."

In 1869 he left Rochester, where he had resided
since 1847, and became editor of a Washington
weekly, the " New National Era," started for the
especial benefit of the colored people.   Their ablest
men contributed to it ; but it was not a pecuniary
success, either under his management or that of his
sons, to whom he handed it over in 1872.   It was
discontinued in 1875, after it had cost him nearly ten
thousand dollars.   Subsequent investments have
been more fortunate.

During his three years of editorship, Grant attempted to annex San Domingo ; and Charles Sumner maintained that the President had violated the
Constitution, by using our navy to keep in power a
usurper who wanted to sell his country, and also by
threatening to make war upon Hayti, which opposed
the scheme as dangerous to its own independence.
The measure failed to secure the support of our people, and our politics would certainly not have been
made any purer by the imposition upon Congress of

the task of governing a province in which there was scarcely a single native who could speak English or read any language. Douglass has favored the scheme as necessary to ensure a good government there ; and this he found, as he states in an unpublished lecture, to be " the opinion of the most intelligent men in the island." His visit was made on board of our man-of-war, the Tennessee, as secretary to a Commission composed of Senator Wade, Dr. S. G. Howe, and ex-President White, of Cornell. He was treated, as Mr. White informs me, with every honor by the Commissioners as well as by the naval officers ; but as they returned to Washington by a Potomac steamer, on March 27, 1871, he was forbidden a place at the supper-table, whereupon Mr. White and Dr. Howe refused to take one. This made it unfortunate that he was not invited to dinner with the Commissioners at the White House, though the omission did not seem to him so important as it did to Sumner.

He was appointed a councillor or member of the upper house of the legislature of the District of Columbia, soon after by Grant, who was indebted to him for the colored vote in 1872. He met the representations of Sumner and other friends of liberty, that Grantism had become synonymous not only with despotism but with corruption, by asserting that the Democratic party was still the negro's enemy. In the speech with which he opened the campaign in April, at New Orleans, he told a story of a man who was riding a mule that put its foot into the stirrup in its efforts to throw him. Then he said : " Faith, and if you are a trying to get on, it is time for me to get off." Thus Greeley was the saddle into which the Democratic party was trying to climb, and it seemed time to jump off.

The national colored convention at New Orleans "pretty largely agreed with me ; " and he continued to take an active part in the campaign until its close. His activity was not seriously interrupted by the burning, early in June, of the house which he still retained in Rochester—a loss especially to be regretted, because it involved that of the only complete files in existence of his "Weekly" and "Monthly." Many other materials which would have been of great value to history as well as biography, perished in the flames. Among the States where he appeared on the stump, that summer or fall, were North Carolina, Virginia, and Maine. New York put his name, as Elector at large, at the head of her ticket ; and the honor of carrying the electoral vote of the State to Washington was given soon after to a member of the race which had once been forbidden by law to handle an ordinary mail-bag.

Unwilling as Douglass was to follow even Sumner blindly, he never ceased to be grateful to the Senator who had been foremost in the battle for the oppressed. They dined together at least once a week, and were often seen walking arm-in-arm in the Senate Chamber. One man, who was sent there by Rhode Island, used to say, " When I see Fred Douglass come in among us, I am ashamed to be sitting in my place ; and it is not because I care anything for Sambo either." No white man at Washington cared more for Sambo then the Senator whom Douglass defended to the face of a President who called Sumner mad. He delights still to remember how his " No " in the Senate, " went up to the dome ; " and, even while opposing his views in the New Orleans convention, he said :

" There is now a man at Washington who represents the future, and is a majority in himself—a man at whose feet Grant learns wisdom. That man is Charles Sumner. I know them both. They are great men ; but Sumner is steady as the North Star: he is no flickering light. For twenty-five years he has worked for the Republican party, and I hope I may cease forever, if I cease to give all honor to Charles Sumner."

He has also said that, " As a man of integrity and truth, Charles Sumner was high above suspicion ; and not all the Grants in Christendom will rob him of this well-earned character."

The colored people of Tennessee now invited their leader to tell them what he knew about farming ; and he began his speech at their fair, at Nashville, September 18, 1873, by saying, " I have been all my life long doing extraordinary things for the first time some of which had been better undone." He proceeded to make many practical suggestions : for instance, that " the primary conditions of peace, purity, and order in your household," consisted in an " ample supply of wood and water." He reminded his brethren that the pressing question was " whether the black man will prove a better master to himself than his white master was to him." . . . " We are to prove that we can better our own condition." One way to do this is, " Accumulate property. This may sound to you like a new gospel. You have been accustomed to hear that money is the root of all evil, etc." . . . " On the other hand, property, money if you please, will purchase for us the only condition upon which any people can rise to the dignity of genuine manhood, for without property, there can be no leisure : without leisure, there can be no thought : without thought, there can be no invention : without invention there can be no progress."

On his way back from speaking thus, he and his son, Frederick, resisted an attempt to order them out of the cars ; and their success justified his words at the fair, " Our destiny is in our own hands."

His exhortations to his people to save money lost much of their effect in consequence of the failure, that fall, of the Freedman's Savings and Trust Company. This bank had been established in 1865 at Washington, for the benefit of the colored people, under the supervision of Congress. In 1872 it had thirty-four branches in various States, and had received more than as many millions of dollars in deposits. It had, however, made some bad loans ; and its president, Frederick Douglass, had said in a letter, dated April 30, 1871, " I have married a corpse." He finally felt it his duty to impart his suspicions to the Finance Committee of the Senate ; and they agreed with him that it was better to close the bank. I have heard that it might have weathered the storm, if no shock had been thus openly given to its credit. There is no doubt that Douglass acted to the best of his judgment in the interest of the depositors, whom he was bound to protect ; and it is difficult to see whether they would have lost more or less if he had acted otherwise. The result was unfortunate, not only to his own influence, but to that of the Republican party over the freedmen ; and these latter suffered by the conversion of an encouragement to industry and economy into a temptation to idleness and extravagance.

It is pleasant to turn from this disaster, and remember that this was the year in which he was elected a member of the lower branch of the District Legislature, and in which he first told how he had escaped from slavery. The story was going the rounds of the press in April, and that summer he wrote the John Brown lecture, which was delivered for the first time in Charlestown, Mass., on December 9, 1873. Six days later he was one of the speakers at the meeting held by the Woman Suffrage Association of New England, in Faneuil Hall, on the one hundredth anniversary of the Boston Tea Party.

The victory of the Republicans in 1872 was the most sweeping they have ever gained. Since then they have had only a small majority, or none, in the popular vote for President; but that year their majority of votes was about one-ninth. Grant carried thirty-one States, out of which only nineteen went for Garfield in 1880; and the change in the number of electors was from 286 in 1872 to the 185 of whom some were claimed by the Democrats in 1876. This falling off was largely due to losing most of the negro vote; and it is worth while to remember that this loss took place immediately after a great Republican victory, while not only the White House but the Capitol was in full possession of a party which had been doing its utmost to protect the freedmen against the Ku Klux, and while federal troops were upholding the candidates supported for governor and members of the legislature by the colored people of Louisiana, against the nominees of the "white man's party."

Why the negro lost the franchise, while his own party was at the height of power and doing its utmost to sustain him, may easily be imagined from what is said by the " first colored member of the Ohio Legislature and late Judge Advocate of the Grand Army of the Republic," Mr. G. W. Williams, in his " History of the Negro Race in America." Vol. ii, pp. 527-8.

" It was to be regretted that the negro had been so unceremoniously removed from Southern politics; but such a result was inevitable. The Government gave him the statute-book when he ought to have had the spelling-book, placed him in the legislature when he ought to have been in the school-house. In the great revolution that followed the war, the heels were put where the brains ought to have been. An ignorant majority, without competent leaders, could not rule an intelligent Caucasian minority. Ignorance, vice, poverty, and superstition could not rule intelligence, experience, wealth, and organization." . . . " It was an immutable and inexorable law which demanded the destruction of those governments. It was a law that knows no country, no nationality." . . . " But a lesson was taught the colored people that is invaluable. Let them rejoice that they are out of politics."

Douglass admits in the " North American Review," for July, 1884, that the colored voter had been carried " to an altitude unsuited to his attainments," and General S. C. Armstrong declares of the people for whom he is laboring that " Their present unfitness, as a class, to use their power is such that they will not be allowed, even in the States in which they have the majority, to assume political control." It was found necessary by a Republican Congress to disfranchise them, in company with the other inhabitants of the District of Columbia in 1874, and the

suffrage has not been restored there. Men who had
helped the freedmen to the ballot were bitterly disappointed at finding it used by unscrupulous white
adventurers, as a weapon for robbing tax-payers in-
discriminately. It is certainly a great pity that Congress did not keep within the line drawn by President
Lincoln three days before his death, when he suggested that "The elective franchise might be conferred on the very intelligent of the colored men, and
on those who served in our cause as soldiers." It is
particularly unfortunate to have had the power of
Mr. Douglass as a political leader weakened by disregard of his own principle, "The true basis of
rights is the capacity of individuals."

He did not falter in the faith declared in a letter
which was the only one selected to be read aloud at
the Centennial Celebration of the Concord Fight, on
April 19, 1875, and which rejoiced in our possession
of "a liberty in presence of which no privileged
classes of wealth or religion, race or color can long
endure." When he spoke soon afterward at the one
hundredth anniversary of the formation of the Abolition Society of Pennsylvania, he said : "I know of no
one period in the world's history for which I would
exchange the present." And he urged the need of
giving to the black man "knowledge to use his suffrage in such a manner as to preserve his own liberty
and the highest welfare of the Government." In a
speech to his own people on July 5, 1875, at Hillsdale, near Washington, he warns them "to be on their
guard against the swarm of white beggars who
sweep the country in the name of the colored race."

A few months earlier, he and other colored men

passed a resolution threatening that the South would be full of " rapine, blood, and fire," if the Senate did not pass the Civil Rights Bill, since found by the Supreme Court to violate the Constitution in giving to the national Government functions which belong to the States.

March, 1876, he spoke at a meeting got up nominally for serenading Senator Morton, of Indiana, but really for rebuking those Republicans who had refused to give a seat in either House of Congress to a mulatto, whose title and character were severely criticized by the independent press. That June the committee on credentials of the Republican National Convention reported against recognizing what was called " the Boss Shepherd and Fred Douglass delegation." IIis wish to have either Morton or Conkling nominated was not fulfilled ; and the zeal with which he took part in sending Butler to fight for negro suffrage in Congress, was soon repaid by the General's getting himself made Democratic governor of Massachusetts. Whatever we may think about the purity and wisdom of the Stalwarts, we must honor the motives which have made the Douglass follow their banner no less loyally after it ceased to float over White House and Capitol, or even to lead the march. And we can all agree with him " that person is at least as sacred as its incident, property." The only question about either is to what extent protection is the business of Congress.

CHAPTER XIII.

MARSHAL AND RECORDER.

No politician, who aimed at keeping the colored people subservient to his ambition, would venture to show as much dissatisfaction with their religious views, as was expressed at this time by Douglass. It is impossible to realize how independently he has thought, and how disinterestedly he has spoken, unless this point is made duly prominent. Before looking at him as a holder of office, we must know how high he stands above such a readiness to conform to received opinions, as has always been the shortest and easiest way to promotion and patronage.

Sympathy with recent movements in theology has deepened the impression made by what he calls the "pregnant and striking fact that American slavery never was afraid of American religion." We have seen how he treated some well-known texts at Nashville ; and in a lecture on "William the Silent," written near the close of the war, he said : "For whatever else we may be indebted to religion, we owe it nothing for the idea of religious toleration. Nothing is so imperious, exacting, unreasoning, and intolerant as faith, when it takes full possession of the human mind." His speaking of the passage of the Fifteenth Amendment, as due to "our common humanity,"

333

rather than to divine grace, called out so much
censure that he wrote in a letter to the " Washington
Republican," in June, 1870 :

" If the instigator of this sham trial, in place of getting up
these church meetings to try distant heretics like myself, would
honestly go to work, and endeavor to reform the character, manners, and habits of the infestering thousands of colored people,
who live in the utmost misery and destitution in the immediate
vicinity of Big Bethel, he would do more to prove his church
sound than by passing any number of wordy resolutions about
thanking God."

Early in 1874 he took part in dedicating the hall
of the Free Congregational Society in Florence,
Massachusetts, and spoke very plainly about the faith
in which he had lived while a slave.   Soon after, he
was invited to speak before the Free Religious Association in Boston, in company with its president, Rev.
O. B. Frothingham, Mr. F. E. Abbot, of the " Index,"
Colonel Higginson, Dr. Bartol, and Rabbi Sonne-
schein.   His letter, which was published in company
with one from the founder of the Brahmo Somaj, is
as follows :

"WASHINGTON, D. C., May 15, 1874.
" *Dear Mr. Potter :—*
" I have delayed attention to your kind invitation thus long in
the hope of being able at last to return you an affirmative
answer, but circumstances are against me.   I cannot be present
at your Free Religious Convention in Boston. This is, of course,
of smaller consequence to others than to myself, for I should
come more to hear than be heard.   Freedom is a word of
charming sound, not only to the tasked and tortured slaves who
toil for an earthly master, but for those who would break the
galling chains of darkness and superstition.   Regarding the

Free Religious movement as one for light, love, and liberty, limited only by reason and human welfare, and opposed to the works of those who convert life and death into enemies of human happiness, who people the invisible world with ghastly task-masters, I give it hearty welcome. Only the truth can make men free, and I trust that your convention will be guided in all its utterances by its light and feel its power. I know many of the good men and women who are likely to assemble with you, and I would gladly share with them the burden of reproach which their attacks upon popular error will be sure to bring upon them. Very truly yours,

"FREDERICK DOUGLASS."

His letters to friends furnish these passages :

" I once had a large stock of hope on hand, but like the sand in the glass, it has about run out. My present solace is in the cultivation of religious submission to the inevitable, in teaching myself that I am but a breath of the Infinite, perhaps not so much. I was very sorry not to be able to attend the Free Relig-ious Convention in Boston last week. I shall hereafter try to know more of these people." . . . "I sometimes (at long inter-vals) try my old violin ; but after all, the music of the past and of imagination is sweeter than any my unpracticed and unskilled bow can produce. So I lay my dear, old fiddle aside, and listen to the soft, silent, distant music of other days, which, in the hush of my spirit, I still find lingering somewhere in the mysteri-ous depths of my soul."

The most complete utterance of his views is a lec-ture which was delivered before the Bethel Literary and Historical Society in Washington, and has not been published. The subject is the saying, incor-rectly credited to Galileo, "It Moves." Among the opening sentences are these :

" I do not know that I am an evolutionist, but to this extent I am one. I certainly have more patience with those who trace mankind upward from a low condition, even from the lower animals, than with those who start him at a high point of perfection and conduct him to a level with the brutes. I have no sympathy with a theory that starts man in heaven, and stops him in hell." . . . "An irrepressible conflict, grander than that described by the late William H. Seward, is perpetually going on. Two hostile and irreconcilable tendencies, broad as the world of man, are in the open field; good and evil, truth and error, enlightenment and superstition."

Another passage I quote at some length, because it is decidedly the ablest I know of on this side.

" It may not be a useless speculation to inquire whence comes the disposition or suggestion of reform, whence that irresistible power that impels men to brave all the hardships and dangers involved in pioneering an unpopular cause. Has it a natural or a celestial origin? Is it human, or is it divine, or is it both? I have no hesitation in stating where I stand in respect of these questions. It seems to me that the true philosophy of reform is not found in the clouds, in the stars, nor anywhere else outside of humanity itself. So far as the laws of the universe have been discovered and understood, they seem to teach that the mission of man's improvement and perfection has been wholly committed to man himself. He is to be his own savior or his own destroyer. He has neither angels to help him, nor devils to hinder him. It does not appear from the operation of these laws, nor from any trustworthy data, that divine power is ever exerted to remove any evil from the world, how great soever it may be. Especially does it never appear to protect the weak against the strong, the simple against the cunning, the oppressed against the oppressor, the slave against his master, the subject against his king, or one hostile army against another, although it is usual to pray for such interference, and also for the conquerors to thank God for the victory, though such thanksgiving assumes that the Heavenly Father is always with the strong and against the weak, and with the victors against the vanquished. No power in nature asserts itself to save even innocence from the consequences of violated law. The babe and the lunatic perish alike when they throw themselves down, or by accident fall, from a sufficient altitude upon sharp and flinty rocks beneath, for this is the fixed and unalterable penalty for the transgression of the law of gravitation. The law in all directions is imperative and inexorable, but beneficial with all. Though it accepts no excuses, grants no prayers, heeds no tears, but visits all transgressors with cold and iron-hearted impartiality, its lessons, on this very account, are all the more easily and certainly learned. If it were not thus fixed, inflexible, and immutable, it would always be a trumpet of uncertain sound, and men could never depend upon it, nor hope to attain complete and perfect adjustment to its requirements, because what might be in harmony with it at one time, would be discordant with it at another. Or if it could be propitiated by prayers or other religious offerings, the ever shifting sands of piety or impiety would take the place of law, and men would be destitute of any standard of right, any test of obedience, or any stability of moral government.

The more thoughtful among orthodox believers concede that the laws appertaining to matter are unchangeable and eternal. They have ceased to pray for rain or for clear weather, but to save something from the wreck which this admission must make in their theological system, they except the spiritual nature of man from the operation of fixed and unchangeable law. But, plainly enough, they gain nothing by this distinction. If the smallest particle of matter in any part of the universe is subject to law, it seems to me that a thing so important as the moral nature of man cannot be less so. It may be further objected to the orthodox view of this question, that, in effect, it does away with moral and spiritual law altogether, and leaves man without any rule of moral and spiritual life. For where there is no law, there can be no transgression, and hence no penalty. This is not the only difficulty in the way of our acceptance of the common theology, and where it manifestly stands in contradiction to sound reason. If they admit that there are moral laws, but affirm that the consequences of their violation may all be removed by a prayer, a sigh, or a tear, the result is about the same as if there were no law.   Faith, in that case, takes the place of law, and belief, the place of life.   A man, on this theory, has only to believe himself pure and right, a subject of special divine favor, and he is so.   Absurd as this position is to some of us, it is, in some vague way, held by the whole Christian world about us, and Christians must cling to it, or give up the entire significance of their prayers and worship.   I discard this office of faith for many reasons.   It seems to me that it strikes at the fundamental principle of all real progress, and ought, by some means or other, to be removed from the minds of men.   I think it will be found that all genuine reform must rest on the assumption that man is a creature of absolute, inflexible law, moral and spiritual; and that his happiness and well-being can only be secured by discovery and perfect obedience to such laws."

In 1875 he protested against making a white man, who was secretary of the American Missionary Association, president of Howard University, in place of some black man who would keep the institution unsectarian ; and five years later he spoke thus to his own people, as may be seen from the last page of his " Life and Times : " " My hope for the future of my race is further supported by the rapid decline of an emotional, shouting, and thoughtless religion. Scarcely in any direction can there be found a less favorable field for mind or morals than where such a religion prevails." . . . "Its tendency is to substitute faith for virtue, and is a deadly enemy to our progress."   He spoke at the May meeting of the F. R. A., in 1883, when he remarked that he supposed he had been invited merely to give a color to the occasion. In "Harper's Weekly," that year, for December 8, there is an article in which he speaks of " The Condition of

the Freedmen," in language which he had also used
in a speech at Topeka, Kansas. He is satisfied of the
existence of " a visible and growing improvement,"
both as to honesty and chastity ; and this he attributes largely to the fact that " The old, emotional
camp-meeting religion is subsiding among them, and
thought is taking the place of feeling." " These old-
fashioned preachers," he adds, " minister to passion,
decry the intellect, and induce contentment in ignorance and stupidity, and hence are a hinderance to progress." The young people who have learned to read
and write have no further use for " the old, cast-off,
theological hats and coats of fifty years ago." . . .
" It is evident that morals and manners have gained
by the change, and will continue to gain as the lamp
of knowledge grows bright among them." Busts of
Strauss and Feuerbach ornament his study ; and
when, as he was about to go to Hayti, in 1889, a
handsome Bible was presented to him by a colored
congregation in Washington, he took care, while receiving the gift with the utmost cordiality, not to
touch on topics which he had been able to handle in
the orthodox way, on a similar occasion forty-two
years before.

Nothing which he said about theology or politics
seems to have created so much excitement in Washington, as a lecture delivered there in 1875, and entitled " Our National Capital." He begins by referring to the ill success of his " William the Silent," as
a reason for speaking of what he knows from observation. Then come amusing pictures of the native-
born Washingtonian gentleman, the local white
trash, the spoilsmen from abroad, and the member of

Congress, who "has two cats in his room and only one mouse in his closet, who gives a constituent a letter of recommendation for a position, and then runs ahead of him by another street to say that what he has written was only for buncombe and should receive no attention." He himself has been "usually approached by the dark side of our fellow-citizens," or else by white men who tell wonderful things about what they or their fathers did when it cost something to be known as an Abolitionist. "Through this class I have learned that there were a great many more underground-railroad stations at the North, than I ever dreamed of in the time of slavery, and when I sorely needed one myself." "Every man in Washington," he says, "is assigned to one of two classes: the class which is used by everybody, or the class that uses everybody." He also complains of the lack of business energy, which has made this perhaps the only city in the United States, where land has been worth no more for fronting on a navigable river. But his severest censures fall upon the cruelty with which horses and mules are treated by negro drivers without rebuke. He concludes by acknowledging that, besides improving in many other ways, "Washington, from being one of the most oppressive and illiberal cities of the Union toward the colored race, has now become one of the most enlightened and liberal."

Nothing in this lecture prevented the people of the District from coming by the thousand to hear the oration which he delivered, in the presence of the President, the Cabinet, Judges of the Supreme Court, Senators and Representatives, at Washington, on April

14, 1876, at the unveiling of the freedmen's statue of Lincoln. This has been called his ablest work. It is printed in full in the appendix to ".Life and Times," as well as in a separate pamphlet, and is more remarkable for uniform elevation of view and impartiality of judgment, than for exceptionally brilliant passages.

According to the system of rewarding fidelity to party with appointment to office, his claim was strong; and a letter of April 2, 1873, mentions the possibility, but remarks that, "The honor would be the main consideration in any case, for it is not likely that any salary would be paid me as far above my expenses as I can make my income by lecturing." Hayes had scarcely been counted in and inaugurated, when he withdrew the federal troops from South Carolina and Louisiana. Public opinion has sanctioned this measure; but there was danger that the colored people might think their interests overlooked ; and their foremost representative was accordingly given the honorable and lucrative office of marshal of the District. The "Nation" speaks of the appointment as "picturesque but not reformatory." The local lawyers tried to have it rejected by the Senate ; but a confirmation was promptly secured by Conkling, on March 18. The opposition revived a month or two later, when the marshal ventured, while complying with an invitation to be present at the opening of the international exhibition, which followed the Centennial one in Philadelphia, to deliver the lecture on Washington in Douglass Hall, Baltimore. The news, that they had been made fun of before a negro audience in Baltimore, was too much for the Washingtonians. Their papers were in " a tempest of passion," as may be

seen from the letter, in justification of the lecture, in
the Autobiography (pp. 469–71). Very few of either
the white or the colored people of the District dared
to say a word for the lecturer ; his bondsmen were
urgently solicited to withdraw their names, and thus
disqualify him ; President Hayes received petition
after petition for removal ; but the Marshal retai .ed
his place.

He was not allowed to introduce guests at the
White House on state occasions, which had been done
by his predecessors under Grant and Lincoln ; and
he was urged by some colored friends to resign on
this account ; but he refused to do so. He has, I
think, fully justified himself by urging that the privilege was no part of the functions and duties conferred upon him by law, but merely a usage of so
recent origin, that a President might alter it without
giving offense ; and he does not consider that he was
personally slighted by Mr. or Mrs. Hayes.

He had found himself on his appointment "in a perfect snow-storm of letters of congratulation." Then
came a swarm of applicants for office ; and a son of
his old master was among the seekers for a place
under him. He writes that, "I have more than fifty
cats for one mouse, and I am tired of saying ' no.' "
One of his deputies, Colonel Perry H. Carson, tells
me that he worked like a tiger, and was on the spot
early and late. He kept the office long enough to be
present at Garfield's inauguration ; but not long
enough to have Guiteau in custody ; and he did not
take part in putting any one to death.

Early in 1878 he was invited by a colored friend to
revisit St. Michael's, where he had been a slave. His

old master, Thomas Auld, was then very sick, but
sent a messenger for him. As he came to the
bedside and was addressed as " Marshal Douglass,"
he replied, " not Marshal, but Frederick to you as
formerly." They shook hands ; the sick man burst
into tears ; and both were for a while speechless.
Then it was that Douglass asked what he now thought
of his slave's running away. After a moment's hesitation, the answer came, " Frederick, I always knew
you were too smart to be a slave, and in your place
I should have done as you did." " Captain Auld,"
was the reply, " I am glad to hear you say this. I did
not run away from you, but from slavery." He also
admitted, as already mentioned, that he had been
mistaken in one of the charges made in his first book ;
but not that he had done him injustice knowingly.

This visit to St. Michael's took place shortly before
Decoration Day, 1878, when he spoke from the Stal-
wart standpoint in Union Square, New York City,
and did not forget to refer to " the old Bay State, the
heart and brain of New England, the home of Sumner, Andrew, and Wilson." Passages have been
already quoted from his addresses at a meeting held in
Washington, on June 3, 1879, in memory of William
Lloyd Garrison. During that same month the people
of Rochester placed a marble bust of " her most distinguished citizen," in the hall of her University.

A serious difference in opinion among leading
colored men was brought about by a general emigration of their people in Mississippi, Louisiana, and
other States, Northward and Westward. The fact
that this exodus began in February, 1879, when there
was peculiarly little excitement about politics, shows

that the chief cause was not Democratic intimidation, but financial distress. The freedman found, after settling accounts with planters and store-keepers at the end of the year, that he was not getting fair pay for his work. The emigrants testified, to quote the words of Marshal Douglass, that :

"Work as hard, faithfully, and constantly as they may, live as plainly and as sparingly as they may, they are no better off at the end of the year than at the beginning. They say that they are the dupes and victims of cunning and fraud in signing contracts which they cannot read and cannot fully understand; that they are compelled to trade at stores owned in whole or in part by their employers; and that they are paid with orders and not with money. They say that they have to pay double the value of nearly everything they buy; that they are compelled to pay a rental of ten dollars a year for an acre of ground that will not bring thirty dollars under the hammer; that land-owners are in league to prevent land-owning by negroes; that when they work the land on shares they barely make a living; that outside the towns and cities no provision is made for education, and, ground down as they are, they cannot themselves employ teachers to instruct their children."

How much poverty had to do with this emigration is plain from such facts as that thousands landed from steamers at St. Louis without any money for going further, and that two-thirds of the sixty thousand, who reached Kansas during twelve months, were pitiably destitute, and had to have an association organized for their relief. There were comparatively few of these refugees at Washington; but their condition was so deplorable, that Douglass lost no time in appealing to his friends for money. Among those who responded liberally was Mrs. Elizabeth Thompson, who has presented our nation with Carpenter's

picture of the "Signing of the Emancipation Proclamation," and expended large sums for many other
worthy objects.

The same spirit of philanthropy, which made
Marshal Douglass quick to relieve the sufferings of
the emigrants, made him slow to recommend those
who remained behind to follow them.   Other colored
orators expatiated on the advantages of just laws, impartial tribunals, free suffrage, high wages, and advanced civilization at the North.   How he replied in
half a dozen speeches, may be seen from the paper
which was read at Saratoga, on September 12, 1879,
before the American Social Science Association.   It
is reprinted fully in their journal, for May, 1880, and
with some omissions in his "Life and Times."   He
begins by stating the great fact that, "The prosperity
and civilization of the South are at the mercy of the
hated and despised negro."   He is so perfectly adapted
to the climate that "For him, as a Southern
laborer, there is no competitor or substitute."   Social
prejudices, as well as climate, keep whites from working in the South ; and the black man must always be
"the arbiter of her destiny."   He has begun to emigrate under circumstances described in a passage
already quoted in part.   But, when his friends at the
North are called upon to contribute funds for increasing the number of emigrants :

"It may well enough be said that the negro question is not
so desperate as the advocates of this exodus would have the
public believe ; that there is still hope that the negro will ultimately have his rights as a man, and be fully protected in the
South ; that in several of the old slave States his citizenship and
his right to vote are already respected and protected ; that the

same, in time, will be secured for the negro in other States.
. . . "The Fourteenth Amendment makes him a citizen,
and the Fifteenth makes him a voter.   With power behind him
at work for him, and which cannot be taken from him, the negro
of the South may wisely bide his time."

It is unfortunate for the colored people of the South
to have the North begged to give money to help them
emigrate ; for this encourages the belief that they are
not able to take care of themselves.   It involves a
surrender of their right to be protected where they
are ; it encourages a restlessness which would keep
them poor ; and it tempts them into regions where
they would have to compete with laborers much
better adapted to the climate as well as to the state
of society.   It is also to be remembered that "In the
South the negro has at least the possibility of power ;
in the North he has no such possibility."

"As an assertion of power by a people hitherto held in bitter
contempt ; as an emphatic and stinging protest against high-
handed, greedy, and shameless injustice to the weak and defenseless ; as a means of opening the blind eyes of oppressors
to their folly and peril, the exodus has done valuable service.
Whether it has accomplished all of which it is capable in this
particular direction for the present, is a question which may well
be considered.   With a moderate degree of intelligent leadership among the laboring class at the South, properly handling
the justice of their cause, and wisely using the exodus example,
they can easily exact better terms for their labor than ever
before.   Exodus is medicine, not food ; it is for disease, not
health ; it is not to be taken from choice, but necessity.   In
anything like a normal condition of things, the South is the best
place for the negro.   Nowhere else is there for him a promise
of a happier future.   Let him stay there if he can, and save both
the South and himself to civilization.   While, however, it may

be the highest wisdom under the circumstances for the freedmen to stay where they are, no encouragement should be given to any measures of coercion to keep them there. The American people are bound, if they are or can be bound to anything, to keep the north gate of the South open to black and white, and to all the people. The time to assert a right, Webster says, is when it is called in question. If it is attempted by force or fraud to compel the colored people to stay, then they should by all means go; go quickly, and die, if need be, in the attempt. Thus far and to this extent any man may be an emigrationist, and thus far and to this extent I certainly am an emigrationist. In no case must the negro be "bottled up" or "caged up." He must be left free, like every other American citizen, to choose his own local habitation, and to go where he shall like. Though it may not be for his interest to leave the South, his right and power to leave it may be his best means of making it possible for him to stay there in peace. Woe to the oppressed and destitute of all countries and races, if the rich and powerful are to decide when and where they shall go or stay."

This address was read at Saratoga, but not by its author, who thus lost the opportunity to defend himself against some criticisms which were made by Professor Greener, upon the views, as he says, of "the greatest negro whom America has ever produced."

The members of the Association agreed, for the most part, with the essayist. The exodus did not last long; and whatever attempts are made to renew it will be regulated by due attention to considerations which have been summed up thus by Douglass. "A negro in a snow-bank makes a ridiculous picture; the colors don't blend."

His efforts in the interest of all classes at the South were badly repaid by fire on October 14, 1879, when the barn on the estate to which he had just removed, on a hill over-looking Washington, was burned by some white trash, jealous of negro superiority. He felt for some time too insecure to sleep at night ; but he held his ground, and has long since ceased to be molested.

He was still popular enough among his own people to be chosen president of their convention at Louisville, in July, 1880, and he was prominent in that year's campaign, although his health had been bad ever since his return from San Domingo in 1871. On August 4, 1880, he made an effective speech at Rochester for Garfield against Hancock, who had, he said, promised more than he could perform, in pledging himself to execute the great amendments. " He has stolen our thunder, but will find it too heavy for him." The best thing in this speech is the hint to the colored people that, " With money and property comes knowledge and power ; what we call money is only stored labor ; a poverty stricken class will be an ignorant and despised class ; and no amount of sentiment can make it otherwise." He had given the same advice, three days before in that city, to a great concourse of his own people, met on what he rightly calls " the colored man's day," to remember gratefully how Great Britain became, " the mother of our abolition movement." This speech is, in great part, given at the end of " Life and Times," and the extract closes with his " hopes that that better day for which the more thoughtful amongst us have long labored, and the millions of our people have sighed for centuries, is near at hand."

He made a visit the next winter to Florida ; and there was such a rush of even the poorest members of

his race to see him that a hotel-keeper at Jackson-
ville asked him to use his influence to keep them out
of the parlor. "No," was the reply; "wherever I
am, they can come." On February 23, 1881, he was
back in Washington, delivering a magnificent eulogium on the star-spangled banner, as he presented the
flag given to the Roscoe Conkling Club of Boys in
Blue by the Senator whose name they bore.

The "North American Review," for April, 1881, has
an article on "The Color-line," by Marshal Douglass, who appeals, not only to his own experience in
Europe, but to that of Remond, Ward, Garnett, Bruce,
and others, in proof of the fact that there is "no
color-prejudice in Europe, except among the Americans who reside there." He saw none of it in our
own great men, like Lincoln, Seward, Chase, Hale,
Wilson, and Sumner ; its existence in this country
may be fully accounted for by the previous enslavement of the negro ; and the hatred against him is so
much like that against the Jews in Berlin, Irishmen
in London, Christians in Constantinople, and China-
men in San Francisco, or like the intolerance once
felt by Catholics against Protestants, that " We may
well enough affirm that this prejudice really has
nothing whatever to do with race or color." " The
color is innocent enough," he adds, "but things
coupled with it make it hated. Slavery, ignorance,
stupidity, servility, poverty, dependence, are undesirable conditions. When these cease to be coupled
with color, there will be no color-line drawn." . . .
"Prejudice of race and color is only natural in the
sense that ignorance, superstition, bigotry, and vice
are natural." . . . "It has no better defense than

they, and should be despised and put away from human relations as an enemy to the peace, good order, and happiness of human society."

His term as marshal expired in 1881, and in May of that year he was appointed to a lucrative office, exacting but little personal labor, that of Recorder of Deeds for the District of Columbia. On decoration day soon after, he delivered an address on John Brown, at Harper's Ferry before the members of the colored college in that town. On the platform sat the attorney who led the prosecution. "What an overturning, what wonderful progress, that I should be called upon to deliver such an address at Harper's Ferry," says an unpublished letter. On June 12, he revisited the Lloyd plantation in a revenue cutter, as is related very touchingly in the " Life and Times " (pp. 492–500) ; and in November he spoke at Easton, the county seat where he had been imprisoned in 1836, when he was led into town, with his hands tied, by the mounted constable who had arrested him for trying to run away. He presided on September 26, 1881, at a meeting of colored people held in Washington in honor of the President who was buried that day while the nation mourned. In his brief speech he mentioned as an instance of the greatness of the loss to his race, the fact that the assassination had prevented the fulfilment of a plan for " sending some colored representatives abroad to other than colored nations." He had himself been invited to take an important position of this kind, but had preferred to remain at home.

In January, 1882, the Park Publishing Company, of Hartford, issued the " Life and Times of Frederick

Douglass," written by himself, with an introduction by Judge Ruffin, of Boston. It contains a fine portrait, but the other illustrations are of little value. This book does not give so full an account of his life before 1843 as " My Bondage and My Freedom," but it is our chief authority for subsequent years. It is very interesting throughout and contains several recent speeches ; but the arrangement is not systematic.

In this year, on August 4, he lost his wife, and wrote to one of his friends, " The main pillar of my house has fallen."

We have seen him working with Father Mathew ; but he said this year at Providence, " While as a temperance man, I should be glad to see every grogshop in the land abolished, I am not inclined to adopt the prohibition doctrine." Of one of the leading organizations which support it, he said, on September 1, 1884 : " Though, as I think, it is manifestly wrong and abundant in mischief, its members are among the most conscientious and philanthropic of the American people." As he was going to one of the many places where he has been received with public honors, a colored man, who talked as fast as Dickens's Mr. Jingle, forced himself into his company and went with him to the house where he was to be the guest of a graduate of Oberlin. This must, he thought, be one of the committee ; but they supposed him to be some personal friend of their visitor. While the latter was brushing his hair, the Oberlin man came in with a bottle, saying : " I know nothing about brandy myself, but your friend says this is excellent." " Now, what do you suppose I want of brandy ? I never use it." "Why, your friend said you always did when you had been travelling." Exit Jingle.

The twentieth anniversary of Lincoln's proclamation was celebrated in Washington, on January 1, 1883, by a banquet given to Douglass by colored citizens of the United States. His speech dwelt on the great improvement made by the race in those twenty years; and he acknowledged this in the address which he made on the twenty-first anniversary of Emancipation in the District, April 16. On the latter occasion, he also declared that the colored people "cannot remain half slave and half free." "You must give them all, or take from them all. Discussion of their wrongs must go on until the public schools shall cease to be caste schools;" . . . "until the colored man's pathway to the ballot-box, North and South, shall be as smooth and as safe as the same is for the white citizen;" . . . "until the courts of the country shall grant the colored man a fair trial and a just verdict;" . . . "until color shall cease to be a bar to equal participation in the offices and honors of the country;" . . . "until the trades-unions, and the workshops of the country shall cease to proscribe the colored man, and prevent his children from learning useful trades;" . . . "until the American people shall make character, and not color, the criterion of respectability." In closing he said: "There is but one destiny, it seems to me, left for us, and that is to make ourselves, and be made by others, a part of the American people, in every sense of the word. Assimilation, and not isolation is our true policy." . . . "We cannot afford to set up for ourselves a separate political party, or adopt for ourselves a political creed apart from the rest of our fellow-citizens. Our own interests will be subserved by a generous care for the interests of the nation at large. All the political, social, and literary forces around us tend to unification."

He took the same hopeful tone as he began his address on September 24, to the National Convention of Colored Men, at Louisville, where he presided ; but he went on to say that such conventions are needed, because the colored man "is still surrounded by an adverse sentiment which fetters all his movements." . . . "His course upward is resented and resisted at every step of his progress." . . . "The color-line meets him everywhere, and, in a measure, shuts him out from all respectable and profitable trades and callings." . . . "He is rejected by trades-unions of every trade, and refused work." . . . "Not even our churches have yet conquered this feeling of color-madness." . . . "What is called lynch-law is peculiarly the law for colored people, and for nobody else." . . . "Our meeting here was opposed by some of our members, because it would disturb the peace of the Republican party." . . . "Depend upon it, men will not care much for a people who do not care for themselves." He then went on to recommend that Congress should investigate the working of the shop-order system, should aid common schools and endow colored colleges, should reimburse the losers by the Freedman's Bank, should do full justice to colored claiments of bounties and pensions, should enforce the Civil Rights Bill, and should protect colored voters at the polls. He added that in making these demands, "We leave social equality where it should be, with each individual man and woman. No law can regulate it." But he did call attention to the fact, that "We shall never cease to be a despised and persecuted class, while we are known to be excluded by our color from all important positions under government." In conclusion he said : "We hold it to be self-evident that no class or color should be the exclusive rulers of this country. If there is such a ruling class, there must of necessity be a subject class, and when this condition is once established, this government of the people, by the people and for the people, will have perished from the earth."

Scarcely had this address been delivered, when the Civil Rights Bill was pronounced unconstitutional by the Supreme Court, on the ground that Congress had no power to forbid discriminations, in public conveyances, inns, or theatres, on account of color, unless made in consequence of State legislation. Such legislation may be counteracted by Congress ; but where the laws are just it must be left to each State to carry them out, unless rebellion justifies federal interference. Douglass left points of law to be discussed by his friend, Colonel Ingersoll, and pleaded against the injustice of denouncing the measure as a "Social Rights Bill." . . .

"To say that because a man rides in the same car with another, he is therefore socially equal, is one of the wildest absurdities." . . . "Social equality is a matter between individuals. It is a reciprocal understanding. I don't think, when I ride with an educated, polished rascal, that he is thereby made my equal." . . . "If it is a bill for social equality, so is the Declaration of Independence ; " . . . "so is the Sermon on the Mount; so is the Golden Rule ; " . . . " so is the Constitution ot the United States ; and so are the laws and customs of every civilized country in the world ; for nowhere, outside of the United States, is any man denied civil rights on account of his color."

His marriage with Miss Helen Pitts, early in 1884, has done much to make his later years bright and happy. It was in her company that he attended the funeral of Wendell Phillips, on Wednesday forenoon, February 6, in the Hollis Street Church, where Miss Louisa Alcott sat between them ; and that afternoon he saw the eloquent champion of all the oppressed lie in state, guarded by colored soldiers, in Faneuil Hall. He had made a special journey in order to take part in paying these last honors ; and whatever differences in opinion had existed between them were entirely forgotten as he poured out his gratitude, in behalf of his race as well as of himself, in the address which was delivered soon after at Washington, and has been printed in the "Life and Times of Wendell Phillips," by George Lowell Austin, 1884. He has not lost sight of either the merits or the defects of Garrison. Never, from first to last, did he speak of Phillips except in a love too deep and warm to make criticism possible.

During the political campaign of 1884, the Jerry Rescue celebration was revived at Syracuse, in order to give a good opportunity for a Blaine speech by Douglass. The defeat of his party that year was afterward attributed by him to the fact, that, " It made national help more important and prominent than national purity ;" "appealed to the pocket and not to the heart of the nation," and was "loud for the protection of things, but silent for the protection of men." While speaking thus, on April 16, 1885, the anniversary of Emancipation in the District, he said: "The inaugural address of President Cleveland was all that any friend of liberty and justice could reasonably ask for the freedmen." . . . "No better words have dropped from the east portico of the Capitol, since the inauguration days of Abraham Lincoln and General Grant." Whether the party was as good as the President was another question ; but "Let it do justice to the negro, and it will certainly succeed itself in power four years hence and long years after." He added, however, that the Republican party was still that of the colored man ; and that their right to the franchise would be the chief issue in the campaign of 1888, unless full justice was done them previously. He spoke as a leader of his people at the dedication, in February, 1886, of a memorial to General Hunter, who had been one of the first to give them a place among our nation's defenders. The short article which he contributed to the "North American Review" for April in that year, on "The Future of the Colored Race," is delightfully hopeful and confident.

What his own relations were with Mr. Cleveland, is shown by a letter important enough to be given in full :

"WASHINGTON, D. C., April 6, 1886.

"HON. F. W. BIRD.

"*My Dear Sir :*—I am obliged by your note of yesterday, requesting me to state the facts connected with my removal from the office of Recorder of Deeds for the District of Columbia. I assure you that there was nothing summary or unpleasant about it. I am a Republican, and did all I could to defeat the election of

Mr. Cleveland. He was under no political obligation to me whatever; yet I held the office of Recorder nearly a whole year under his Administration, an office by law held not for any term but solely at the pleasure of the President. He could have removed me at his pleasure at any time after his inauguration. When he asked for my resignation, he simply asked me to set a time when it would be agreeable to me to tender it. I did set the time, and when that time arrived I sent in my resignation. His manner toward me was in every way courteous, and I have nothing whatever to complain of. While in office, President Cleveland treated me as he treated other office-holders in the District. He was brave enough to invite Mrs. Douglass and myself to all his grand receptions, thus rebuking the timidity—I need not say cowardice or prejudice—of his predecessor. I am a Republican, and if living shall do all I can to elect a Republican in 1888; but I know manliness wherever I find it; and I have found it in President Cleveland, and I should despise myself if I should let any one think otherwise. Whatever else he may be, he is not a snob; and he is not a coward. Yours very truly,

" FRED'K DOUGLASS."

CHAPTER XIV.

THE NATION'S PROBLEM.

RELEASE from the cares of office enabled Douglass to give his thoughts more fully than had recently been possible to such questions as, how his brethren are prospering at the South ; what they have a right to ask from the national Government for their more complete protection and education ; which party is doing them the best service ; and what steps ought to be taken for their relief by individuals outside of politics.

In the address which he made on April 16, 1886, in memory of the abolition of slavery in the District of Columbia, he mentioned the significant fact that the occasion was celebrated for the first time by the colored people in two rival gatherings. His own hope that negroes would be better treated after they had ceased to help the Republican party rule at the South, had been sadly disappointed. "Their condition seems no better and not much worse than under previous administrations. Lynch law, violence, and murder have gone on about the same as formerly, and without the least show of federal interference or popular rebuke." . . . "There have also been the usual number of outrages committed against the civil rights of colored citizens on highways and by-

358

ways, by land and by water; and the courts of the country, under the decision of the Supreme Court of the United States, have shown the same disposition to punish the innocent and shield the guilty, as during the presidency of Mr. Arthur." . . . "The truth is that neither the Republican party nor the Democratic party has yet complied with the solemn oath taken by their respective representatives to support the Constitution and execute the laws enacted under its provisions." . . . "Has any of our Republican presidents since Grant earnestly endeavored to establish justice in the South?"

Referring to the charge that "Negroes are by nature the criminal class of America," he said:

"I admit the charge, but deny that nature, race, or color has anything to do with the fact. Any other race, with the same antecedents and the same conditions, would show a similar thieving propensity. The American people have this lesson to learn, that where justice is denied, where poverty is enforced, where ignorance prevails, and where any one class is made to feel that society is an organized conspiracy to oppress, rob, and degrade them, neither persons nor property would be safe." . . . "While I hold now, as I held years ago, that the South is the natural home of the colored race, and that there must the destiny of that race be mainly worked out, I still believe that means can be and ought to be adopted, to assist in the emigration of such of their number as may wish to change their residence to parts of the country, where their civil and political rights are better protected than at present they can be at the South."

He had no sympathy with those colored men who wished to take an independent position in politics. "The Republican party is not perfect; it is cautious even to the point of timidity ; but it is the best friend we have."

He took the same ground on revisiting Boston, where, on Saturday, May 22, two days after delivering the John Brown lecture in the Music Hall, he was the guest of those leading Republicans who compose the Massachusetts Club. The dinner was at Young's Hotel, and he said :

" I have so seldom dined in my life, that I am at a loss to know how to make an after-dinner speech. I have heard say that such speeches should be witty ; and I am no wit. I have heard say that they should be short. I never made a short speech in my life with which I was satisfied ; and I don't know that I ever made a long speech with which anybody else was satisfied."

After expressing his wonder at finding himself in such company, and hearing no one say " Douglass, get out," he continued thus :

" I am sometimes asked ' How are your people getting along at the South ?' I am at a loss sometimes to know to whom they refer. Who are my people at the South ? I am in a position to speak more impartially, perhaps, than any man in this room as regards the merits of the two races, for I occupy a middle position." . . . " It would be as appropriate to ask, ' How are the white people of the South getting along ?' as to ask how the colored people are getting along. The two should go together : one cannot get along without the other." . . . " Men ask me if I don't think that the condition of the freedmen is hopeless. I tell them ' Never !' I have seen too much progress."

After referring to what had been suffered by his people and also by himself, he said, " Now, I look around in vain for anybody to insult me." He was, however, very desirous that much more stress should be laid, in the campaign of 1888, on the duty of the nation toward the freedman, than was actually the case. He deeply regretted the decision against the constitutionality of the Civil Rights Bill, and said : " I am one of those who pray to my God every day for a Supreme Court of the United States that shall be as true to liberty as ever Judge Taney was to slavery."

On Monday evening, May 24, he spoke at the Woman Suffrage meeting in Tremont Temple, and began with the words, " It is a long time since it was my privilege to address a convention of reformers in Boston." After referring to the opposition, which had been made to the speaking of women in public, he said :

" In bearing this cross, and maintaining this conflict, woman has risen in grandeur and glory, like the rainbow above the storm. In securing the right to think and speak, the right to use her voice and her pen, she has secured the means of victory in all other right directions; for speech is the lever that moves the world." He rejoiced in her attainment of a higher education and larger opportunities for supporting herself; and he held that " There is not one reason, not one consideration of justice and expediency, upon which man can claim the right to vote, which does not equally apply to woman." . . . " If the law takes no thought of sex when it accuses her of crime, why should it take thought of sex when it bestows its privileges ? " . . . " If man could represent woman, it follows that woman could represent man, but no opponent of woman suffrage would admit that woman could represent him in the government." . . . " Believing, as I firmly do believe, that human nature as a whole, contains more good than evil, I am willing to trust the whole, rather than a part, in the conduct of human affairs." . . . " What could be more absurd upon the face of it, than to pretend that to put woman on a plane of political equality with man, is to degrade her, when the whole argument for making man the exclusive possessor of the ballot is based upon his superiority to woman ? Does the possession of the suffrage degrade man ? If not, it will not degrade woman." He also remarked that if those people, who say women do not wish to vote, really felt sure of it, they would not take so much pains to prevent them from having the opportunity; and he also showed that two other objections, namely, that wives would quarrel with their husbands about politics, and that wives would merely follow their husbands, really answer each other. In conclusion, he urged that the suffrage would be " a vast advantage to woman herself. Her dignity and importance, as a member of society, would be greatly augmented. She would be brought into responsible and honorable relations with the government; her citizenship would be full and complete; and instead of being merely a subject, she would be a sovereign. And now I ask, what right have I, what right have you, what right has anybody who believes in government of the people, by the people and for the people, to deny to woman this full and complete citizenship ? What right have I, what right have you, what right has anybody thus to humiliate one-half of the human family ? "

Douglass now made up his mind to carry out purposes formed long ago, and visit not only France and Italy, but Egypt. Shortly before he left, he came to Boston as the guest of the Wendell Phillips Club, who gave him a dinner at the Revere House on Saturday evening, September 11, 1886. Among the other guests were those veteran Abolitionists, Dr. Bowditch, Oliver Johnson, and James M. Buffum ; and there, too, was the Democratic Mayor of Boston, in company with Judge Ruffin, Lewis Hayden, and other leading colored men. The chief guest opened his speech thus :

"If I have done anything for the colored people, it is in a great measure due to my having had the good-fortune, when I escaped from slavery, to become acquainted with William Lloyd Garrison, and with Wendell Phillips, and with our friend Oliver Johnson, and with Dr. Bowditch. The home of Dr. Bowditch, I may say, gave me the first shelter I received in this city. I have often been asked where I got my education. I have answered, from the Massachusetts Abolition University, Mr. Garrison, president."

He went on to say :

"I have been grieved at one thing, and I think we should set our faces against it. We are imitating the extravagancies of the white people among whom we are : and it is going on at a fearful rate. I meet with colored men on all sides smoking, and sometimes drinking. That is not the way to rise in the world. For my own part, I neither smoke, nor chew tobacco, nor take snuff, nor drink whiskey ; and I should be delighted if I could make the same statement with regard to my whole people."

In conclusion, he said :

"I shall take this demonstration of your club with me abroad, and if I have occasion to speak in England, (I am not going as an advocate,) I shall remember your injunction to extend your sympathy to all men oppressed ; and I shall not hesitate to declare my own entire sympathy with that grand old man, Mr. Gladstone, in his endeavors to remove the reproach of oppression from England and to extend the desired liberty to Ireland."

"My year's trip abroad," as he calls it in an unpublished lecture, led him, after looking once more at the Tower of London and Westminster Abbey, to France, where impatience at the way his baggage was treated "made me for the moment a free-trader." He spent two months in Paris, "a city of taste and terrors, of heroes and horrors, of beauty, barricades, and bottles." He was shocked at the non-observance of Sunday ; but he never met a single drunken or disorderly person on that day, which fact he attributes to the national character. No building impressed him so deeply as the church whose bell was the signal for the massacre of Saint Bartholomew ; and notl.ng gave him such pleasure as that utter absence of color-prejudice, which had surprised Dr. Bowditch more than fifty years ago. This Douglass says is " in part, because the negro has never been seen there as a degraded slave, but often as a gentleman and a scholar." He visited the grave of " a man whose great heart was broad enough to take in the whole world, and who, in my estimation ranks among the greatest of the human race," Victor Hugo. IIe praises the fine appearance of the law-makers, as well as the courtesy with which the members of that Senate treat each other. He was also pleased to see the horses driven without check-rein or blinders. He often heard Father Hyacinthe, and " was deeply impressed by his character and preaching," although he could not " understand all his words."

He was much struck by the relics, at Avignon, of the time when " Religion stood no such nonsense as what we call free thought." . . . " A difference of religion, in the days of this old palace, was sufficient to justify the utmost cruelty ; and difference of color to-day, in some quarters, is about the same thing. But light has dawned upon the papal palace of Avig-non." . . . " It is no longer the home of saints, but the home of soldiers." . . . " Martial law has taken the place of ecclesiastical law ; and there is no doubt as to which is the more merciful of the two." So, on reaching Rome, he found it "neither pleasant to the eye nor to the thought," to meet "the vacant, bare-legged, grimy monks, who have taken a vow neither to work nor to wash;" and he was much more inter- ested in the ruins of the past than in the ecclesiastical splendors of the present. Not one of the beautiful objects in Genoa held him so long as an old violin, that with which Paganini had played on the hearts of thousands as never man had played before. It was precious to Douglass, because it had been "the favorite instrument of the most famous musical genius of his time," and, "though silent and motionless now, could once, under the wonderful touch and skill of its master, fill the largest halls of Europe with a con- cord of sweet sounds, and cause even the dull hearts of courts, kings, and princes, to own their kinship to common mortals."

Egypt was a disappointment in some respects. He had to admit that her temples and pyramids were not built by negro kings; and it took him two weeks to recover from the terrible strain of climbing to the great pyramid's top. The grandeur of the prospect went far to repay him, however; especially the view over "the silent, solemn, measureless desert." He had already felt, in travelling along the Suez canal, "such a deep sense of unearthly silence, such a sense of vast, profound, unbroken sameness and solitude," as enabled him to understand how it was that Moses and the prophets, John, the Baptist, Paul, and Mahom- et thought God peculiarly near them in the desert, and became founders of new religions.

He also visited Athens, and had pleasant meetings

with his old friends in England and their children, before returning to Washington, where we find him on February 12, 1888, the seventy-ninth anniversary of the birth of Abraham Lincoln, telling how "he went up before his Maker with four millions of broken fetters in his arms." Of himself, he spoke thus:

"I came down here from the North; I was not born in the North; but I went North on a mission some fifty years ago. It was not healthy for me to come down here for some twenty-five years after I went North." In going on to describe his first interview with Lincoln he said: "I was a little disturbed, and a great deal agitated; but there was no real cause for trepidation or for alarm. I was going to see a great man." . . . "I have noticed that the higher we go up, in the gradations of humanity and moral greatness, the further we get from prejudices."

Soon afterward, on Saturday, March 31, he spoke before the International Council of Women, who had set that day apart in order to hear from the pioneers in their cause. A portion of this speech has been already quoted. Other passages run thus:

"One year ago I stood on the Pincio in Rome, and witnessed the unveiling of the statue of Galileo. It was an imposing sight. At no time before had Rome been free enough to permit such a statue to be placed within her walls. It is now there, not with the approval of the Vatican. No priest took part in the ceremonies. It was all the work of laymen. One or two priests passed the statue with averted eyes, but the great truths of the solar system were not angry at the sight, and the same will be true when woman shall be clothed, as she will yet be, with all the rights of American citizenship." . . . "Whatever the future may have in store for us, one thing is certain—this new revolution in human thought will never go backward. When a great truth once gets abroad in the world, no power on earth can imprison it, or prescribe its limits, or suppress it. It is bound to go on till it becomes the thought of the world. Such a truth is woman's right to equal liberty with man. She was born with it. It was hers before she comprehended it. It is inscribed upon all the powers and faculties of her soul, and no custom, law, or usage can ever destroy it. Now that it has got fairly fixed in the minds of the few, it is bound to become fixed in the minds of the many, and be supported at last by a great cloud of witnesses, which no man can number and no power can withstand."

On Monday evening, May 28, he spoke before the New England Woman Suffrage Association, in Tremont Temple, Boston, where he argued that the question, why woman is forbidden to vote, is not answered by pleading that the suffrage is not a right but a privilege. In conclusion, he said that " If the whole is greater than a part, if the sense and sum of human goodness in man and woman combined is greater than that of either alone and separate, then the government that excludes women from all participation in its creation, administration, and perpetuation maims itself." His zeal in this cause has not carried him so far as to approve of the formation of separate suffrage associations by colored women. He holds that real reforms must keep themselves above the color-line.

Earlier in 1888, he had made a journey through the South, and had been escorted into Charleston by a company of soldiers whose name was brighter than their complexion, the Douglass Light Infantry. Soon after returning, he wrote to one of the leaders in a movement for encouraging emigration of colored people to the North-west, a letter which is dated April 10, and runs thus :

" I have long hesitated to give my endorsement to any movement looking to the removal of considerable numbers of the
colored people of the South, to the North and West. I have
felt that it was better that they should endure, and patiently
wait for better conditions of existence where they are, than to
take the chance of seeking them in the cold North, or in Africa,
or elsewhere. I had hoped that the relations subsisting between the former slaves and the old master class would gradually improve ; but while I believed this, and still have some such
weak faith, I have of late seen enough, heard enough, and
learned enough of the condition of these people in South Carolina and Georgia, to make me welcome any movement which
will take them out of the wretched condition in which I now
know them to be. While I shall continue to labor for increased
justice to those who stay in the South, I give you my hearty
' God-speed ' in your emigration scheme. I believe you are
doing a good work."

Ten days later, at the emancipation celebration in
Washington, he spoke thus, in answer to the charge
that the negro is a failure as a citizen and is in every
way doing badly :

" I admit that the negro, and especially the plantation negro,
the tiller of the soil, has made little progress from the barbarism of slavery to the civilization of freedom ; that he is in a
deplorable condition since his emancipation ; and that he is
physically worse off in many respects as a freeman than he was
when a slave. But I contend that the fault was not his, but the
fault is with his heartless accusers. The explanation is easily
given ; he is the victim of a cunningly devised swindle—one
which paralyzes his energies, suppresses his ambition, blasts his
hope, and leaves him crushed and helpless. In fact, though he
is nominally free, he is still actually a slave. I here and now
denounce his so-called emancipation as practically a stupendous fraud ;—a fraud upon him, a fraud upon the country, a
fraud upon the world, and a reproach upon the American

people. It was not so meant by the great-hearted Abraham Lincoln. It was not so meant by the Republican party; but whether so meant or not, I contend that this so-called emancipation is practically a lie of the worst kind, keeping the word of promise to the ear and breaking it to the heart. Do you ask a more particular answer to the question, why the negro of the plantation has made so little progress, why his cupboard is empty, why he flutters in rags, why his children run naked, and his wife is barefooted and hides herself behind the hut when a stranger is passing? I will tell you. It is because the husband and father is systematically and almost universally cheated out of his hard earnings. The same class that once extorted his labor under the lash, now extorts his labor by a mean, sneaking, and fraudulent device, which is more effective than the lash. That device is the trucking system, a system which never permits him to see or save a dollar of his hard earnings. He struggles from year to year, but like a man in a morass, the more he struggles, the deeper he sinks. The highest wages paid him are eight dollars a month, and this he receives only in orders on a store, which, in many cases, is owned by his employer. This scrip has a purchasing power on that one store, and that one store only. A blind man can see that by this arrangement the laborer is bound hand and foot, and is completely in the power of his employer. He can charge the poor fellow just what he pleases and give him what kind of goods he pleases, and he does both. His victim cannot go to another store and buy, and this the storekeeper knows. The only security the wretched negro has under this arrangement is the conscience of the storekeeper—a conscience educated in the school of slavery, where the idea prevailed in theory and practice that the negro had no rights which white men were bound to respect, an arrangement in which everything in the way of food or clothing, whether tainted meat or damaged cloth, is deemed good enough for the negro. For these he is often made to pay a double price. But this is not all, or the worst result of the system. It puts it out of the power of the negro to save anything of what he earns. If a man gets an honest dollar for his day's work, he has a motive for laying it by and saving it for future emergency. It will be as good for use in the future, and perhaps better a year hence than now; but this miserable scrip has in no sense the quality of a dollar. It is only good at one store and for a limited period. Thus the man who has it is tempted to get rid of it as soon as possible. It may be out of date before he knows it, or the storekeeper may move away and it may be left worthless on his hands." . . . "In England, to her credit let it be spoken, this trucking system is abolished by law. It is a penal offense there; and it should be here. It should be made a crime to pay any man for his honest labor in any other than lawful money."

Copious quotations are then given from the tenant laws of the South; and the orator proceeds thus:

"Now let us sum up some of the points in the situation of the freedman. You will have seen how he is paid for his labor— how a full-grown man gets only eight dollars a month, out of which he must feed, clothe, and educate his children. You have seen how even this sum is reduced by means of an infamous truck system of payment. You have seen how easily he may be charged with a price one-third higher than the value of the goods that he buys. You have seen how easily he may be compelled to receive the poorest and most worthless commodities at the highest prices. You have seen how he is never allowed to see, save, or handle a dollar. You have seen how impossible for him to accumulate money or property. You have seen how completely he is chained to the locality in which he lives. You have seen, therefore, that having no money, he cannot travel or go anywhere to better his condition. You have seen by these laws that, even on the premises which he rents, he can own nothing, possess nothing, but what must belong to the landlord. You have seen that he cannot sell a sheep, a pig, a goat, or even a chicken, without the consent of the landlord, whose claim to all he has is superior and paramount to all other claims whatsoever. You have seen that he works for the landlord rather than for himself. You have seen all this and more; and I ask again, in view of it all, how in the name of human reason could the negro be expected to make progress, or rise higher in the scale of morals, manners, religion, and civilization than he has done during the twenty years of his so-called freedom? Shame! Eternal shame on those writers and speakers who taunt, denounce, and disparage the negro, because he is to-day found in poverty, rags, and wretchedness!"

It is further complained that our National Government allows him to be disfranchised, while "His color exposes him to be treated as a criminal;" and that by this neglect, as well as by the decision of 1883, he is "swindled of his citizenship." The best remedy would have been to make Logan or Conkling President; but, as neither was living, and there was no probability of the nomination of Judge Harlan, the only member of the Supreme Court who thought the Civil Rights Bill constitutional, the preference of Douglass in April, 1888, was for Senator Sherman.

He was present at the convention which nominated Harrison and Morton, that June; and soon after he made an address to his brethren, in which he remonstrated earnestly against joining the newly-organized "colored Democratic party." The leaders in that movement asserted that "The Republican party has failed to protect negro suffrage at the South;" and Douglass replied that :

"It is not true that the Republican party has not endeavored to protect the negro in his right to vote. The whole moral power of the party has been, from first to last, on the side of justice to the negro; and it has only been baffled, in its efforts to protect the negro in his vote, by the Democratic party."

Of another argument, brought up by the black Democrats, the black Republican spoke thus :

" Suppose it be granted that Mr. Cleveland is a just man, and desires to protect colored citizens in the exercise of their constitutional rights. What is he, and what is any man in the Presidential chair, without the support of his party ? As against his party, he is only as a feather against a whirlwind. In the hands of his party, Mr. Cleveland is as clay in the hands of the potter."

The address is long enough to occupy about ten pages of this volume, but it does not make the slightest allusion to a question which, as Douglass said in another of his campaign speeches " has been the leading topic, and undoubtedly will continue to be the leading topic of this canvass." This, of course, is the tariff ; and when he does take it up, he makes no attempt to prove that colored people have any large share in the protected industries. He does maintain that the tariff keeps all wages up ; and he says :

" Suppose the American manufacturers do derive larger gains than any other class, suppose protection does support manufacturing monopolies in America, is it not obvious that free trade will build up similar monopolies abroad ? " . . . " Let the American people turn their attention to raising cotton, cattle, and grain for Europe, and how long do you think it would be before the manufacturers of Europe would put up the prices of all their articles ? "

What is the exclusive topic of one address is, however, the main theme of the other. Both insist on the duty of electing a Republican President, in order to restore suffrage to the freedman. One speech dates his disfranchisement from 1877, but the other says of

Georgia that "Under the shot-gun rule, the Democrats carried the State against Grant and Colfax," who were candidates in 1868. Both addresses consider the character of the parties more important than that of the candidates ; but it is said, on the basis of personal knowledge of President Harrison :

" He embodies and illustrates the highest and best elements of American character." . . . "During the last few weeks, Mr. Harrison has surprised those of his countrymen, who did not as I did, know him, by the fertility of his mind, the breadth and comprehensiveness of his statesmanship. His more than half a hundred speeches stand like a wall of granite, and utterly defy assault."

Perhaps the most important contribution made by Douglass to this campaign was a letter, written in October, to oppose one of the best nominations made that year by either party for Congress, that of Colonel T. W. Higginson. His brilliant services, not only as a speaker but as a soldier, to the slave, only brought out a declaration that his " election, considering his antecedents, would be much more detrimental to our cause than would be the election of an old-time pro-slavery Democrat." . . . " Of course, if I had a thousand votes, I would give them all to General Banks, the nominee of the Republican party."

Before writing thus, he had been obliged, by previous engagements, to decline an invitation to deliver an oration in Faneuil Hall, on November 13, the day when the monument to Crispus Attucks was unveiled on Boston Common. In this letter, written on October 5, 1888, he says he is " happy in the thought, that the Commonwealth of Massachusetts is about to commemorate an act of heroism in a race seldom credited with heroic qualities." He did speak at the celebration in Philadelphia, on December 6, of the fifty-fifth anniversary of the settlement of Rev. Dr. Furness ; he was able to compare his recollections with Whittier's on the poet's birthday, December 17 ; and he contributed to the "Cosmopolitan," for August, 1889, a paper entitled " Reminiscences," and forming part of a series about " The Great Agitation."

The last speech which Douglass has published, so far as I know, and certainly one of the most important, was delivered in Washington on April 16, 1889, at the invitation of the Bethel Literary and Historical Society, which, as he says, " comprises the most cultivated class of our people." He begins by saying :

" At no period since the abolition of slavery in the District of Columbia, have the moral, social, and political surroundings of the colored people of this country been more solemn and foreboding than they are this day." . . . "Nature has given me a buoyant disposition." . . . "No man can see the silver lining of a black cloud more joyfully than I. But he is a more hopeful man than I am, who will tell you that the rights and liberties of the colored people in this country have passed beyond the danger-line." . . . "It is an ominous fact, that at no time in the history of the conflict between slavery and freedom in this country, has the character of the negro, as a man, been made the subject of a fiercer and more serious discussion in all the avenues of debate, than during the past and present year." . . . "When the negro was a slave, he was almost as completely outside of the nation's thought, as he was outside of the nation's law and the nation's religion. But now all is changed. His freedom makes him discussed on every hand. The platform, the pulpit, the press, and the legislative hall regard him, and struggle with him, as a great and difficult problem, one that requires almost divine wisdom to solve. Men are praying over it. It is always a dangerous symptom when men pray to know what is their duty."

Douglass then protests against representing his race as a cause of discord :

" I deny and utterly scout the idea, that there is now, properly speaking, any such thing as a negro problem before the American people. It is not the negro, educated or illiterate, intelligent or ignorant, who is on trial, or whose qualities are giving trouble to the nation." . . . " The real question, the all-commanding question, is whether American justice, American liberty, American civilization, American law, and American Christianity can be made to include and protect, alike and forever, all American citizens." . . . " It is whether this great nation shall conquer its prejudices, rise to the dignity of its professions, and proceed in the sublime course of truth and liberty marked out for itself during the late war, or shall swing back to its ancient moorings of slavery and barbarism. The trouble is that the colored people have still to contend against ' a fierce and formidable foe,' the ghost of a by-gone, dead and buried institution.

" One thing which they ought to do, in order to hold their own against this enemy, is to give up cultivating what they call ' race pride,' a sentiment too much like that which is ' the lion in the way ' of our progress." . . . " Do we not know that every argument we make, and every pretension we set up in favor of race pride, is giving the enemy a stick to break our own heads ? " . . . " You will, perhaps, think this criticism uncalled for. My answer is that truth is never uncalled for." . . . " In some of our colored public journals I have seen myself charged with a lack of race pride. I am not ashamed of that charge. I have no apology or vindication to offer. If fifty years of uncompromising devotion to the cause of the colored man in this country does not vindicate me, I am content to live without vindication. While I have no more reason to be proud of one race than another, I dare to say, and I fear no contradiction, that there is no other man in the United States prouder than myself of any great achievement, mental or mechanical, of which any colored man or woman is the author. This not because I am a colored man, but because I am a man ; and because color is a misfortune, and is treated as a crime by the American people."

He also protests against the preference shown by the colored people for dwelling by themselves, and carrying on separate churches, schools, benevolent and literary societies :

" There are buildings which will hold a few, but which will break down under the weight of a crowd. The ice of the river may be strong enough to bear a man, but would break through under the weight of an elephant. The ice under us in this country is very thin, and is made very weak by the warm fogs of prejudice." . . . " Our policy should be to unite with the great mass of the American people in all their activities, and resolve to fall or flourish with our common country. We cannot afford to draw the color-line in politics, trade, education, manners, religion, fashion, or civilization. Especially we cannot afford to draw the color-line in politics. No folly could be greater. A party acting on that basis would be not merely a misfortune, but a dire calamity to our people."

It is admitted that the terror excited among the blacks by Cleveland's election " turned out to be groundless ; " but it is complained that after the inauguration,

" He said no word and did no act, expressed no desire to arrest the hand of violence, to stay the effusion of innocent blood, or to vindicate in any manner the negro's constitutional right to vote." . . . " Well, now the American people have returned the Republican party to power ; and the question is, what will it do ? " . . . " For a dozen years and more the Republican party has seemed in a measure paralyzed in the presence of

high-handed fraud and brutal violence toward its newly-made citizens. The question now is, will it regain its former health, activity, and power? Will it be as true to its friends in the South as the Democratic party has been to its friends in that section, or will it sacrifice its friends to conciliate its enemies?"
. . . "Not only the negro but all honest men, north and south, must hold the Republican party in contempt, if it fails to do its whole duty at this point. The Republican party has made the colored man free; and the Republican party must make him secure in his freedom, or abandon its pretensions.

"It was once said by Abraham Lincoln that this Republic could not long endure half slave and half free; and the same may be said with even more truth of the black citizens of this country. They cannot remain half slave and half free. They must be one thing or the other. And this brings me to consider the alternative now presented between slavery and freedom in this country. From my outlook, I am free to affirm that I see nothing for the negro of the South but a condition of absolute freedom, or of absolute slavery. I see no half-way place for him. One or the other of these conditions is to solve the so-called negro problem. There are forces at work in both of these directions, and for the present that which aims at the re-enslavement of the negro seems to have the advantage. Let it be remembered that the labor of the negro is his only capital. Take this from him, and he dies from starvation. The present mode of obtaining his labor in the South gives the old master-class a complete mastery over him. I showed this in my last annual celebration address, and I need not go into it here. The payment of the negro by orders on stores, where the store-keeper controls price, quality, and quantity, and is subject to no competition, so that the negro must buy there and nowhere else —an arrangement by which the negro never has a dollar to lay by, and can be kept in debt to his employer, year in and year out—puts him completely at the mercy of the old master-class. He who could say to the negro, when a slave, you shall work for me or be whipped to death, can now say to him with equal emphasis, you shall work for me, or I will starve you to death.

This is the plain, matter-of-fact, and unexaggerated condition of the plantation negro in the Southern States to-day."

He is further wronged, it is said, by being prevented from emigrating as well as from keeping weapons in his cabin. If he becomes a criminal, " The law puts him on the auction block and sells him to the highest bidder." . . . " No adequate means of education has been provided for him ; his vote avails him nothing ; he, of all men is easiest convicted of crime ; he does not see or receive a dollar in payment of wages ; and, by the opinion of the Supreme Court, the Fourteenth Amendment affords him no protection."

But the nation is stronger than the oppressors. " They may rob the negro of his vote to-day, but the negro will have his vote to-morrow. The spirit of the age is with him." . . . " If the Republican party shall fail to carry out this purpose, God will raise up another party that will be faithful."

" There is still another ground for hope for the freedom of the Southern States. It is that the good citizens of these States cannot afford and will not consent always, to lag far behind the old free States in all the elements of civilization." . . . " They have rich resources to be developed, and they want both men and money to develop them and enhance their prosperity. The wise and loyal people in these States know very well that they can never be prosperous, that they can never have their share of emigration, from at home or abroad, while they are known and distinguished for intolerance, fraud, violence, and lynch law. They know that while this character attaches to them, capital will hold aloof from them, and population will shun them, as it would shun a land blasted by pestilence." . . . " They know that industrious and enterprising men, searching for homes, will turn their backs upon the South, and make their

way to the West and North, where they can hold and express
their opinions without fear of the bowie-knife and shot-gun of
the assassin. Thus the self-interest of the people of these
States will yet teach them justice, humanity, and civilization."
. . . "The spirit of justice, liberty, and fair play is abroad in
the land." . . . "It has an agent in every bar of railroad iron,
a servant in every electric wire, a missionary in every traveller."
. . . "States, parties, and leaders must, and will in the end, ad-
just themselves to this overwhelming and irresistible tendency."

These last words indicate the true solution of a
problem, which we know to be both difficult and urgent. Its importance is manifest, even in the comparatively simple form in which it meets us at the
North. Here at least, there is no conceivable reason
why all colored people should not be treated according to the merits of each individual. It is not only
the plain duty, but also the interest of us all, to have
every colored man take the place for which he is best
fitted by education, character, ability, manners, and
culture. If others insist on keeping him in any lower
and poorer place, it is not only his injury, but our
universal loss. Yet which of our white congregations would take a colored pastor? How many of
our New England villages would like to have colored
postmasters, or doctors, or lawyers, or teachers in the
public schools? A very slight difference in complexion suffices to keep a young man from getting a
place as policeman, or fireman, or conductor, even on
the horse cars. The trades-unions are closed against
him, and so are many of our stores; while those
which admit him are obliged to refuse him promotion on account of the unwillingness of white men to
serve under him. Colored girls find dressmakers

who would employ them to be "as scarce as hens'
teeth." It is hard for them to get places behind
counters or in factories : and there is some prejudice
against them as domestic servants. One poor girl in
Iowa, who had been highly educated, could get no
employment except in a drudgery under which she
speedily died. Rich people who wish to hire suitable houses in Boston find the color-line drawn against
them. A candidate for office in the capital city of
Kansas found seven-eights of the white Republicans
desert him, because his skin was darker than theirs ;
and a Philadelphia writer on this subject, Mr. A. K.
McClure, declares that such prejudice was much
stronger in his own State, in 1886, than in South
Carolina. The recent refusal of the Episcopal Convention to recognize negro ministers as equal to their
brethren, has called out far too little protest in
Northern churches ; and there are frequent instances
of denial of civil rights in our Western cities. We
see, however, that there has been great improvement
throughout the North during the last fifty years.

May we not hope, that there has been some improvement in the South also, and that Charles Dudley
Warner is right in saying that "There is generally
good-will" toward the negro, "desire that he shall
be educated and become thrifty." The South has
not yet wholly ceased to be unjust. Many freedmen
are lynched, or sentenced to excessively long terms
of suffering under the atrocious system of farming
out convicts. Laborers continue to be swindled,
travellers to be molested, and ballot-boxes to be kept
out of reach. The extent to which these abuses prevail is often exaggerated, however ; the condition of

the freedmen has, I think, on the whole, improved
greatly since they were emancipated ; and I believe
that many of their white neighbors and employers
would say, with Mr. Grady, " We want to bar them
from no avenue in which their feet are fitted to
tread." The sincerity of such language is proved by
the fact, stated by Dr. Haygood as well as by the
National Bureau of Education, that every southern
State now provides as liberally for educating colored
children as white. The schools are separate ; and
this gives employment to thousands of colored teachers. The South will undoubtedly continue to educate and elevate the freedman ; for he will always
form so large and so necessary a part of her population, that he cannot safely be left in ignorance.
Her need of skilled labor is increasing rapidly ; and
even the field-hand would be much more valuable if
he could be taught to treat animals more kindly,
remember orders more faithfully, and abstain entirely
from pilfering. The health of the white people requires that the negro cabin be kept clean ; and the
maintenance of chastity there is necessary for the
protection of woman throughout the land. The need
of making the black man more intelligent and conscientious has already been so far recognized by the
South, that she has remodelled her entire school system
for his benefit ; and her desire to make him more
valuable as a member of the community, cannot long
permit him to be lynched or otherwise maltreated.
Her memory of the misrule of the carpet-baggers
will grow fainter ; and she will finally be able to see
that even the illiterate voter is not so dangerous a
citizen in a republic as the man who has not this

reason to interest himself in its welfare. The South
may be much slower than we could wish in reaching
these conclusions ; but no others will be found permanently satisfactory to her ; and it is by no means
certain that her pace will be quickened by a display
of federal bayonets.

This is substantially the view " of many thoughtful
colored men, who care more for race than for party,
and more for country than for race." These last
words are quoted from a letter. in the " Boston
Post" of August 17, 1889, by Mr. Archibald H.
Grimké, who is confident that the old regime under
which his brethren now suffer at the South, "is
crumbling under the action of new moral ideas," and
"new industrial forces." These are creating "a
nobler public opinion ;" and " The New South is in
very truth the Œdipus who is destined to solve the
southern riddle." Both the New South and the Old
are determined not to let outsiders interfere, nor to
suffer "a return of negro domination." "Between
the existing order and that terrible disorder, no sane
man would hesitate to choose the existing order with
all its evils. For myself, I would prefer the existing
order a thousand times, to that swarm and saturnalia
of fools and scamps which the appalling ignorance
and poverty of the blacks made possible fifteen
years ago."

The first duty of the North is to purify herself
from those prejudices which now encourage oppression at the South. The need of industrial education
among the freedmen is still so great that institutions
which furnish it deserve liberal endowments, not only
from rich individuals but from the Government,

though we need not think of offering charity to
States which have doubled their school funds since
1880. The interests of the colored laborer should be
considered in revising the tariff. The only way of
solving the color-problem is by the cordial co-operation of all classes and races at the South. Any
attempt to set race against race will injure the blacks
even more than the whites. They have interests
enough in common to insure the ultimate elevation
of the negro to the high place necessary for the common welfare.

An opportunity to study the negro character from
a new standpoint was given to Douglass, as he was
appointed Minister to a country in which he has
always felt deep interest. As he wrote to his friend,
Dr. Bowditch, on July 4, 1889, "With many misgiv-
ings, I accepted the mission to Hayti. I distrusted
my qualifications for the office ; but coming to me as
it did, unasked, unsought, and unexpected, and with
the earnest wish of the President that I would accept
it in the interest of the peace, welfare, and prosperity
of Hayti, I felt I could not decline it. I shall leave a
comfortable house and a healthy climate, and shall
probably have to occupy trying positions ; but I go
forth hopefully." . . . " Hayti is but a child in national life, and though she may often stumble and
fall, I predict that she will yet grow strong and
bright."

Just as he was about to leave Washington, he wrote
a letter which was read in the Tremont Temple, Boston, at the Reunion of the Abolitionists, on Monday,
September 23, to celebrate Lincoln's first proclamation of emancipation. " You meet " he says, " in Bos-

ton, at a time still critical if not alarming. Slavery
has left behind it a spirit that still delights in human
blood. Outrage, murder, and assassination are the
inheritance of the freed men and women of the
South. Neither our government nor our civilization
seems able to stop the flow of blood. As in the time
of slavery, the Church is silent."

The sensational stories, set afloat soon after, about
the unwillingness of naval officers to take a colored
passenger, are proved to be false by the testimony
of Secretary Tracy and Mr. Walter Blaine, as well as
of Douglass himself in a letter from Port au Prince.
He arrived there, on October 8th, after a smooth passage, which was made very pleasant for his companions by his animated accounts of his early life. On
being asked why he left his comfortable home for a
benighted and turbulent country, he said : " I am
tired of having Hayti thrown in my face : I am going
now to see for myself." Four days after landing, he
was able so far to carry out his plans as to take possession of the Villa Tivoli, which, according to the
" New York Evening Post " is " an unpretentious residence on the heights overlooking the lower town
and the bay, and like all these villas, even the best of
them, rather dilapidated, and enclosed by a jungle
of tropical growth aflame with gorgeous blossoms ;
palms shading the avenue between the gateway and
the wide veranda, before which is a little fountain,
the soothing fall of whose water is suggestive of cool-
ness and shade." The Haytian Minister at Washington, Mr. Preston, says that the rumors which have
been circulating about the unwillingness of the rulers
of the black republic to receive Douglass cordially,

had no foundation, except in the disappointment of
certain New York merchants, who had tried in vain
to hire him to act as their agent in pressing claims
upon the Haytian Government. I have heard that
they offered him heavy bribes, soon after his appointment ; but he answered, that all proposals, for his
undertaking any kind of business in Hayti, must be
sent to him through the State Department.

The new President, Hyppolite, said in his inaugural address, that "Hayti ought to be proud of the
sympathy with this administration, which has been
shown so abundantly by the United States," and that
" The greatest proof of regard which that country
has given us, is unquestionably her sending to Port
au Prince, as Minister Resident and Consul General,
Hon. Frederick Douglass, that illustrious champion
of all men of African descent, himself one of the
most remarkable scions of that race whose representatives in America we are proud to be."

While spending his vacation in this country, last
summer, Mr. Douglass told me that he had found
everything in Hayti delightful, except the climate ;
and on September 10, he sent me the following letter :

" DEAR MR. HOLLAND :—

" In answer to your question in respect of my relations with
the government of Hayti and whether they were cordial or
otherwise, I have to state that, while the office of United States
Minister Resident and Consul General to Hayti was vacant,
and prior to my nomination to that position by President Harrison, an honor accorded to me without any solicitation on my
part or on that of my friends, the policy of sending a colored
citizen to represent our country at that important post was seriously discussed, and such appointment condemned in the col-

umns of certain papers published in New York City and elsewhere. After I was appointed, the subject was continued and discussed with even more emphasis and bitterness. Notwithstanding the fact that Hayti is known as the ' Black Republic ' and that her people are of the African race, it was contended that she did not want a colored representative in her capital in the high quality of Minister Resident and Consul General of the United States, but that she very much preferred to have a white man sent to her in that quality. As for me, personally, it was contended that I was especially objectionable ; and that I was so, not only on account of my color, but on account also of my political opinions. It was given out that I had at one time (that is twenty years ago) favored the annexation of Santo Domingo to the United States, a measure to which Hayti was strenuously opposed, and that the latter would be likely to resent the presence in her capital of a Minister who had supported a policy which she deemed offensive and dangerous. It made no difference to these writers, that annexation had ceased to be a living question, and that it had long since been abandoned both by the Government of the United States and by Santo Domingo. It was found to be a convenient circumstance by which to stir up bad feeling in Hayti against me, and it was no fault of theirs if it did not succeed. Some of these papers went so far as to intimate very unpatriotically, that I was especially sent to Hayti for the purpose of advancing some scheme of annexation, not only of Santo Domingo but of Hayti. They were not troubled in these utterances by the absurdity of the pretence, that color would be an objection to me in a black or colored republic. They took no note that, at the time I favored the annexation of Santo Domingo, it was only because that country was supposed to desire it. They could not see that being herself pretty deeply colored, and her citizens considerably under the ban on account of color in the United States, Hayti would naturally be pleased to see one of her own complexion honored by the appointment to the Haytian Mission. All that they seemed to aim at, or to desire, was to create the impression that a white man, and not a colored man, was the proper description of man to be sent to Hayti. It was amusing to witness the high professions of respect on the part of these journals for the feelings and preferences of Hayti, professions that struck me, considering their source, to be too vehement to be sincere, and too unusual to be ascribed to nature. There was ample room to suspect a motive for this opposition less creditable and generous than any wholesome concern for either the interest or the feelings of Hayti. Quite a flood of light fell upon the whole subject, when it was said that the New York merchants were unanimously opposed to sending a colored representative of the United States to Hayti. It at once became plain that an American and not a Haytian motive was at the bottom of this color opposition.

"But whatever may have been the motive, whether it arose from my color, my character, or my known record as a public man, the opposition was spirited, vigorous, persistent, and mischievous ; for nothing was said against me that was not reproduced and repeated in Hayti. A people less generous and intelligent than those who control affairs there might have been made to feel that the United States had designedly insulted them by sending me to their country. But, fortunately, they did not so think or act. Having, however, predicted that I would be unacceptable to the people and Government of Hayti, it was perhaps natural that these prophets of evil should endeavor to create the impression that their predictions had been realized. Hence it was said in the same papers, that I was having a hard time in Hayti, that I had been 'snubbed' by that Government, that I was about to resign, and much else of the same sort. Undue advantage was taken after my arrival in Hayti, of the fact that some delay occurred in my presentation to President Hyppolite. The facts in the case will explain all this. I arrived in Hayti on the 8th of October, 1889. At that time the country was just emerging from one of the most exciting revolutions which had occurred there in many years. The government of General Solomon had been overthrown the year before ; and there had succeeded to it the government of General Légitime, which was never recognized by the United States. This government had lasted but a few months, when its President was driven from power and banished from the country. The city of Port au Prince was under martial law ; and sixteen thousand troops were in its streets. The Government I found there was simply titular and provisional ; but a convention to frame a new constitution was in progress in the neighboring city of Gonaïves. This convention was charged with the duty of electing a President of the Republic and thus inaugurating a permanent government. This they did by electing General Florvil Hyppolite President for a term of seven years. Even after this election, the necessary delay in receiving my letter of credence hindered my prompt presentation to the newly elected President, to whom I was subsequently accredited. During the interim between my arrival in Hayti and my presentation to President Hyppolite, Mr. Thompson, my predecessor, who had long before sent in his letter of resignation (which had been accepted by our Government), and who, as I had supposed, had previously to my arrival departed from Hayti, as he had requested permission to do, still remained, and for a time, in view of the fact that I had not presented my letter of credence, nor been formally received by the Government, allowed himself to be considered as the then present representative of the United States Government, notwithstanding my presence in the Haytian capital and my assumption there of the duties and control of the United States Legation. This circumstance, no doubt, gave rise to the rumor in the United States of unpleasant relations between myself and the Government of Hayti. The delay in my reception was just long enough to be used in New York, with all proper exaggeration, to create the impression that my relations with the Haytian Government were not cordial, and to justify the conclusion to which those papers had already come, that a white man should have been sent to Hayti in my stead. Happily, this embarrassment did not last long. As soon as my letter of credence arrived, I was duly presented to His Excellency, President Hyppolite, and from that time onward my relations with the Haytian Government were entirely cordial, and no respect due to my person or to my country was ever afterward withheld by the Government or by the people of Hayti. FREDERICK DOUGLASS."

Shortly before sending the above letter, Douglass visited a camp-meeting near Baltimore, on Sunday, September 7, and made a speech in which, after referring to the time when "The American eagle laid bad eggs," he said :

"Our American friends are apt, when they want to say anything against us, to remark : 'Look at Hayti; these negroes cannot govern themselves there; why here ?' There is something about Hayti which we have to deplore, and so there is about the United States. Let us go back 100 years and look at Hayti, and we find it surrounded by slavery and the whole Caribbean Sea reddened by the curse. The negro was a slave everywhere, under every nation in the islands of the West Indies. But in the midst of that slavery, in the midst of that doom and despair, they had the manhood to rise from the dust and shake off the fetters and drive out the men who tyrannized them. Since then Napoleon, with his 30,000 invaders and troops from England, have tried to throw them back; but, with the help of 'Yellow Jack,' they have held their ground. These degraded, stupid negroes were able not only to assert their liberty, but to organize a government which they have carried on for eighty-seven years. They have sent their Ministers to all Christian lands, and Hayti has never been known to break a treaty. Some of the papers said, not long since : 'Send a white man as Minister to Hayti, for the people of that country would resent a negro.' Well, there is always a demand made for a white man, when there is $5000 attached to the office. I have been shown every courtesy and I have not the slightest reason to complain. I believe the press has become reconciled to my presence in the office, except those that have a candidate for it, and they give out that I am going to resign. At them I fling the old adage, 'Few die, and none resign,' and that I am going back about Oct. 1."

In speaking at the Abolitionist Reunion in Boston, on September 22, 1890, Douglass said :

"A word about Hayti. We are not to judge her by the height which the Anglo-Saxon has reached. We are to judge by the depths from which she has come. We are to look at the relation she sustained to the outside world, and the outside world sustained to her. One hundred years ago every civilized nation was slave-holding. Yet these negroes, ignorant, down-trodden, had the manhood to arise and drive off their masters and assert their liberty. Her government is not so unsteady as we think."

He also, that morning, defended our pension system, which had been criticised by a previous speaker; and he added: " The Abolitionists were right in their attitude to the Church. Slavery and the Church were side by side : the Church was at peace with slavery : men were sold to build churches, women sold to pay missionaries, and children sold to buy Bibles. We did right to oppose it."

The great event of the occasion was his speech that evening, in Tremont Temple. The immense audience greeted him with round after round of applause. Then followed a general laugh, as he held up a big packet of manuscript and dropped it, with the words : "All my thunder has been stolen by the friends who have already spoken ; so I lay this thunderbolt aside." He then insisted that " There is no race problem before the country, but only a political one, the question whether a Republican has any right to exist south of Mason and Dixon's line." There is still a great deal of prejudice, even in the North, against

colored people ; but he has found out that the only
way to cure it, is to treat them kindly. This he proved
by the fact that at Pittsfield, New Hampshire, forty-
eight years before, Mrs. Norris had been helped, by
doing him a kindness, to shake off her prejudice
against his color and his views so thoroughly as to be
the first to shake hands with him after his lecture. It
had been said, by the clergyman who preceded him,
that it was not the Garrisonians who abolished
slavery, nor the Republicans either, but Almighty
God. "The good Lord had had a chance for a long
time before the abolition. I believe that there is a
moral government ; and that God reigns. I am no
pessimist ; I give thanks to the good Lord, and also
to the good men through whom He has worked.
Prominent among them was Garrison, and scarcely
less so was Phillips. It was they and their associates who made Abraham Lincoln and the Republican party possible. What abolished slavery was the
moral sentiment which had been created, not by the
pulpit, but by the Garrisonian platform. The
churches did not do much to abolish slavery ; but
they did much to keep the agitation down." He saw
no danger of negro supremacy at the South, nor any
cause of alarm to the white people "who have a
thousand years of civilization piled up in their three-
story heads." "I am just as white myself as I am
black ; and I am not afraid of the negro getting the
upper hand in me." Finally he rose to a power of
pathos, which carried away the whole audience, as he
said, in pleading for the Blair and Lodge bills, "If
you build the negro a church on every hill, and a
schoolhouse in every valley, and endow them all for

a hundred years, you will not make up for the wrongs you have done him. Who is it that asks for protection at the polls and for equal education? The men who came forth to clutch with iron fingers your faltering flag, and shed their blood for you, who protected the women and children of the South during the war, who have tilled your soil with their horny hands, and watered it with their tears!"

Four weeks later he made an address to the Bethel Literary and Historical Association, in Washington, and, after asserting the right of colored men to vote and marry as they choose, closed with noble words which we may accept as his farewell before departing once more to Hayti, on December 7 :

" I have no doubt whatever of the future. I know there are times in the history of all reforms, when the future looks dark." . . . " I, for one, have gone through all this. I have had fifty years of it, and yet I have not lost either heart or hope." . . . " I have seen dark hours in my life, and I have seen the darkness gradually disappearing, and the light gradually increasing. One by one, I have seen obstacles removed, errors corrected, prejudices softened, proscriptions relinquished, and my people advancing in all the elements that make up the sum of general welfare. And I remember that God reigns in eternity, and that, whatever delays, disappointments, and discouragements may come, truth, justice, liberty, and humanity will ultimately prevail."

CHAPTER XV.

How and why the Minister to Hayti failed to obtain one of the objects of his mission, the cession of the Môle St. Nicholas to the United States, has been fully explained by him in the "North American Review" for September and October, 1891; and the articles have since been republished in the second edition of his "Life and Times." One of the reasons why Hayti refused us even a lease of the harbor, which he calls her Gibraltar, was resentment at our national prejudice against the color of her citizens. "Hayti is black," said he at Chicago, "and we have not yet forgiven Hayti for being black, or forgiven the Almighty for making her black." The fleet which was sent by our Government to frighten the Haytians excited only their indignation; as it did that of Douglass, who resigned accordingly, on July 30, 1891.

While the first edition of this biography was in press, Douglass wrote me thus about the meeting of Abolitionists in September, 1890, "I am very glad to find that I did not appear at the late reunion in Boston as a worn-out and broken-down public speaker, tolerated rather than desired by the thousands assembled, though the time is at hand, when, like the thousands who have gone before me, I must cease to

393

disturb the public eye and ear. The reunion was
both a pleasure and a disappointment. There were
many old friends I was delighted to see, but more
absent that I wanted much to see once more in this
life. But what a meeting it was! White heads,
wrinkled faces, dim eyes, trembling limbs, bent
forms, turned downward towards the earth! Such is
the complexion to which we all come at last. Yet
the meeting was to me a soul-reviving feast."

Of the severity with which Garrison blamed his
giving up disunionism (see p. 204), Douglass wrote
me thus:

"The first remark with which my statement was met
by Mr. Garrison was this, 'There is roguery somewhere.'
There was no mistaking the meaning; and, coming from any
one else, it would have been resented on the spot. . . . I
do not think that the grand, old anti-slavery pioneer went
to his grave thinking there was any 'roguery' in me. If
he did, I was not alone in this bad opinion of his. No
man who ever quitted the Garrisonian denomination was permitted to leave without a doubt being cast upon his honesty.
That was one of the Liberator's weapons of war; and it was a
weapon which never rusted for want of using. There are spots
on the sun; but it shines for all that; and Garrison with all his
harshness of judgment is Garrison still, and one of the best
men of mothers born."

Signs of decaying physical vigor were to be plainly
seen on March 16, 1892, when he lectured to an immense audience on Hayti, in the Tremont Temple in
Boston. He began by showing the value to this
country of an alliance with the Black Republic. Her
greatest curses are the frequent revolutions; but
these are constantly encouraged by residents of the
United States, who want to sell worthless ships and

weapons. The foreign legations are allowed to shelter defeated leaders; and " This right is merciful to the few, but cruel to the many." President Hyppolite was warmly praised by the orator, who admitted the superstition of the Haytians, but urged that there are many men in this country who, as he did, liked to have the first sight of the new moon over the right shoulder, and did not like to be one of thirteen at table. The Haytians won freedom by fighting for it as their right, and defended it against Napoleon. They taught the world the danger of slavery; and they struck for the freedom of every black. It was Hayti's brave example that first of all startled the Christian world into a sense of the negro's manhood. Her progress during the last twenty years, for instance, in founding hundreds of new schools, justifies belief that " Whatever may happen of peace or war, Hayti will remain in the firmament of nations, and, like the star of the North, will shine on, and shine on for ever."

Three months afterwards, he delivered his lecture on " Self-Made Men " as a commencement address at Tuskegee, Alabama. Among the new passages was this statement of a complaint he had often made, about the destitution into which the freedmen were launched in 1865, " Even the Israelites were better off than we. When they left Egypt, God told them to spoil the Egyptians; and I believe the Jews have been in the jewelry business ever since." He was delighted at the classic culture he saw there, and had just seen at Fiske University, Tennessee; but he took care to remind his hearers how much their welfare, as well as that of their race, would depend on their success.

not in reading Greek, but in working at trades and on the soil. "The earth has no prejudice against color. Crops are yielded as readily to the touch of the black man's hand as to that of his white brother." He insisted that they must save their earnings, if they would be respected, and closed thus: "Go on! I shan't be with you long. You have heights to ascend, breadths to fill, such as I never could and never can. Go on! When you are working with your hands, they grow larger; it is the same with your heads. The negro's head is small now. Why, a good-sized white man's hat will often slip right down over a negro's shoulders. But by-and-by you will develop great three-story heads with intelligence looking out of the windows." He often told them that they must not look to prayer to save them from being lynched or banished. They must make themselves respected as a valuable part of the free population of the South. "Seek to acquire knowledge as well as property; and, in time, you may have the honor of going to Congress; for if the negro can stand Congress, Congress ought to be able to stand the negro."

The dedication of a statue to that leader of the practical men, who really abolished slavery, John P. Hale, on August 3d, brought Douglass to Concord, New Hampshire. Weakness of body made him brief; but he took particular pleasure in saying that his friend's greatness and goodness were revealed in his unusual attractiveness for children. It must have been like his own. He also insisted that it was the policy, as well as the duty, of the Republican party to make the negro more prominent than the tariff in the Presidential campaign; and this position was fully stated by him in " Zion's Herald " for September 28th. His protest against the lynching at the South had already appeared in the July " North American " ; and his letter, published in the " Boston Herald," August 22d, says: " Any part that I take in the discussion during this campaign will be founded, not on hard money or honest money, the tariff, the McKinley Bill or any other kind of bill. I don't see anything for us but to make sentiment favorable to the race ; and let us make it aggressively." In this letter, he blamed James G. Blaine as " the marplot of his party," for keeping the negro question in the background, in 1884, when the Blaine men tried, not only to check his own sympathy with the oppressed, but " to tie the tongue of that noble and brave woman, Anna Dickinson, one of the best and purest women this world has ever had in it, and one of the truest at all times to us." He was far enough above party prejudice to admit, as soon as Cleveland was reëlected, that the country was not going to ruin, and that the condition of the colored people was not likely to have "a violent change for the worse." His sagacity also led him to predict that the victors would not give up protection, or depreciate the currency.

He speaks of his campaign work in 1884 and 1888, though not in 1892, in the edition of his autobiography, published early in 1893 ; and here he says, after lamenting Garfield's assassination, " The madness of Guiteau was but the exaggerated madness of other men. It is impossible to measure the evil which this craving madness may yet bring upon the country. Any civil-service reform which will diminish it "

.   .   .   "should be supported by every patriotic citizen." He tells us, that while marshal and recorder he was not "less outspoken against what I considered the error of rulers" than before. "My cause, first, midst, last, and always, whether in office or out of office, was and is that of the black man, not because he is black, but because he is a man, and a man subjected in this country to peculiar wrongs and hardships." His account of his last visit to Europe contains an interesting sketch of Gladstone in Parliament. His visit to the grave of Theodore Parker reminded him that he made his first speech in Roxbury against slavery, in the pulpit of a lover of Garrison who was not a Garrisonian, but the "generous brother" of all Abolitionists.   He felt   some   curiosity at   seeing "people going up to the black statue of St. Peter,—I was glad to find him black—I have no prejudice against his color,—and kissing the old fellow's big toe."

The latest event mentioned in the book just quoted, is the appointment of its author by President Hyppolite to represent Hayti as her commissioner at the World's Fair. In that capacity he took the lead in dedicating her tasteful pavilion, on the ninetieth anniversary of her declaration of independence, January 2, 1893. That same day, the lecture on Hayti was repeated to an audience of fifteen hundred, in a more central part of Chicago. We also hear of his dancing the Virginia reel, and playing "Home, Sweet Home" on his beloved fiddle, at the hanging of the crane, when the New England Log Cabin was opened on the Midway Plaisance. On August 9th, he made an impassioned protest, in the Suffrage Congress, against the objections of a professor from North Carolina to allowing colored men to vote independently; on the 16th, Haytian Day, he did the honors of her pavilion; and on the 25th, Colored American Day, a hundred and forty thousand of his friends followed his advice by attending, instead of staying away as some disappointed seekers for offices at the Exposition desired. Two thousand prosperous and intelligent colored people listened eagerly to his oration. " Our presence here in such numbers is a proof," said he, " of our wisdom and our good-nature." . . . " That we are outside of the World's Fair is only consistent with the fact that we are excluded from every respectable calling, from workshops, manufactories, and the means of learning trades. It is consistent with the fact that we are outside of the Church, and largely outside of the State."

The violin of his grandson, Joseph H. Douglass, furnished some fine music that afternoon, and also on the evening of May 9, 1894, when the orator spoke for the last time in Boston, to an audience in which were many of the surviving Abolitionists. Speaking of the willingness of the slave-holder to baptize, but not to emancipate, he said, " Well, the poor negro wasn't consulted; he looked around for his body—his master had it; for his soul, but the Lord had it; for himself—he wasn't there." He regretted the habit of treating colored people as subjects for ridicule, and protested against all attempts to banish them from the South, which they had helped to restore to the Union as well as reclaim for cultivation. He was busy to the last in plans for settling them in a factory town in Virginia, and rebuilding an industrial school which had been burned at Manassas.

The last scene was singularly characteristic. He had spent most of Wednesday, February 20, 1895 in the National Council of Women, at Washington, and had been escorted to the platform by a committee appointed in his honor. He had dined with his wife at Cedar Hill, once the property of General Lee, and was standing in the hall, waiting for his carriage to take him to lecture in one of the African churches, and talking about the speakers he had just heard. When he clasped his hands and dropped on his knees, Mrs. Douglass thought he was only mimicking somebody, as he had delighted to do. Suddenly he sank down on the floor; and she saw that he was dying. It was heart disease. He passed away without pain, at seven o'clock, aged seventy-eight.

He left two sons, Lewis Henry and Charles Remond, a daughter, Mrs. Rosetta Sprague, her three children, and the grandson whose musical skill has been already mentioned.

The largest African church in Washington was crowded for five hours, the next Monday, with colored people, thronging to see their champion lie in state. Beside him stood Hayti's coat of arms, in palms, roses, lilies, and orchids, presented by her minister. Baltimore and other cities sent delegations to the funeral that afternoon. Among the bearers were four Senators, an ex-Senator of Mississippi, and an ex-Governor of Louisiana. The presidents of Howard University and of the Woman's Council were among the speakers, as were Miss Susan B. Anthony and a colored bishop. The closing prayer was by

Rev. Anna H. Shaw. John W. Hutchinson, whose singing worked powerfully against slavery, fifty years ago, sang:

> " As man may, he fought his fight,
> Proved his truth by his endeavor.
> Let his name in golden light
> Live for ever and for ever!

Refrain.

> Lay him low, lay him low,
> Under the clover or under the snow;
> How we loved him none can know;
> Lay him low.

* * * * * * * *

> Bend in love, O azure sky!
> Shine, O stars, at evening time,
> Watch our Frederick calmly lie,
> Clothed in faith and hope sublime."

The Mayor, ex-Mayors, and Aldermen of Rochester, New York, helped to carry the body, next day, to Mount Hope Cemetery, after the funeral sermon had been preached in the Central Presbyterian Church by the Unitarian pastor, Rev. Wm. C. Gannett, a prominent member of the Free Religious Association, which still numbered among its vice-presidents the veteran who had been a mighty champion, not only of freedom for the body, but of unrestricted liberty for the soul.

His memory will live in many brilliant sentences, some of which are:

" Speech is the lever that moves the world." " Enforced morality is artificial morality." " A difference of opinion, like a discord in music, sometimes gives the highest effects of harmony." " The limits of tyrants are prescribed by the endurance of those whom they oppress." "Human government is for the protection of rights, and not for the destruction of rights." "The binding quality of law is its reasonableness." "The world moves, but only by fighting every inch of its disputed way." "I know of no rights of race superior to the rights of humanity." "The true basis of rights is the capacity of individuals." "Person is at least as sacred as its incident, property." "What we call money is only stored labor." "It may be with men as some one has said about tea: if you wish to get its strength you must put it into hot water."

Looking at Douglass as an orator, his life may be divided into four periods.

First come the twenty-four years of preparation, before he mounted the platform in 1841. During this time, he became familiar with slavery in its best aspects, as well as in some of its worst. Only a woman could have realized all its horrors; but he felt them keenly enough to be able to make their iniquity plain to his hearers; and he had the great advantage of knowing how bad the system was in its best possible form. He also discovered that the only solid foundations of liberty are knowledge and courage. His last four years as a slave were made unusually pleasant, because he had dared, at the risk of the gallows, to fight hand to hand with his master; and promotion, from a field-hand to a city mechanic, rewarded his first attempt to run away. He taught himself to read and write, and also to speak effectively. His residence for almost three years at New Bedford showed him how deeply the North was stained with prejudices which would not let him enter a church on equal terms with white worshipers, and which prevented him from taking up the trade which he had followed successfully in Baltimore. In spite of

many hardships, he realized so fully the superior
advantages of working in free competition over labor
under compulsion, that he was prepared to resist all
the blandishments of socialism, even when presented
by those white people who had been among the first
to recognize his rights. His joining the Garrisonians enabled him to become prominent as a speaker
much earlier than would, in all probability, have been
the case if he had preferred the voting Abolitionists ; but he could not in any case have remained
very long unknown and silent in Massachuestts.
His education did not advance as rapidly as it would
have done if he had not been obliged to be his own
teacher, for the most part, even in New Bedford ;
but this isolation had some compensation in his
developing unusual capacity for thinking for himself.

This was plain during the second period of his life,
which began with his ranking himself among the
Garrisonians, in August, 1841, and closed with his
renouncing disunionism in May, 1851. All these years
he was busy as a lecturer against slavery, and especially so during the first six. His first exploit was in
helping his people gain the suffrage in Rhode Island ;
and he next took part in that agitation against the
return of a fugitive named Latimer, which has embodied itself permanently in our literature, in Whittier's magnificent poem, " Massachusetts to Virginia."
For four years the black knight roamed to and fro,
from Maine to Indiana, always ready to break a lance
with any champion of slavery. Sometimes he had to
collect his audience by going through the town, ringing a big bell, and crying the meeting. Or else he
would take his stand under a tree, or at the corner of

a side-street, and persuade people who had set out for church to stop to hear him. Once, at least, he fought for his life against an armed mob ; sometimes he had the full sympathy of thousands of eager listeners ; and sometimes he found only a handful of timid adherents in the almost empty hall. Opposition and indifference could not lessen his zeal, but only made him exert more eagerly his matchless power of pathos mingled with ridicule. His parodies of the slave-holders' cant had an effect which is not to be revived by merely reprinting the words ; and it is impossible to do any justice to his success in calling forth tears of sympathy. His fiercest denunciations were provoked by a clerical conservatism, largely due to the disunionism represented on the banner which he and his friends formally accepted, at Boston, in 1844, and carried at the head of a great procession through Hingham. While joining eagerly in this agitation for a dissolution of the Union, he resisted the attempt of some leading Garrisonians to merge abolitionism in socialism ; and his boldness in defying the authority of his superiors kept the great reform true to its orignal aim.

His devotion to it made him, when challenged to prove that he had really been a slave, tell the place and his master's name. The little book was such a great success that he could not be safe in the United States. He crossed the ocean ; and found that the color-prejudice was only an Americanism. Ireland gave him one long ovation. He was at war for a year with the Scotch clergy, on the question, whether slave-holders ought to be fellowshiped ; and this gave him a reputation which was increased by a single combat in London, with a Doctor of Divinity from New York. His English friends would have kept him among them, but he preferred to fight in the forlorn hope ; and so they bought his freedom. He was also enabled by them to start a newspaper ; but this was opposed by Garrison, and postponed for six months, part of which were spent in a western tour, involving some sharp debates with men who appealed to the ballot-box against slavery. Before the close of 1847, Douglass made up his mind that it was his duty to publish the " North Star ; " and he took up his residence at Rochester, for there was much hostility in Boston, in spite of his remaining for three years more, loyal to Garrisonianism. He continued to lecture, though not often in New England ; but his main strength was given to the paper, which showed high ability and was carried on for twelve years, in spite of occasional pecuniary difficulties. The movement in behalf of women found one of its earliest advocates in the " North Star ; " much stress was laid on the need among the blacks of industrial training ; and the editor's house soon became one of the most useful stations on the Under-ground Railroad.

He took less interest than many other colored men in the organization of the Free Soil party ; and that same year, 1848, he denounced all supporters of the Constitution of the United States as enemies of God and man. He found out gradually his error, as he carried on controversies, first with a negro clergyman named Ward, and then with the great philanthropist, Gerrit Smith. Before finally casting in his lot with the men who actually abolished slavery, he was able to quell a pro-slavery riot in New York, with Ward's help ; but the united efforts of Phillips, Garrison, Parker, and Douglass could not prevent Faneuil Hall from being taken from them by a noisy mob, soon after the passage of the Fugitive Slave Bill in 1850.

Our hero's life thus far is told in six chapters : and five more are given to the fourteen years, ending with the complete conquest of slavery in 1865. This third period is by far the most important in the light of history; for Douglass was now working in harmony with Sumner, Wilson, Chase, Seward, Lincoln, and other leaders of the party which actually freed the slaves. His devotion to the cause of his race was as pure and lofty as ever ; and he met the hostility of the disunionist Abolitionists, by saying: "I would unite with anybody to do right, and with nobody to do wrong." . . . "I love and honor William Lloyd Garrison," . . . and "have not the slightest wish to be embroiled in personal controversy with anti-slavery men of any sort." His reception by the Free Soilers, in the convention of 1852, was enthusiastic ; but the people of Rochester forced him to live year after year among them like a hermit ; and ten years went by without his revisiting Boston. Ohio and Illinois were more hospitable than Massachusetts, and listened to him eagerly, when the attempt to enslave Kansas excited such indignation in the North as suddenly transformed what had hitherto seemed only an insignificant faction into a mighty party. His newspaper went on under a new name until it was merged in a "Monthly," which lasted almost to the end of the war. He also published a number of pamphlets at this period ; his Autobiography assumed a new and highly interesting form ; and he began to write out his lectures before delivery. His style had always been powerful, as well as picturesque; and it was now liable to little criticism, except on account of repetitions. His mastery of English was complete, in spite of lack of knowledge of other languages, or perhaps in consequence of concentration upon one vocabulary.

The intimacy which he had formed, while still a disunionist, with John Brown, continued until it was broken off by a refusal to go to Harper's Ferry ; and discovery of the correspondence obliged Douglass to make a brief visit to England, where he did much to dispel the prejudices of Abolitionists against our Constitution. The indignities inflicted on him in Boston and Albany by mobs of would-be savers of the Union, did not hinder him from taking sides with the Government as soon as war broke out ; and he published a pathetic Appeal to Great Britain, against recognition of the Confederacy. Freely as he blamed Lincoln's tardiness, he was among the warmest admirers of the proclamations of emancipation ; and the plan of raising colored regiments was enthusiastically supported, in spite of occasional complaints that it was not carried out in good faith. His personal relations with our great President were friendly, and this enabled him to break through the exclusiveness which had hitherto stained the White House. The energy with which he supported the war from the first, was kept up until he was able to tell a delighted audience, in Faneuil Hall, that the parable of Dives and Lazarus was all true. The rich man of the South was in torments, and calling out in vain for the sending back of Lazarus, who was safe in Abraham's bosom.

The twenty-five years after April 1865, occupy but three chapters; for this last period is by no means so rich as its predecessor in great events. It has been one of those happy times, when but little takes place which is intensely interesting; and Douglass has had little chance to make history, though he has done much to make presidents. It was largely due to him that the freedmen secured the ballot and gave it faithfully to the Republican party; and their disfranchisement has called out his earnest but not very successful protests. The questions about the annexation of San Domingo, and the exposure of the Freedman's Bank, have already ceased to be important; his services as Marshal and Recorder belong, like his reconciliation with his dying master, his last book, and his journey to Europe, to biography, not history; and the negro exodus of 1879 would have little interest, if there were not some danger of a second edition. His denunciations of the store-order fraud, lynching, sale of convict labor, and other wrongs upon the Southern negro, ought not to be forgotten until all such abuses are abolished; but his most valuable suggestion is that the white men of the South cannot afford, for their own sakes, to let fraud and violence continue unpunished; and that the need of attracting capital and immigration will yet teach justice and humanity. It is by no means certain that his mission to Hayti will do more good than his constant advice to his brethren to give their children trades, to practice industry, and to avoid all extravagance, even in religion.

The five closing years, described in the first part of this chapter, belong with those just considered to that golden period of his life, when he was not so exclusively occupied as before with the defense of an oppressed race. During these thirty years he spoke even more impressively, though less and less passionately; and his mighty eloquence poured forth freely in behalf of the disfranchised sex, of down-trodden Ireland, of the maltreated Chinese, and of dumb animals. We even find him rising so far above party prejudice as to write thus, in behalf of what he calls the cause of truth and justice. " It is my opinion that but for the unwarrantable intermeddling of our citizens Queen Liliuokalani would now be on the throne. The stories afloat intended to blacken the character of the Queen do not deceive me. The device is an old one, and has been used with skill and effect ever since Caleb and Joshua saw the grapes of Canaan. We are the Jews of modern times, and when we want the lands of other people such people are guilty of every species of abomination and are not fit to live. In our conduct to-day we are but repeating our treatment towards Mexico in the case of Texas. Our citizens settled in Texas under promise of obedience to the laws of Mexico, but as soon as they were strong enough they revolted and set up a government for themselves to be ultimately added to the United States. In whatever else President Cleveland may have erred, history will credit his motive and commend the object he has aimed to accomplish. I am Republican, but I am not a ' Republican right or wrong.' "

This letter goes with his outgrowing the orthodoxy

which, while a slave, he had aspired to preach, with his renouncing the disunionism, which he had learned from the man he loved and honored most deeply, and which he had himself advocated most earnestly, and also with his discovering, while still suffering under his master's cruelty, that the best way to save himself from being whipped again was to resist desperately. All this goes to prove that he had a white man's independence and originality of intellect. He was whiter than those who despised him on account of the color of his skin. How much courage he inherited from fire-eaters, was manifest in the fierceness with which he fought against white men at Baltimore. He owed his escape from slavery to his steadiness of nerve; he charged, club in hand, against a mob in Indiana; and he stayed three months within reach of the Fugitive-Slave Law, after publishing a narrative which made his capture probable. When we also remember how passionately he loved knowledge, and consider further that he amassed a handsome fortune by his foresight and economy, it is easy to see that he had the best traits of the Anglo-Saxon race. He was born to be a great leader; and the brilliancy of his conversation was not more remarkable than its perfect freedom from indecency or vulgarity.

It must have been from his mother's race that he inherited his love of music and mimicry, his openhanded generosity, his warmth of religious feeling, his habitual courtesy, and that loyal gratitude in which he readily overlooked defects in other champions of the oppressed. Few men have been so great and at the same time so lovable, or have left behind them so few enemies and so many friends.

APPENDIX.

LIST OF PUBLICATIONS BY FREDERICK DOUGLASS.

Letters in the " Liberator," 1842–7 and 1859.

" Narrative of the Life of Frederick Douglass, an American Slave, Written by Himself," Boston, 1845. (Various Editions afterward.)

" Correspondence between Samuel H. Cox and Frederick Douglass," New York, 1846.

Speech at Soirée at London Tavern, March 30, 1847, in " Report of Proceedings," London, 1847.

" The North Star, " Rochester, 1847–50.

" Vie de Frédéric Douglass, Traduite par S. K. Parkes," Paris, Pagnerre, 1848.

" Letter to Thomas Auld," 1848.

" Lectures on American Slavery, Delivered at Corinthian Hall, Rochester," Buffalo, 1851.

" Frederick Douglass's Paper," Rochester, 1850–60.

" The Heroic Slave," in " Autographs for Freedom," 1852 or 1853.

Extract from a Speech made at New York, May, 1853, in " Autographs for Freedom," 1854.

" The Claims of the Negro, Ethnologically Considered, an Address at Western Reserve College," Rochester, 1854.

" My Bondage and My Freedom. Part I, Life as a Slave; Part II, Life as a Freeman," New York and Auburn, 1855.

" The Anti-Slavery Movement, a Lecture before the Rochester Ladies' Anti-Slavery Society." Rochester Daily American Office, 1855.

" Two Speeches, one on West India Emancipation and the

other on the Dred Scott Decision," Rochester, American Office, 1857.

" Douglass's Monthly," Rochester, 1858–64.(?)

" Eulogy of the late Hon. Wm. Jay," Rochester, 1859.

"Sclaverei und Freiheit. Autobiographie von Frederick Douglass. Uebersetzung von Ottilie Assing," Hamburg, 1860.

" The Slave's Appeal to Great Britain," 1862.

" What Shall be Done With Four Million Slaves, if the are Emancipated ? " Essay quoted in " The Black Man, his Antecedents, his Genius, and his Achievements," by W. W. Brown, 1863.

" Men of Color to Arms," 1863.

" Speech before the American Anti-Slavery Society, at its Third Decade, New York, 1864.

Lecture at Dedication of the Douglass Institute, Baltimore, in the " Liberator," for October 13, 1865.

Reply to President Johnson, 1866, also in " Life and Times," 1882.

" The New National Era," 1869–72.

Address at Arlington, on Decoration Day, 1871, also in " Life and Times," 1882.

" Oration at the Unveiling of the Freedmen's Monument to Abraham Lincoln," Washington, 1876, also in " Life and Times," 1882.

Letter in the " Washington Evening Star," 1877, also in " Life and Times," 1882.

Address on Decoration Day in New York, 1878.

" The Negro Exodus from the Gulf States," in " Journal of Social Science," No. XI, May, 1880, also in " Life and Times," 1882.

" The Color-line," in the " North American Review," April, 1881.

Addresses at Elmira, August 1, 1880, on " West India Emancipation," and at Washington, September 26, 1881, on " Garfield," in " Life and Times," 1882.

" Life and Times of Frederick Douglass, Written by Himself," Hartford, Conn., Park Publishing Co., 1882.

Speech at the Civil Rights Mass-meeting, October 22, 1883, Washington, C. P. Farrell, 1883.

" The Freedmen," in " Harper's Weekly," December 8, 1883.

" The Future of the Negro," in the " North American Review," July, 1884.

Address on Wendell Phillips, in " Life and Times of Wendell Phillips," by G. L. Austin, Boston, 1884.

" Three Addresses on the Relations Subsisting Between the White and Colored People of the United States," delivered September 24, 1883, April 16, 1885, April 16, 1886, Washington, Gibson Bros., 1886.

" The Future of the Colored Race," in the " North American Review " for April, 1886.

" Speech on the Seventy-ninth Anniversary of the Birth of Lincoln," Washington, Gibson Bros., 1888.

Speech at the International Council of Women in Washington, in the " Woman's Journal,"April 14, 1888.

Speech before the N. E. Woman Suffrage Association, in the " Woman's Journal," June 2, 1888.

" The Nation's Problem," a Speech delivered on April 16, 1889.

" Reminiscences," in the " Cosmopolitan " for August, 1889.

Among lectures and speeches which were, perhaps without exception, reported more or less fully at the time of delivery, and which may in some cases have been published in pamphlet form, are the following :

Speech at Plymouth County Convention, Hingham, November 4, 1841.

Speech on Dorr Constitution at Providence, December, 1841.

Speeches against the Liberty Party, before M. A. S. S., Boston, January 26 and 27, 1842.

Speeches at Latimer Meetings, New Bedford, November 6, 1842.

Disunionist Speech, before M. A. A. S., Boston, January 27, 1843.

Lecture on " Slavery as Actually Existing in the South," Boston, March 6, 1843.

Speech before A. A. S. S., New York, May 10, 1843.
Speech before M. A. S. S., Boston, January 24, 1844.
Speech at Hingham, August 2, 1844.
Speech against Annexation of Texas, Boston, January 26, 1845.
Speech in New York, May 8, 1845.
Speech before New England Convention, Boston, May, 1845.
Speech at Repeal Meeting, Dublin, September, 1845.
Speech in Glasgow, April 21, 1846.
Addresses in London on Slavery, May 18, on Peace, May 19, on Manhood Suffrage, May 20, on Temperance, May 21, and at the Douglass Reception, May 22, 1846.
Speech at World's Temperance Convention, London, August 7, 1846.
Speech before Anti-Slavery League, London, September 14, 1846.
Speech before A. A. S. S., New York, May, 1847.
Speech before Western Anti-Slavery Society, New Lyme, O., August 18, 1847.
Speech at Oberlin, O., August, 1847.
Speech before A. A. S. S., New York, May 9, 1848.
Address on Industrial Education at the Colored Convention, Cleveland, O., September, 1848.
Address before A. A. S. S., New York, May 9, 1849.
Defense of A. A. S. S., against a mob, New York, May 7, 1850.
Attack on Fugitive Slave Bill, Boston, October 14, 1850.
Speech at Cincinnati, May 5, 1852.
Debate with Garrisonians in A. A. S. S. Convention, Rochester, N, Y., May 12, 1852.
Fourth of July Oration, Rochester, 1852.
Address to the Free Soil Convention, August 11, 1852.
Kansas Speech, in Chicago, September, 1854.
Address to the Legislature, at Albany, March, 1855.
Lecture on " Self-made Men."
" The Constitution of the United States : is it Pro-slavery, or Anti-slavery ? " Glasgow, March 26, 1860.

War speeches, Rochester, April 27, 1861, and often afterward.

Lecture on " The Rebellion, its Cause and its Remedy," Syracuse, November 14, 1861.

Lecture in behalf of the Emancipation League, Boston, 1862.

Protest against Sending Negroes back to Africa, Cooper Institute, New York, February 12, 1862.

Fourth of July Oration, at Himrod's Corners, N. Y., 1862.

Emancipation Speech in Boston, January 1, 1863.

Address Urging Colored Men to Enlist, Philadelphia, June 17, 1863.

Lecture on " The Mission of the War,'' Boston, February 10, 1864.

Lecture on " William the Silent."

Lecture on " The Composite Nation," Parker Fraternity Course, Boston, 1867.

Address at Watkin's Glen, N. Y., August 1, 1867.

Lecture on " Santo Domingo."

Address to Convention of Colored Citizens at New Orleans, April, 1872.

Campaign Speeches during this and other Presidential Contests.

Lecture on " John Brown," Charlestown, Mass., December 9, 1873.

Speech at Woman Suffrage Meeting, Faneuil Hall, Boston, December 15, 1873.

Decoration Day Address, Rochester N. Y.

Lecture entitled " It Moves."

Speech at Centennial of the Abolition Society of Pennsylvania, 1875.

Fourth of July Oration at Hillsdale, 1875.

Address at Pinchback Mass-meeting, Washington, March, 1876.

Lecture on " Our National Capital," Washington, 1876, and Baltimore, 1877.

Speech on the Death of Garrison, Washington, June 2, 1879.

Address at Colored Convention, Louisville, July, 1880.

Campaign Address at Rochester, August 4, 1880.

Speech to Conkling Club, Washington, February, 1881.

Speech on Twentieth Anniversary of Emancipation Proclamation, Washington, January 1, 1883.

Address on Twenty-first Anniversary of Emancipation in the District of Columbia, April 16, 1883.

Blaine Speech at Syracuse, October 1, 1884.

" Thoughts and Recollections of the Anti-Slavery Conflict,' a Lecture.

Address at Dedication of Hunter Memorial, Washington February, 1886.

Speech at Dinner of Massachusetts Club, Boston, May 22, 1886.

Woman Suffrage Address, Boston, May 24, 1886.

Speech at Dinner of Wendell Phillips Club, Boston, September 11, 1886.

Two Lectures on his Trip to Europe and Egypt, one of which is entitled, " Paris, Rome, and Cairo."

Address on Relations of White and Colored People, delivered at Washington, April 16, 1888.

Speech on the Issues of the Presidential Election, 1888.

Address to the Colored Citizens of the United States, 1888.

Two Speeches at Abolitionist Reunion, Boston, September 22, 1890.

Address before Bethel Association, Washington, October 21, 1890.

LATEST PUBLICATIONS.

" Haiti and the United States," in the " North American Review," September and October, 1891.

" Lynch Law in the South," in the " North American Review," July, 1892.

" The Negro in the Present Presidential Campaign," in " Zion's Herald," September 28, 1892.

" Life and Times of Frederick Douglass." New Edition. Boston : De Wolfe. Fiske & Co., 1892.

" Lecture on Haiti," Chicago, 1893.

INDEX.

417